CHINA

———— Route followed by Mr. Huc
⚓ Ta-Bien-lou, Point of entrance into Chin...
▲ Tching-tou-fou, Capital of the Province See-Tche...
▲ Ou-Tchang-fou, Capital of the Province of Hou-...
▲ Nan-Tchang-fou, Capital of the Province of Kiam...

Li of China.

English Miles 69 = One Degree.

Printed in colours by Schenck & McFarlane, E...

LOOKING EAST

LOOKING EAST

William Howard Taft and the 1905
U.S. Diplomatic Mission to Asia

The Photographs of Harry Fowler Woods

Margo Taft Stever
James Taft Stever
Hong Shen

Edited by Kevin Grace

ORANGE *frazer* PRESS
Wilmington, Ohio

ISBN 978-1939710-222
Copyright©2015 University of Cincinnati

Published for the University of Cincinnati Press by:

Orange Frazer Press
P.O. Box 214
Wilmington, OH 45177
Telephone: 937.382.3196 for price and shipping information.
Website: www.orangefrazer.com
Book and cover design: Alyson Rua and Orange Frazer Press

Library of Congress Cataloging-in-Publication Data

Stever, Margo.
  [Kan dong fang. English]
  Looking east : William Howard Taft and the 1905 U.S. diplomatic mission to Asia : the photographs of Harry Fowler Woods / Margo Taft Stever, James Taft Stever, Hong Shen ; edited by Kevin Grace.
      pages cm
  Originally published in Chinese.
  Includes bibliographical references and index.
  ISBN 978-1-939710-22-2
1. Taft, William H. (William Howard), 1857-1930--Travel--Asia. 2. Taft, William H. (William Howard), 1857-1930--Travel--Asia--Pictorial works. 3. United States--Foreign relations--Asia. 4. Asia--Foreign relations--United States. 5. United States--Foreign relations--1901-1909. 6. Woods, Harry Fowler, 1859-1955. I. Stever, James Taft. II. Shen, Hong, 1954- III. Grace, Kevin editor. IV. Woods, Harry Fowler, 1859-1955. V. Title. VI. Title: William Howard Taft and the 1905 U.S. diplomatic mission to Asia.
  E762.S7413 2015
  973.91'2092--dc23
                    2014046231

Printed in China

The endsheets are from a 19th Century map of China in the holdings of the Archives and Rare Books Library, University of Cincinnati.

CONTENTS

vii   Acknowledgments

ix   Message from University of Cincinnati President Santa J. Ono

xi   Message from Zhejiang University President Lin Jianhua

xiii   Foreword by Kevin Grace

xvii   "Double Exposure"

003   **Chapter 1** Looking East: William Howard Taft and the 1905 Mission to Asia, The Photographs of Harry Fowler Woods

113   **Chapter 2** Francis W. Frost: Letters to His Father from China

204   **Chapter 3** William Howard Taft: Letter from China to His Wife, Nellie

228   **Chapter 4** Interviews

259   **Chapter 5** Conclusion

276   Afterword

278   The Authors

280   Bibliography

288   Index

ACKNOWLEDGMENTS

The authors would like to thank the following people whose advice and wisdom were invaluable in the research and writing of this book. First and foremost, we would like to thank Donald W. Stever, who helped with every aspect of the project, and without whom the "Looking East" exhibition and book would not have been possible; Hope Taft, who inspired and guided the "Looking East" photography exhibition; and Professor Hong Shen, who originally suggested working on the book project after inviting Margo and James Taft Stever to give a talk and to feature the "Looking East" exhibition at Zhejiang University. We would also like to thank President Lin Jianhua of Zhejiang University for his personal interest in and warm support for the present book project; professor and poet Jianqing Zheng, who originally encouraged us to submit an abstract to the international symposium at Zhejiang University; Anna Reid Jhirad, for her invaluable advice and assistance with writing for the exhibition; Angelina Mak, for helping with copyediting the Chinese version of the book; Paula Armbruster, for her discerning suggestions after reading sections of the text; Ira Wunder, President of I. Wunder Photographics, for his work on the digital restoration of the Woods photographs; Professor Jonathan Spence, for generously offering his views on the photographs and the historical period; Professors Michael Hunt and Stacy Cordery, for providing their rich and colorful insights in the interviews included in this book; Eric Besch, for allowing us to publish for the first time the detailed and informative F.W. Frost letters and for his interview on his family background for the Frost letters; Martha Smiley, for her interview on Christian missionaries in China during 1905; the staff of the Manuscript Division of the Library of Congress, Washington, D.C., for their untiring assistance during specific periods of research over the last decade; Bob Lees, for his generous effectiveness in acting as a liaison in bringing together the University of Cincinnati and Zhejiang University to work on this and other academic projects; Dean Xuemao Wang of the University of Cincinnati, for lending his organizational skills and effort in initiating the publication of the English language edition by bringing key people together in meetings at Zhejiang University and the University of Cincinnati; Kevin Grace of the University of Cincinnati for his work in gathering together all the pieces of the book and for his writing about the Taft family and the university; and Jeffrey Harrison, for his poem, "Double Exposure," about Harry Fowler Woods and the 1905 journey.

The "Looking East" exhibitions and book project included the digitizing and restoration of hundreds of photographic snapshots included in five albums, the originals of which were donated to the Beinecke Rare Book Library at Yale University. The "Looking East" traveling exhibitions were donated and now reside at the William Howard Taft National Historic Site in Cincinnati and Zhejiang University in Hongzhou. The exhibition and book were made possible, in part, with generous financial assistance from: the Louise Taft Semple Foundation; Zhejiang University, the University of Cincinnati; the David G. Taft Foundation; the Ohio Humanities Council; the Thendara Foundation; the Donald and Margo Stever Fund; the Jacob G. Schmidlapp Trust, Fifth Third Bank Trustee; Japanese Chamber of Commerce Fund; the Ohio Historical Society; the William P. Anderson Foundation; the Betty D. Anderson Family Fund; the Cincinnati USA Regional Chamber; Honda of America, Mfg., Inc.; and the Yokkaichi America Corporation.

MESSAGE FROM UNIVERSITY OF CINCINNATI PRESIDENT SANTA J. ONO

LOOKING BACK, LOOKING FORWARD THROUGH *LOOKING EAST*

A look back at the 1905 yearbook for the University of Cincinnati reminds us just how much has changed in the 110 years since William Howard Taft's voyage to Hawaii, Japan, the Philippines and China. The pages of the 1905 *Cincinnatian* show no names or faces of Asian heritage among the UC faculty or students. Faculty connections to France, Germany, Spain, Italy, Greece, Peru and other international destinations are mentioned, but the only Asian references appear to be in a satiric section with a line referring to Port Arthur and the Russo-Japanese War and another to a "Chinaman." Taft's listing as a faculty member in the law school notes his leave of absence for the year for apparent good reasons as he served as the U.S. Secretary of War.

Fast forwarding to UC today, we find a sharp and encouraging contrast. UC has become a global university. In recent years, our international student enrollment has risen to record highs along with our total enrollment. Of our nearly 3,000 international students who travel from abroad to study at UC, more than three-quarters come from Asia, with the majority from China followed by India. Of UC's total enrollment of approximately 43,000 students, a little more than three percent have Asian, Hawaiian or Pacific Islander heritage. That does not include those who identify themselves as multiracial. Our alumni live all around the world.

For me, Taft's historic trip to Asia and our nation's relationship to Asia take on personal, not just academic, significance. I am the son of Japanese immigrants who moved to the United States in the 1950s and I became a naturalized U.S. citizen. My wife's parents were born in China and relocated to Canada. While the efforts of Taft, Alice Roosevelt, and their fellow-travelers in East Asia met with mixed success, they did widen the door to intercultural dialogue and greater understanding. Sixty years later in 1965, the anti-Asian immigration and naturalization policies of the United States were finally set aside.

Our university today has blossomed into a truly global university that seeks ever-wider opportunities to partner with higher education, business, and civic institutions in China and around the world. We encourage our students and faculty to venture forth to experience and learn firsthand about the many cultures of our planet. This is the best way we can honor and build on the legacy of Taft, his fellow-sojourners and their unprecedented journey of 11 decades ago.

MESSAGE FROM ZHEJIANG UNIVERSITY PRESIDENT LIN JIANHUA

Looking East: William Howard Taft and the 1905 U.S. Diplomatic Mission to Asia provides an interesting account of a little known episode in Sino-American diplomatic relations at the beginning of the 20th century, together with vivid snapshots taken by H.F. Woods. In 1905, W.H. Taft, the United States Secretary of War, and Alice Roosevelt, personal envoy of her father, President Theodore Roosevelt, led a high-grade American government delegation to visit China and to have face-to-face talks with Chinese rulers such as Empress Dowager Cixi and Yuan Shikai, with the result that a serious crisis in Sino-American diplomatic relations was successfully resolved.

The success of this China visit by the delegation has an important significance even today. It teaches us a lesson that the open conflicts between two sovereign countries should be, and can be, resolved with active diplomatic means, such as exchange of visits and peaceful negotiations by high-level officials. Military confrontation is never the best choice in solving a crisis. When the movement of embargo against American goods started in the coastal areas of China back in 1905, in strong protest against the discrimination and maltreatment of Chinese immigrants in the United States, many American merchants suffered a heavy loss in China trade. In retaliation, the U.S. administration had once considered the possibility of taking military measures in attacking the city of Canton. Fortunately, President Roosevelt rejected this extreme proposition. Instead, he sent the Taft delegation to China and in so doing, successfully maintained, or even improved, the peace and friendship between the two countries.

I am delighted to learn that the University of Cincinnati, alma mater of William Howard Taft, has published the English-language edition of this book, in cooperation with Zhejiang University Press. When I was president of Chongqing University a few years ago, I had personal experiences of cooperation with President Santa Ono of the University of Cincinnati in creating a joint teaching program, which was both successful and pleasant. In the publication of this book, I hope that Zhejiang University will be able to establish the same cooperative relationship with the University of Cincinnati.

FOREWORD

The Taft Family and the University of Cincinnati

On a patch of lawn between the College of Law and the Carl Blegen Library on the University of Cincinnati campus, there is a bronze statue of William Howard Taft. Portrayed in judicial robes and holding a law book in his right hand, Taft looks happy, his walrus moustache slightly crinkled below the cheeks raised in a smile topped by a satisfied gaze. Dedicated in 1992, the statue is fitting for two very important reasons. From the founding of the University of Cincinnati in 1870 (the professed 1819 founding date indicates that the original Cincinnati College which began in that year, and its Law School, were later absorbed by UC), the Taft family has been deeply involved in the welfare of the university, from its initial planning in which Alphonso Taft made his opinions known in terms of educational methods to William Howard Taft effecting the merger of Cincinnati College's Law School with UC's College of Law and to various Taft funds that enrich scholarship and teaching.

The second reason is that Taft, serving his community and country as a judge, as a law school dean both at UC and Yale University, as secretary of war and governor of the Philippines, and, as president of the United States and chief justice of the Supreme Court, was most content as a teacher and jurist. In laboring as president from 1908 to 1912, he answered the call of his wife, Theodore Roosevelt, and the Republican Party. But he was not a happy chief executive. Those particular years in Washington, D.C. were ones of duty. But, he loved the law. He loved teaching about it, writing about it, and administering it. Garbed in his bronze statue gown, Taft's personality and ardor are evident.

Taft's father, Alphonso, was a member of the Law School faculty

→ The statue of W. H. Taft at the University of Cincinnati.

of Cincinnati College in the years following the Civil War. In his own career, Alphonso was also a diplomat, a jurist of some repute and he worked in Ulysses Grant's presidential cabinet variously as Attorney General and Secretary of War. Solicited by the city of Cincinnati in 1869 to help form the nascent University of Cincinnati, Taft made public speeches on behalf of the effort, and once it was founded, was named to the first Board of Directors.

William Howard followed in his father's footsteps. He graduated from Woodward High School in Cincinnati, took his undergraduate degree at Yale, and then attended the Cincinnati Law School where Alphonso had taught. After admission to the bar in 1880 and working for a time as a Hamilton County prosecutor before being elected to the Ohio Supreme Court, Taft became dean of the Cincinnati Law School in 1896. He served as both judge and dean for a few years as he worked to merge his institution with the University of Cincinnati. In 1900 he began his national endeavors under President William McKinley with the Philippines position before becoming Secretary of War under Roosevelt in 1904. And back in Cincinnati, there was a contingent of students who wished for him to become president of UC. Four years later, he would be President of the United States.

→ Taft as Dean of the Cincinnati Law School.

William Howard Taft often returned to Cincinnati to visit his brothers and friends. In 1917, he promoted the sale of war bonds in a community-organized drive in the Queen City, and on October 28, 1925, along with his brothers Charles Phelps Taft, Henry W. Taft, and Horace D. Taft, he dedicated Alphonso Taft Hall, the home of UC's College of Law. All four sons of Alphonso were graduates of the Cincinnati Law School. Among the audience that day were two other UC graduates, Vice President Charles G. Dawes and Speaker of the House Nicholas Longworth. Of course, at that same time, Taft was the Chief Justice. It was a notably influential time for UC alumni in national affairs.

→ The Taft brothers at the 1925 dedication of Alphonso Taft Hall on the U.C. Campus.

In his dedication speech, Taft stated that a grounding in general education was essential for lawyers, *"No man can sit in a court of justice and not realize how men suffer, how injustice is done that cannot be remedied…"*

The Taft family legacy at the University of Cincinnati is a commitment of service and support. In 1922, Mrs. Charles P. Taft established Taft Fellowships for scholarship and in 1930 the Charles Phelps Taft Memorial Fund was established to endow teaching and research in the humanities, a fund that enriches learning to this day. And in 1961, Louise Taft Semple created a trust fund for the Department of Classics, continuing Taft family support since the 1930s that made UC Classics a renowned leader in archaeology and history.

It is inconceivable that the University of Cincinnati would be the world-class institution it is today without the involvement of Alphonso Taft and his progeny. And in this volume, there is considerably more evidence of the Taft ideals of service and global responsibility.

Note: A line on the map represents the itinerary of the 1905 U.S. delegation. Another shows the route of the Taft party after the delegation split into two groups in Hong Kong. The third line is the route that Alice Roosevelt and her party traveled.

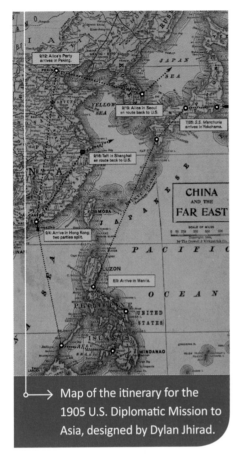

→ Map of the itinerary for the 1905 U.S. Diplomatic Mission to Asia, designed by Dylan Jhirad.

→ The cover of the Harry Fowler Woods' China photo album.

Double Exposure

by Jeffrey Harrison

My great-grandfather's photo albums
from his trip around the world in 1905,
their suede covers printed with his name
in gold capitals, and their brittle pages
torn loose and out of order, show him
in the Philippines with William Howard Taft
(round as the world, big as an elephant),
then *on* an elephant in India,
wearing a pith helmet and staring out
from behind his black, indelible moustache
as if he owned the world…
                              a world
I can't recognize (Hong Kong's bristling
          crystallization of skyscrapers
          dissolved to a sediment of shacks),
and a man I never knew, with whom
          I feel no bond beyond the facts
of my middle name and an inheritance
          of genes now reshuffled as
                    these pages I turn.
                              But wait! Here's one
          of Varnasi, just as I saw it
a year ago—and all at once I'm looking
          with his eyes through the viewfinder
of his camera with the black bellows extended,
          then letting it fall and feeling its weight
against the back of the neck as the scene
          just caught on film—a body in flames
          crumpling as the pyre underneath it
          collapses—burns itself into the brain
which can't contain it, can't stop the fire
from spreading through all the internal organs

and into the limbs, until the knees give way
and he has to sit down.
He sits there
for a long time, dazed, not sure what has happened,
then gets up and leaves me on the stone steps
in the exact spot he rose from, while he
wanders off along the ghats, ghost-like,
in the shadows of temples piled like stalagmites,
to join the multitude of spectral figures
who have traveled here for centuries,
disappearing behind a hazy veil
of smoke rising from the funeral pyres
and the emulsion's silvery sheen.

LOOKING EAST

CHAPTER 1 LOOKING EAST

William Howard Taft and the 1905 Mission to Asia, The Photographs of Harry Fowler Woods[1]

INTRODUCTION

1905 was a defining year in global history. In that year, Albert Einstein developed his quantum theory of light, assisted in confirming the existence of atoms, and turned concepts of space and time upside down. He helped to explicate Brownian motion and created what would become science's most heralded equation ($e= MC^2$) in the history of science.[2]

In 1905, the Japanese shocked the world by pummeling Russia in the Russo-Japanese War, upsetting assumptions about the military inferiority of Asians. Five years after the surprise Boxer Rebellion, the Chinese in 1905 initiated a successful boycott of American goods to protest the treatment of Chinese immigrants in the United States. This was the first step in the arduous road to expel foreign forces and modernize China. In 1905, the United States engaged in a continuing, costly, and ultimately futile struggle with an insurgency in the Philippines in an effort to legitimize its civilizing mission and administrative colonial foothold in Asia.

Against this backdrop of cataclysmic global and societal change, and largely forgotten for close to a century, the 1905 U.S. mission heralded ground-breaking diplomacy in the Philippines, Japan, and China that aided in setting the course of international affairs in the twentieth century. President Theodore Roosevelt sent his trusted negotiator, Secretary of War William Howard Taft, his media star daughter Alice Roosevelt, Freshman Ohio Congressman Nicholas Longworth, and a sizeable cast of politicians and businessmen on what was at that time the largest U.S. diplomatic delegation ever to visit Asia. The entourage consisted of twenty-three U.S. congressman, seven U.S. senators, and a group of civilians including thirteen wives, businessmen, and their servants.[3] Soon after the trip, Alice Roosevelt would marry Nicholas Longworth in a highly publicized White House wedding.[4] Congressman Longworth would later become the distinguished speaker of the House of Representatives. The Taft party steamed into a scenario that carved a controversial but undeniable impact on East-West relations.[5]

From the unprecedented visit of foreigners to the Japanese Imperial Gardens to their audience with the Empress Dowager of China, the participants in this trailblazing diplomatic trip to Asia forged alliances and fomented conflicts that affected the world into the foreseeable future. The following pages explore the historical context of the trip; the familial background of the two U.S. photographers, H.F. Woods and F.W. Frost; the emergence of documentary photography and the hand-held camera; the roots of American expansionism; the importance of sea power; a synopsis of the U.S. mission's visit to San Francisco, Hawaii, Japan, and the Philippines; U.S. views on race at the turn of the twentieth century; the Boxer Rebellion as photographed by Frost and Woods; the Boxer Protocols and Indemnity; the background of the 1905 Chinese boycott of U.S. goods and the Taft party's experience of the boycott, their trip through China and return to the United States.

To those in the United States who did not know its purposes, the trip was called a "boondoggle." From 1900 to 1908, a period during which Taft was governor of the Philippines and secretary of war, his overseas travels to Manila, Rome, Cuba, and Panama, and his journeys within the United States, would cover more than 100,000 miles.[6] Taft himself mused that such a large Congressional delegation had never traveled so far, and he hoped that the sheer number of legislative witnesses would enhance U.S. public interest in the Philippines.[7] This occurred during a period in which the U.S. occupation of the Philippines was increasingly unpopular at home and abroad.[8]

A reluctant candidate for the U.S. presidency, Taft had nonetheless received assurances from Roosevelt by the summer of 1905 that he could count on the President's support for the 1908 Republican nomination. According to Taft biographer Henry F. Pringle, "he received, during 1905 and 1906, every possible assurance—everything short of a public announcement—that he could count on the active support of Theodore Roosevelt."[9] The 1905 trip would showcase Taft's competence as a leader and as a tough negotiator, both characteristics later drawn upon during his 1908 run for the U.S. presidency.

Highlighting the importance of the state of Ohio in U.S. national affairs at the turn of the century, many members of the eighty-three-person delegation were Ohioans, and most of those, including Taft, hailed from Cincinnati. Other Cincinnatians were Nicholas Longworth; banker and philanthropist J.G. Schmidlapp, a personal friend of Taft's who went with him to Rome in 1902;[10] Schmidlapp's daughter, Charlotte; her friend, Mignon Critten; businessman and amateur photographer, Harry Fowler Woods; R. Clough Anderson, who represented one of Cincinnati's most illustrious and wealthiest families; and

T. Sugimoto, a Japanese merchant living in Cincinnati. Congressman Charles Grosvenor, also on the 1905 mission, came from Athens, Ohio.[11]

According to the census records, the population of Cincinnati, built on an ancient alluvial plain, had increased by 150 per cent between 1840 and 1850.[12] Despite its boom-town status during the nineteenth century, the elite of the burgeoning city looked to the eastern United States and, ultimately, to Europe as the determiners of social status and taste. In his book *Nellie Taft: The Unconventional First Lady of the Ragtime Era* (2005), Carl S. Anthony described the dilemma of living in Cincinnati succinctly:

> The truth was, no matter how sophisticated its museums or fine its parks, Cincinnati would always be viewed as a backwater by the social elite of New York and Boston. That tended to make the Cincinnatians strive all the more to prove their sophistication. The Storers, the Findlays, the Tafts, the Sintons, the Longworths, and the Andersons made their tours of Europe, held debutante balls for their daughters, and kept summer homes in New England.[13]

Whether or not this was a realistic view of affluent Cincinnatians and outliers from similar geographic locations, it is true that most of those people had moved from eastern United States and, not too many generations earlier, from Europe or England; consequently, they would have naturally searched for their roots and even their relatives. They would have attempted to explore the remnants of their forgotten past.[14] By the turn of the century, owing to the development of the railroad, Cincinnati, already famous for its hogs, and then the arts, and its beer breweries, had begun to lose ground to the new, more western cities like Chicago.

HARRY FOWLER WOODS, F.W. FROST, AND THE NEW HAND-HELD CAMERA

Amateur photographer Harry Fowler Woods, a Cincinnati businessman and friend of Taft's, and F.W. Frost, a younger member of the group from a New Jersey and New York newspaper family, documented the 1905 mission with hundreds of photographs. Woods organized seven hundred and fifteen images into three leather-bound volumes with diligently typed captions and created two additional albums of his consequent travels. F.W. Frost assembled his photos in albums with documents and invitations from the trip.[15] Whether they are viewed as diplomats of peace, crass imperialists, glorious adventurers, or some combination of these, it is necessary to consider the origins and viewpoints of Harry Fowler Woods and F.W. Frost as individual photographers and as exemplars of the attitudes of the 1905 diplomatic travelers in order to analyze the prisms through which these photos and letters were created. A century is a long time, and much of the detail of their undocumented lives has been lost.

Part of the 1905 trip's mission was to introduce businessmen to Asia in order to engender knowledge of Asian countries and trade. Both Frost and Woods came from families that were generally involved in the industrialization of America in careers such as engineering, communications, and merchandising. Woods qualified for an invitation to travel in three ways—as a friend of Taft's, a member of a well-known Cincinnati family, and a representative from a successful business, the Chatfield and Woods Company. Born Henry Fowler Woods in Cincinnati on March 2, 1859, he was the son of William K. Woods and Elizabeth Martin Sharp Woods. In 1760, his great-grandfather, also William Woods, had been born at Carragallan, Leitrim County, Ireland. William immigrated to the United States and became a merchant and ship owner in Baltimore, Maryland. In 1879, after his father made and lost his fortune and died, his son, also named William, moved to Cincinnati where he took a job in the dry-goods store of Shillito, Burnet & Pullen. Over time, he became a partner and then retired from that business. Afterward, he joined his brother-in-law as a partner in the Chatfield and Woods Company, a pioneer in the paper trade west of the Alleghenies.

In 1880, H.F. Woods joined Chatfield and Woods, the paper company founded by his father and his uncle, Albert Chatfield. Harry became the president of the company in 1918 and served in that capacity until 1928, when he became chairman of the board, a position he held until 1951. In its early years, the company became the biggest manufacturer of paper in the Ohio River Valley. It would ultimately merge with the Mead Paper Company of Dayton, Ohio, which combined with Westvaco to become the MeadWestvaco Corporation. Harry also served as a vice president of the Chatfield & Woods Sack Company and as president of the Security Storage Company.[16]

Harry Woods married Katherine Longworth Anderson, with whom he had three daughters and a son. She was the great-granddaughter of the first Nicholas Longworth, a lawyer, land speculator, and one of the wealthiest men of his time. He had become a world-famous botanist for his work with the wild strawberry, which he was the first to cultivate in his greenhouses to help prevent scurvy, and to develop the first sparkling American wine.[17] Longworth was dubbed "the father of American wine" for his creation of the drink from the Catawba grape, a project he took on partly to alleviate the scourge of alcoholism that had affected so many Ohioans of his time. He was also a renowned art patron and was reputed to have created the most beautiful gardens in the Midwest.[18] Katherine was a cousin of the young Congressman Nicholas Longworth and R. Clough Anderson, both of whom traveled on the 1905 trip. She died in 1938.

During Woods's young adulthood, he was offered the opportunity to travel around the world or attend college, and he chose the former. The extensive travels of H.F. Woods included the 1905 diplomatic trip to Asia, which he and his friend F.W. Frost followed with a tour of Burma, India, Egypt, and Greece. Not long after the 1905 Asia trip, Woods purchased a camp in New York's Adirondack Mountains where he spent much of each summer fishing and exploring in the artistically crafted Adirondack guide boat. As a young adult, H.F. Woods was an avid and talented amateur photographer. He also served as trustee on many boards including the Children's Home, the Cincinnati Art Museum, the Historical and Philosophical Society of Ohio, and Rookwood Pottery, a world famous Cincinnati pottery school founded by his wife's relatives. Woods was named trustee emeritus of both the Children's Home and the Cincinnati Art Museum. Other honors included his naming as the oldest living member of the Queen City Club and a thirty-second-degree Mason. He founded a luncheon group for men, the "Sewing Circle," for discussion of important topics of the day because their wives participated in a sewing group on the same day. Woods died in 1955 at age 95.[19]

F.W. Frost (March 23, 1876–December 14, 1935), a younger member of the Taft party, represented his family's two newspapers; he also stood in for his father, George H. Frost, who had supported Republican causes and involved himself with politics. George H. Frost was an engineer who had attended McGill University to study engineering. George's father, Ebenezer Frost, was a blacksmith who had left Canada and "lit out for the territories,"[20] which at that time was New York. During his diverse and innovative career as an engineer, George had created the *Engineering News Review*, originally composed of "cheat sheets" to help laymen figure out how to build simple structures such as temporary bridges. George Frost was called to the Chicago area to help build road beds and bridges. After finding a deficit of trained engineers, who were engaged in construction for the Civil War, George was inspired to create the newsletter—which would eventually become a big business and continues today as one of the premiere U.S. engineering papers, *Engineering News-Record*. One of his collateral descendants, Eric Besch said: "Many of the metal bridges in North America were being built at this time. So it was a pretty innovative time, and he [George] ended up informally, at first, and then formally documenting a lot of the North American innovation in the engineering realm."[21] After George's retirement, he sold the business to a man named Hill, who partnered with a McGraw, and those two men created the McGraw-Hill printing house, which continues today as a major American publishing venture.

F.W. Frost was too young to get involved in George's business. His father had also bought two local newspapers in Plainfield, New Jersey, where the family had ended up living. F.W. Frost's older brother, Charles Frost, later ran the papers, and F.W. represented those newspapers by doing articles and photography while on the 1905 trip. The papers were ultimately sold to the Gannett family as their first non-New York paper, and that newspaper corporation continues as one of the powerful news groups in the United States. After traveling on the 1905-06 trip with Woods, F.W. Frost married and started an import/export business, F.W. Frost & Company, located at 60 Wall Street. H.F. Woods was best man at Frost's wedding. Frost, who loved to travel, subsequently circled the globe at least twice. He often ventured to Japan and China. According to family documents, he sponsored young and promising students from those countries to study in the United States.

The Frost letters and the Woods and Frost photographs underscore the Westerner's viewpoint of China at the turn of the last century. As artifacts, they signify as much about the Americans on the 1905 mission as they do about the Asian peoples whom they depict. Some of the Frost letters broadcast the Westerner's implicit condescension and "see how superior we are" civilizing discourse that was typical during this period. In Frost's descriptions that underlie his assessment, the most prevalent complaints relate to perceived lack of cleanliness, a low standard of living, noxious smells, bad roads, a general sense of foreignness, and signs of a civilization that had fallen far from its former glory. About Canton (Guangdong), he writes, "But the worst feature of Canton is the stench that constantly assaults you, especially when passing one of the many cook shops, but everywhere the same smell pervades." About Chinese inns, he writes, "A Chinese inn at best is not as desirable place as a summer hotel. They are all ground floor affairs, and the kitchens vile smelling places." [22]

Another traveler, Adjutant General Henry C. Corbin, who headed the U.S. Army's Philippine troops and who had originally offered the Taft party berths on the *Logan* for the trip to Peking, espoused a similar vision of China. According to his

June 7th letter to Taft, he had intended to go on the trip to look over the Legation Guard which had not been inspected for over a year.[23] In a letter to Stuyvesant Fish, Sr., delivered to him by his son, Stuyvesant Fish, Jr., who went on part of the 1905 mission, General Corbin observed:

> Our visit to Peking was one of very great interest. The advanced age of the Empress and the manifest idiocy or nearly so of the young Emperor makes important changes in the government of China very certain, and at no distant day. The evidence of decay is seen on all hands. Even about some of the most sacred temples the weeds are more vigorous than anything else in sight, and in many of the grounds have taken full and complete possession. The great temples and magnificent walls testify to prosperity and enterprise on the part of this people that no longer exists, or, if it does exist, is suppressed and kept beyond sight of the casual observer, and yet the genius of the Chinese people is industry.[24]

Some of Frost's descriptions of the bad smells of China ironically bring to mind Frances Trollope's reviews of Cincinnati, the very hometown of many of the 1905 diplomatic travelers, including Taft, Longworth, and Woods. Written less than seventy-five years before the 1905 trip and originally published in 1832, *The Domestic Manners of the Americans* by Mrs. Trollope, the mother of the famous British novelist Anthony Trollope, included a scathing attack on American hearth and home. Frances Trollope resided in Cincinnati, where she attempted to launch what must have been one of the first shopping malls, dubbed "Trollope's Folly" after its failure. She brought herself out of impending bankruptcy by publishing her travel book and instantly became the best known and most hated writer in the young United States. Accustomed to the more refined English standard of living, she reviled the American backcountry, which she described in often hilarious and graphically negative descriptive swaths.

In one passage, she recalls mounting a certain Sugar-Loaf Hill in Cincinnati, where she hoped for a pleasant view but instead found:

> the brook that we had to cross, at its foot, red with the stream from a pig slaughter-house; while our noses,

instead of meeting "the thyme that loves the green hill's breast," were greeted by odours that I will not describe, and which I heartily hope my readers cannot imagine; our feet, that on leaving the city had expected to press the flowering sod, literally got entangled in pig's tails and jawbones; and thus the prettiest walk in the neighborhood was interdicted forever."[25]

If one of William Howard Taft's distant collateral relatives, the great nineteenth-century American poet and essayist Ralph Waldo Emerson was correct when he wrote, "We estimate a man by how much he remembers," then perhaps the whole human race could be judged by how much it forgets.[26] Not only does F.W. Frost depict in his letters the harsh and, at times, unbearable smells and sights of China during this period, but he also frequently alludes to enchanting glimpses of a once magnificent past. In Peking (now Beijing), Frost documents their trip to the Drum Tower, which he described as "like everything else rapidly going to decay." At the Temple of Agriculture, he says, "you find the same neglect, rank weeds and long grass overgrowing what must have once been magnificent stone-flagged drives and delightful gardens." At the Yellow Temple, he finds, "this place once very beautiful is now in a most dilapidated state, and in this respect the Chinese temples differ mostly from the Japanese."

On their way to the Great Wall, he describes the towns that they passed. "The larger towns had high stone walls and massive gates, and here as well as in Peking were the earmarks of what was once a magnificent highway." Later on, at the Ming Tombs, he states, "But I was impressed here more than anywhere else with the evidences of departed glory. Five broad roads flagged with huge stones are overgrown, and unkempt and handsome marble bridges have fallen down and been washed away leaving only an arch here and there."

What Frost did not know at that time—nor did most Chinese or any other people, for that matter, and what would not be fully discovered until 1937, when Joseph Needham published the first volume of *Science and Civilization*[27]— was the degree to which China had contributed to science, botany, and major cultural advances of humankind. Needham's laboriously assembled seventeen volumes, which marked him as one of the greatest encyclopedists, overflowed with descriptions of China's early inventions and technological developments, including the printing press, explosives, paper, and the suspension bridge.

As Simon Winchester chronicled in *The Man Who Loved China* (2008), a book about Needham's remarkable and idiosyncratic life and discoveries, most people were totally ignorant of the history and pre-history of science and had no idea of the magnitude of Chinese contributions.[28]

A street scene in Peking.

A marble bridge on the way to the Great Wall.

THE EMERGENCE OF THE HAND-HELD CAMERA

The Woods photography albums depict scenes in San Francisco, Honolulu, Japan, the Philippines, and China. Viewed from a historical perspective, some of the photographs define this unique moment in Chinese and U.S. history, which marked the end of the European colonial empires and the dawn of an era of American imperialism. These photographs also represent an early use of photography as a documentary form employing the hand-held camera, which had only recently come on the market. Often featuring spontaneous images that the new cameras made possible, the Woods collection may be as important as the official, frequently staged or ceremonial photographs, taken during portions of the trip by the well-known official photographer, Burr McIntosh. The China images can be considered unusual not only because they furnish documentation of the official U.S. diplomatic trip, but also because they provide a Westerner's perspective through images of people and places, many of which no longer exist.

→ A few of the "camera fiends" on the *S.S. Manchuria*.

Until the appearance of the hand-held Kodak camera in 1888, photography had been a field reserved for professionals. After the second Opium War in 1860, the British and French had gained entry to the interior of China with missionaries, traders, adventurers, and photographers.[29] In crude, makeshift darkrooms, photographs were created through a fragile procedure that included the use of glass negatives and gold for coating the prints. With the introduction in the United States in 1879 of the new dry-plate negative, which allowed for informal and spontaneous "snapshots," and in 1888, of the new lightweight, hand-held camera, photography became a novel and compelling pastime for the average U.S. citizen. As stated by scholar Mary Ison "By 1895 … the price dropped to five dollars, and the taking of photographs became part of the life of the common man."[30]

The difficulties that the early photographers confronted were frequently magnified by the view held by some in China, especially by those who lived in rural areas, that permitting a photograph to be taken would rob the subjects of their souls, and that their ensuing deaths, if not immediate, could take from a month to two years.[31] During the 1905 trip, F.W. Frost documents this kind of superstitious fear when he described the difficulty of taking photos in Guangdong. About the people, he said, "…they do not like to have their picture taken. At the pagoda, I wanted a picture of our party in the chairs, but the coolies dropped the chairs and fled when I pointed my camera, so I did not press the matter." At the Lama Temple, Frost also detailed his encounter with the couple who took care of the temples, and how the woman, who wore "the most wonderful headdress," pleasantly refused to have her photo taken. The prevalence of this superstitious attitude could help explain why Woods did not take more photographs of rural Chinese people.

ROOTS OF AMERICAN EXPANSIONISM

In order to further understand why the *S.S. Manchuria*, peopled with Caucasian, Anglo-Saxon male politicians, some of their wives and servants, army officers, businessmen, and the daughter of the U.S. president felt empowered to cross the ocean to far-flung parts of the globe on what was widely viewed back home as a good-will trip, it is necessary to explore the unprecedented rise of the United States of America in the nineteenth century from a collection of "neo-European settler societies"[32] in a vast wilderness to a position of near-global dominance resulting from a fast-developing industrializing society.

The diplomatic intentions of the 1905 delegation were to assist with the Russo-Japanese peace negotiations; demonstrate accomplishments in the Philippines; shore up the "Open Door" policy in China; advance U.S. trade in Manchuria; and, generally, enhance U.S. competitive standing in the Far East.[33] Under President McKinley, maintaining peace in the Philippines was viewed as a necessity in the struggle to gain a commercial foothold in China.[34] American scholar Michael

Hunt described the forces that drew these Americans from home onto the *S.S. Manchuria* and then to Asia in the following way: "A union of wealth, confidence, and leadership provides the basis for sustained international success, which in turn creates a virtuous cycle, reinforcing confidence, confirming national myths, and giving rise to widely accepted policy codes."[35] At the beginning of the twentieth century, America joined the ongoing imperialist activities already exercised by Britain, Portugal, Spain, France, and the Netherlands.[36]

Among all the dazzling technological developments, discoveries, and shifts in global power alignments that occurred in the late nineteenth and early twentieth centuries, none was greater than the meteoric expansion of the United States.[37] By the end of the nineteenth century, the acceleration of global change created a pervasive sense of destabilization among the most powerful countries. As a result of new technologies such as the telegraph, steamships, railways, and the modern printing press, the global trading and communication systems accelerated the spread of advances and inventions from one continent to another in only a few years.[38] Perhaps, more than any other factor, technological development provided the greatest impetus for America's sudden accession to international dominance.[39] In his book *The American Ascendancy* (2007), Hunt states, "New technologies were a prime source of North Atlantic wealth and power in relation to the rest of the world, an indispensable tool of the emergent nation-state, and the driver behind the relentless modernization of social and economic life."[40]

→ Loading baggage on the *S.S. Manchuria*, San Francisco, California.

A view of the *S.S. Manchuria*, 1905.

One of the main reasons for the 1905 trip on the *S.S. Manchuria*, described in the presses as a "floating palace,"[41] was simply that faster and cheaper travel, with a level of comfort theretofore unknown, suddenly became possible.

Whereas accessibility to travel had before been reserved for the wealthy, by the beginning of the twentieth century burgeoning numbers of middle class were taking advantage of the edification and knowledge of the world associated with exploring distant places.[42]

In only a five-year span after 1879, when Sidney Gilchrist Thomas invented a way to change inexpensive phosphoric ores into steel, eighty-four converters had been built in western and central Europe, and the process had crossed the Atlantic.[43] By 1901, when Andrew Carnegie sold his business to J.P. Morgan's enormous United States Steel Company, Carnegie was at that time manufacturing a larger amount of steel than the combination all of the steel companies of England.[44] Side by side with the development of new technologies during the McKinley era, the rapidly increasing agricultural and industrial output often outpaced demand with disastrous economic results, epitomized by the frequent boom-and-bust cycles.

→ A very extraordinary view of the Steamer *Salazie*, French line.

After providing a theater for showcasing the use of the telegraph, steamship, and train, the Civil War proved their efficacy in streamlining troop movement and modernizing warfare. Specific new technologies for combat included torpedoes, mines, and more accurate and powerful canons.[45] In the late nineteenth century, the arms race made Krupp the biggest European business, an industry built to produce ammunition and armaments by a four-hundred-year-old German dynasty. The war industry, inextricably tangled with nationalism, was virtually impossible to contain.[46] During Reconstruction after the Civil War, the United States was able to take advantage of the many new technological breakthroughs in the exploitation of nearly boundless agricultural land and raw materials. Furthermore, the relative geographic security of the North American continent coupled with general social order contributed to the accelerated pace of industrialization.[47]

From the mid-1800s and after, one of the most shocking results of industrialization was the sharp rise in mental illness in America and the race-based stereotyping of those characterized as insane. In his book *Mad in America* (2003), Robert Whitaker states, "In 1850, the U.S. census counted 15,610 insane in a total population of 21 million, or one out of every 1,345 people. Thirty years later, 91,997 people, in a population of 50 million, were deemed insane, or one out of every 554 people."[48] In thirty years, the population of those in the United States labeled as crazy had doubled. The Anglo-Saxons, who believed that the greatest incidence of insanity plagued the poor, easily identified eugenics as the explanation, and some even recommended that those considered racially weak should be prohibited from breeding.[49]

President Taft and those of his party who sat at his table on the *S.S. Manchuria.*

At the same time, the middle- and upper-class Anglo-Saxons delineated their own category of mental illness called "neurasthenia," first described in 1869 by George M. Beard.[50] With symptoms including alcoholism, stress, uncontrolled activity, and emotional turmoil, neurasthenia became the catch-all prototypical mental diagnosis for the group of nervous Americans who were overeducated, overworked, overwrought, and/or over-refined.[51] According to Beard, even though Europeans seemed to record similar cases, this disease only attacked those Americans with the highest sensibilities. In his view, these hardworking individuals were likely to fall into madness, since the United States lacked the social structures such as titled aristocracy and state churches that existed in Europe to provide a safe haven for those afflicted by the conditions induced by severe individual striving.[52]

In William Howard Taft's family, one of his half-brothers, Peter Rawson Taft, II, who had earned valedictorian in his class at Yale (1867) and who was written up in the newspapers as the best student Yale had graduated up to that time,[53] was diagnosed as neurasthenic. Three months after graduation, he contracted a near-fatal case of typhoid fever, traveled to study in Europe for over a year, became a lawyer, and married Matilda Hulbert, the daughter of a wealthy Cincinnati industrialist. A year after the birth of Hulbert Taft, their only child, Peter was institutionalized at the Cincinnati Sanitarium, Private Hospital for the Insane, with a diagnosis of neurasthenia. During one of the many boom-and-bust depressions of the 1800s, his letters to his father, Alphonso, indicate that he had worked extremely hard to support his family with poor results. In *The Imperial Cruise: A Secret History of Empire and War* [Footnote: (New York, Boston, London: Little, Brown and Company, 20090, 142], James Bradley makes the claim, unsubstantiated by contemporaneous family correspondence or other evidence, that Peter suffered mental collapse as a result of undue "pressure" exerted by his step-mother, Louisa Taft. He also states that Peter died in a sanatorium, which is factually incorrect. In Doris Kearns Goodwin's *The Bully Pulpit: Theodore Roosevelt, William Howard Taft, and the Golden Age of Journalism,*[54] she makes a similarly undocumented assertion that Peter suffered from "nervous exhaustion" because he was trying to meet his father's rigid "expectations." Neither author mentions that Peter Taft contracted a near-fatal typhoid fever infection three years after his graduation from Yale and appears to have suffered for the remainder of his short life from the consequences of that disease and the ill-begotten treatment that he received for it.

In his letters from Germany[55] shortly after his recovery from the acute infection, Peter clearly writes of having severe headaches. For example, in his letter to his father, Alphonso, from Berlin on November 15, 1868, he wrote, "I had expected to remain here until the middle of March, and thence to France. But I have had so much headache during my stay I have concluded to leave

Berlin earlier than I intended. Accordingly, I propose to go to Paris about the first of January…" Also, from Berlin, on November 8, 1868, Peter wrote, "During the past week, I have been driven away from my books, by the headache.[56] It is really quite discouraging to be thus bothered. If these attacks do not cease before next summer, I think I shall make up my mind to go home with you, and try a more decisive course of treatment. If I am going to accomplish anything in this world, the headaches must first be gotten rid of."

Perhaps, as a result of his diagnosis as a neurasthenic and consequent hospitalization, an insurmountable social stigma during that time, his wife divorced him, and at the age of 44, while living as a recluse, he died of tuberculosis. *The Obituary Record of Graduates of Yale University: Deceased during the Academic Year Ending in June, 1890*[57] states that "his health… had never been vigorous since graduation." *The Report of the Trigintennial Meeting with a Biographical and Statistical Record of the Class of 1867, Yale University*[58] adds, "A few months after he graduated Taft had a severe attack of typhoid fever, producing violent delirium, to which serious later results may be traced." His pursuant health and psychological problems such as headaches, poor eyesight, eventual loss of sight in one eye, and irritability could be traced to the effects of the illness, such as brain swelling which sometimes resulted from typhoid fever, or to prescribed medication, usually calomel, a mercury compound, frequently administered in large doses in that era as a treatment.

According to Ishbel Ross, at Peter's funeral, his brother, Harry, recalled the days when Peter was "the sunniest of us all." Ross quotes his brother Horace as stating, "Nothing is stranger than to see what different records men have made from those they were expected to make when we graduated."[59]

Edith Roosevelt, the mother of Theodore Roosevelt, was also diagnosed as neurasthenic.[60] As a child, Roosevelt himself was diagnosed with the dreaded disease, even though he actually suffered from asthma. After bloodletting and other extreme treatments failed to alleviate his symptoms, the family sent Roosevelt, a sickly boy, to Dr. George Beard and his partner Alphonso D. Rockwell. The family doctor, John Metcalfe, recommended Beard.[61] The forces that Beard attributed to neurasthenia seemed to include anything modern— women's intellectual strivings, steamships, the telegraph, weekly magazines, and scientific inventions.[62] Rockwell treated Theodore Roosevelt with electric shocks, which understandably had no effect on his asthma. He determined that Roosevelt was suffering from "the wretchedness of extreme civilization."[63] Beard wrote that neurasthenia was "the price refined upper-class people paid for their evolution into self-controlled and advanced creatures."[64] He pictured Africans, Indians, and Aborigines on the lower slats of the ladder, while the Anglo-Saxons had slogged through barbarism to claw their way up to the higher reaches of "civilization." His views were propounded in his popular book, *American Nervousness: Its Causes and Consequences* (1881). Rockwell would later refine his electric-shock treatments, even creating devices used for electrocutions.[65] Roosevelt's consequent exaltations of masculinity, brotherhood, and heroism, which were perhaps best represented in the victory of the Rough Riders after the War of 1898,[66] but which also permeated his presidency, were possibly partly a reaction to his sickly childhood and early diagnosis as a neurasthenic. As Dalton asserts in her book *Theodore Roosevelt, A Strenuous Life* (2003): "He saw men as knights of the Roosevelt Round Table who, like King Arthur's loyal band, wagered their lives together in battle…"[67] Roosevelt clearly utilized early twentieth-century notions of masculinity in his vision of the necessary civilizing of the "barbaric" cultures.[68] He perhaps best articulated his views on the connection between masculinity and imperialism in his talk "The Strenuous Life," which took place on April 10, 1899, at the Hamilton Club in Chicago:

> The timid man, the lazy man, the man who distrusts his country, the over-civilized man, who has lost the great fighting, masterful virtues, the ignorant man, and the man of dull mind, whose soul is incapable of feeling the mighty lift that thrills "stern men with empires in their brains"—all these, of course, shrink from seeing the nation undertake its new duties; shrink from seeing us build a navy and an army adequate to our needs; shrink from seeing us do our share of the world's work, by bringing order out of chaos in the great, fair tropic islands from which the valor of our soldiers and sailors has driven the Spanish flag.[69]

Although the U.S. debate between imperialists and anti-imperialists had waxed and waned over the years closing the nineteenth century, the quick and almost bloodless winning of the Spanish-American War in 1898 had garnered significant favor within the United States for the expansionist viewpoint. The less popular anti-imperialist group contended that because colonies could not become states, this reality would ultimately threaten republican ideals. Furthermore, anti-imperialists in the U.S. South worried over competition from non-white populations.[70] While Americans did not have a uniform consensus about U.S. imperialism, the conventional wisdom of the day equated an intensified, aggressive international role in controlling remote territories with the promise of achieving social good and accessing previously unexploited resources and sources of untapped revenue.[71]

Despite the relative chronological proximity of the American Revolution, with its hard-fought struggle for independence from Britain, a foreign aggressor state, the sudden birth of the new and somewhat contradictory American imperialistic impulse can be partially explained by the necessity of procuring markets for overproduction of goods, which caused repeated and serious economic depressions.[72] The depressions of the 1870s and 1880s evolved into the crisis of the 1890s and the panic of 1893, which held the country in its grip until 1898.[73] During this last depression, 500 banks and 15,000 businesses failed, and it left 4,000,000 people unemployed.[74] Conservatives and reformers alike were unified in their belief that strong action was required to avert anomie and chaos. In his book *The Tragedy of American Diplomacy* (1959), William Appleman Williams explains, "That an expansionist foreign policy would provide such relief and prevention rapidly became an integral and vital part of all but an infinitesimal segment of the response to the general crisis."[75]

Several events which led to the first Sino-Japanese War (1894-95) alerted Americans to the precarious balance of power in Asia and its possible effect on potential Asian markets.[76] The Manifest Destiny credo, a political ideology, combined religious virtue and social forces to create a rationale for the new American imperialist and the development of his crusader spirit. Josiah Strong, a Congregationalist minister, summarized the tone of the zealous, religiously oriented imperialist. In his view, "America had been hand-picked by the Lord to lead the Anglo-Saxons in transforming the world."[77] A Chinese group visited the United States in the autumn of 1896 with the idea of forming an alliance with a major power that had not yet entered into China with territorial ambitions. The Chinese delegation discussed the possibility of offering railroad concessions, which increased U.S. attention.[78]

As a means of securing markets in China, in December, 1900, President McKinley and Secretary of State John Hay issued the first of two "Open Door Notes," which granted the United States equal access in China to that held by the other great powers. McKinley was concerned about possible exclusion from the enormous market potential of China through formal European territorial partition.[79] Just a year after Hay had turned to William Rockhill, Minister Plenipotentiary to China and, at that time, Roosevelt's foremost China expert, to help create the "Open Door Notes," the Boxer Rebellion erupted.[80] American historian Williams states, "Taken up by President Theodore Roosevelt and his successors, the philosophy and practice of the imperialism that was embodied in the Open Door Notes became the central feature of American foreign policy in the twentieth century."[81] The Open Door concept appeared to be benevolent and idealistic—even protective—toward China, while in actuality the strategy intended for the door to be forced open equally to all the great powers, including the United States.[82] What emerged in America by the turn of the century was a generally accepted image of the country as a "benevolent, progressive policeman."[83]

THE IMPORTANCE OF SEA POWER

While travel to Europe and more exotic places had long been a mainstay of the upper class, with the grand tour featured as part of the education of many wealthy young men, the accessibility, comfort, affordability, speed, and convenience of the new steamers made tourist travel available to increasing numbers of the middle class.[84] Whereas 35,000 journeyed across the Atlantic in 1870, 100,000 tourists were venturing abroad by 1885.[85] By the early twentieth century, the steamship made the transatlantic voyage in a week, twice as fast as during the middle of the nineteenth century. While the costs were reduced from $200 for one-way cabin fare at mid-century to $100 by century's end, the entertainment and culinary amenities were ramped up to mimic luxury hotels.[86] In his article "Travel and World Power," Christopher Endy details motivations for travel:

> As an activity requiring both money and time, going abroad served as a rite of passage into a social elite. Travel bore ritualistic themes that intensified its function as a conduit of higher status. A large part of the so-called art of travel consisted of mastering intricate details on foreign customs and travel etiquette.[87]

Many of the Woods photographs contrast the delicate and exotic indigenous boats of the Philippines and China with the massive, technologically superior warships and marine vessels of Western origin. In his quest for imperialist power, Roosevelt had vested much of his presidency in constructing big ships and building up U.S. sea power.[88] The significant advances in steam-engine technology that occurred before the end of the nineteenth century allowed boats to travel great distances without re-coaling.[89] These technological innovations both enabled and enhanced the imperialistic ventures of the great powers—the 1905 trip, in particular, and American expansionism, in general.

Proponents of U.S. naval development strongly argued for the acquisition of a collection of bases in the Caribbean and Pacific to strengthen the United States for potential confrontation with the major powers such as Germany and Japan.[90] A significant foreign-policy shift that emphasized sea power was heavily influenced by the 1890 publication of the book *The Influence of Sea Power upon History*, written by Alfred Thayer Mahan, a career naval officer, historian, and perhaps one of the most significant figures in shaping American foreign policy during the early twentieth century. Mahan's book, which criticizes America's weak navy, warns that its power would determine the nation's future.[91]

Admiral Train visiting General Corbin on board the steamer, *Logan*, near Chefoo, China.

Not until the 1890s did Americans come to terms with their country as a maritime nation. Before that, they generally believed that the United States was secure. Wind powered their ships, which visited principally friendly ports. Eleven countries had grander navies than the United States.[92] With the development and pervasive deployment of steamships in the 1880s, along with major inventions in technology and advancements in naval engineering, as well as changes in the global balance of power, Mahan conceptualized the need for a revised vision of the U.S. Navy. Because of the steamship's unconditional requirement of coaling stations, Germany and Britain worked to secure colonies around the world, and imperial competition added new destabilization to an already dynamically changing world order.[93]

Between 1890 and 1914, the U.S. ranking among the world's naval powers would rise from twelfth to third. During this period, based on arguments advanced by Mahan and "Mahanians"—such as Theodore Roosevelt, Robert M. La Follette and populist Jerry Simpson—the U.S. Navy reconstituted itself as an offensive rather than defensive force that relied on battleships instead of cruisers.[94] The rationale for this philosophy was succinctly detailed by George W. Baer in his book *One Hundred Years of Sea Power* (1994):

> An argument with Germany and Britain over Samoa, on which stood an American coaling station, revealed that the United States could become entangled in European policies even in the far Pacific. Every island and coastline in the world seemed up for grabs. In the fever of imperialism, isolation was no longer possible, invulnerability no longer taken for granted. The United States and its territorial interests could come under threat by sea. So the Navy rethought its strategy, its force structure and doctrine of operations, and the nature of its service to the nation."[95]

In order to persuade the American public of the necessity for the massive military construction of ships, Mahan had to demonstrate the impending possibility of combat. To accomplish this, he studied and artfully described examples from military history.[96] He pointed out that if the Russians could deploy their Baltic Fleet in the Far East, they, or any other great power, could attack the U.S. Pacific coast if they gained coaling stations in the

Caribbean. Thus, according to Mahan, the protection of the Caribbean (after the construction of an Isthmian canal) would be as critical to U.S. national security as defending the English Channel was to the British.[97]

Mahan believed that in America's past, much of the nation's energy was directed internally toward colonizing the western United States and toward cultivating and populating America's frontiers. He successfully argued that the United States could no longer ignore the sea and would have to look outward beyond her now limited and densely populated continental borders. He proposed that with an adequate navy, the United States could "control" Asian territories such as the Philippines and China because of a perceived lack of resistance, deficiency of power, and degrading conditions that existed in those regions.[98]

○──→ The U.S. warship *Ohio* in Manila.

The 1905 Japanese triumph over the Russian Battle Fleet at Tsushima confirmed for Mahan and his followers that fleet buildup was a necessity.[99] Questions about control over Manchuria were the major cause of the Russo-Japanese War. Progress in naval construction fostered the engineering of the battleship, which was bigger, speedier, and more heavily armed than its predecessors.[100] More ships, which would culminate in Roosevelt's 1907 Atlantic Fleet, required more coaling stations. The major principle of Mahan's strategy could be summed up by "destructiveness was all," or the most accurate and biggest guns in the right places.[101] This principle and the newly constructed bases necessitated the steady construction of more battleships and auxiliaries, including armored cruisers, lighters, scout cruisers, destroyers, colliers, and other support and supply ships.

With the goal of ranking second in naval power worldwide, and mainly in response to fear about potential German encroachment in the Western Hemisphere, the U.S. Navy's General Board advocated building forty-eight battleships with artilleries.[102] The American who undoubtedly had the greatest influence in thrusting the United States onto Asia was Alfred Thayer Mahan.[103] Within eight years, Mahan's book, which was reprinted in fifteen editions, was widely read across the globe. At his death, the American Historical Society applauded him as the scholar who had influenced American political history more than anyone else.[104]

SAN FRANCISCO AND THE CRUISE

At the beginning of the twentieth century, the U.S. Congress enjoyed a recess that spanned three months from the spring to the fall.[105] For many senators and congressmen who did not have other jobs, the prospect of accompanying Secretary Taft on a peace mission to such exotic places must have seemed particularly alluring. According to Taft, because the Philippines government was poor, they were unable to provide for more than "passage money" for the Congressmen, but the remaining costs, including sleeping-car accommodations and meals along the way, were left up to the individual passengers. The official party numbered around fifty people, and the unofficial members, about thirty more, paid their own way.[106] F.W. Frost wrote that his bill from August 13th to September 12th, from beginning the southern cruise, was only $30. He stated, "I think that is the cheapest traveling I will ever do."

Taft and the main group of six of his party set out from the Baltimore and Ohio Station on-board a private car, "the Colonial." Congressman Longworth met them in San Francisco.[107] Soon after their departure, when Secretary of State Hay died, Alice Roosevelt expressed concern that her father would call off the trip.[108] Traveling from Washington, D.C., Alice Roosevelt commemorated the party's arrival in San Francisco on July 4th, the anniversary of U.S. independence, by setting off fireworks from the train platform and taking potshots at telegraph poles with her hand-held revolver.[109] She attended a luncheon at the glamorous Bohemian Club beneath the giant redwood trees.[110] She wiled away the night-time hours as Longworth's apprentice poker player, and some gossiped that she tricked her chaperones to venture out one night from the Palace Hotel to Chinatown.[111] According to Alice, "One evening I escaped my chaperones for a trip to Chinatown, of which I saw only the fringes. At that time a girl had to go on such an expedition very much on the side."[112]

With part of the group on July 7th, Secretary Taft inspected military posts around the San Francisco Bay on the United States tug *Slocum*. That afternoon, he delivered a speech to a "vast audience" in which he expressed his views on the Chinese Exclusion Acts. To avoid offending the Chinese empire with a policy that he assured would not hurt the United States, Taft said, "Keep out the coolies, let in the merchants and students."[113] Because of the intense heat, Alice Roosevelt was forced to leave the open Greek Theater at the University of California where Taft spoke, but she recovered after resting at her hotel. In the evening, both attended a reception given for Secretary Taft and party by Eleanor Martin.[114]

Less than a month before, on June 15th, at the eighty-first commencement of Miami University in Oxford, Ohio, Secretary Taft exhorted an unusually large audience of Americans to treat Chinese fairly with respect to the exclusion laws. He expressed a premonition about a boycott arising in China if the United States didn't change its way of handling Chinese immigration:

> Is it just for the purpose of excluding or preventing per-
> haps 100 Chinese coolies from slipping into this country
> against the law we should subject an equal number of
> Chinese merchants and students of high character to
> an examination of such an inquisitorial, humiliating,
> insulting and physically uncomfortable character as to
> discourage altogether the coming of merchants and stu-
> dents? … One of the great commercial prizes of the
> world is the trade with the four hundred million Chi-
> nese. Ought we to throw away the advantage which we
> have by reason of Chinese natural friendship for us and

continue to enforce an unjustly severe law, and thus create in the Chinese mind a disposition to boycott American trade and drive our merchants from Chinese shores,
simply because we are afraid that we may for the time
lose the approval of certain unreasonable and extremely popular leaders of California and other coast states?
Does the question not answer itself: Is it not the duty of
members of congress and of the executive to disregard
the unreasonable demands of a portion of the community, deeply prejudiced on the subject, in the far west
and insist on extending justice and courtesy to a people
from whom we are deriving and are likely to derive such
immense benefit in the way of international trade?" [115]

After spending four days in San Francisco—a city that would in a mere nine
months be largely destroyed by the famous 1906 earthquake and fire—the Taft
party boarded the *S.S. Manchuria* on July 8th and crossed the Pacific for five days
to a brief stopover in Hawaii, annexed in 1898, and then onward for ten more
days to Yokohama, Japan.[116] U.S. Senator Francis G. Newlands, who traveled
with the 1905 mission and whose wife was one of Alice Roosevelt's chaperones,
had introduced the joint resolution for Hawaii's annexation in the House of
Representatives, and the joint piece of legislation that finally passed the 55th
Congress, House Resolution 259, was called the "Newlands Resolution." After
the explosion of the U.S. Battleship *Maine* and the eruption of the Spanish-
American War, the perceived necessity of establishing a fueling station and naval
base in the mid-Pacific had impelled the drive for the Hawaiian annexation.[117]

With the convergence of groundbreaking developments in photography and
the crucial exigencies of U.S. diplomacy in Asia, the Taft party powered onward,
with more photographers on board than had ever previously accompanied such
a group.[118] One notable emergence from the 1905 voyage is the combination
of odd technologies and forces—the hand-held camera, the idiosyncratic and
original American style of Alice Roosevelt, the genesis of a nationwide media,
and the steamship—all these allowed for the birth of America's first media
darling and the new concept of the American celebrity. In her article "The
First Daughter of the Land," Stacy A. Cordery explains, "Theodore Roosevelt
conquered the presidency, but his daughter gained fame without a career. More
particularly, she was a success at being famous; she was 'known for her well-

knowness.'"[119] In order to provide a more nurturing environment for her children, Taft's wife, Nellie, took them for a vacation in England rather than participate in the adventures of the 1905 mission.[120]

Palace Hotel, San Francisco, California.

On board the *S.S. Manchuria*, the delegation engaged in activities that would seem odd by today's standards—a mock trial; a sheet and pillow-case party; daily sittings for the official photographer, Burr McIntosh; evening betting on the day's run; and fancy-dress balls.[121] In his diary, James A. LeRoy, Taft's political adviser, attested to Taft's love of parties. During the sheet and pillow-case party, the participants reportedly dressed up in bedclothes and cheesecloth masks and danced around the deck.[122] According to F.W. Frost, "If anyone aboard was under the impression when starting that those who make our national laws cannot unbend, he was very soon undeceived for a jollier and more unconventional family party would be hard to find."

Jiu-jitsu, on the *S.S. Manchuria*.

The group also listened to lectures, played bridge games, and engaged in miles of walking around the deck. One of the daily newspaper articles doting on their homegrown princess featured Alice Roosevelt jumping fully dressed into a water-filled canvas tank with Congressman Bourke Cockran following close at her heels. Some reporters inflated their romance by writing erroneously that Nicholas Longworth made the jump.[123] As Henry Pringle put it in his book *The Life and Times of William Howard Taft* (1993), "The *S.S. Manchuria* steaming westward in July, was a congressional ark with Taft as its Noah."[124]

Born on February 12, 1884, Alice Lee Roosevelt had shared only two days in this world with her mother and grandmother, Edith Roosevelt, both of whom shockingly died around the same time as Alice's birth of different ailments in a terrible confluence of totally unanticipated tragedies. First overwhelmed with grief and then saddled with his new marriage to a childhood girlfriend, Theodore Roosevelt never talked to Alice about her mother. Perhaps owing to her own special blend of self-pity and rebelliousness, Alice seemed to delight in angering her father and stepmother and delighting the press with her antics.[125] As she herself stated in her autobiography *Crowded Hours* (1933), "I really liked my Congressional fellow voyagers, yet I think I felt it to be my pleasurable duty to stir them up from time to time."[126]

One of the greatest obsessions of the American press, which documented Roosevelt's every move with painstaking detail, was whether and when Congressman Nicholas Longworth would propose to her. Longworth dined at Secretary Taft's table in the saloon chair next to Alice Roosevelt's.[127] According to Stacy Cordery, he had already proposed before the trip began. In her book *Alice: Alice Roosevelt Longworth, From White House Princess to Washington Power Broker* (2007), Cordery states, "After this June night, Alice felt herself engaged to be married—and he [Nick] must have responded positively, reading between the lines of his letter to her of June 20."[128]

→ A Group on the *S.S. Manchuria*. Miss Roosevelt, Col. Edwards, Nicholas Longworth, Miss McMillan, R.C. Anderson, H.F. Woods.

According to Professor Hong Shen, one of Taft's lengthiest letters to his wife Nellie from the 1905 trip reads like the general prologue of Chaucer's *Canterbury Tales* by rendering a sketch of every pilgrim in the group. In that letter, Taft offered a different assessment of their courtship. He reported that Alice Roosevelt "speaks with great uncertainty as to whether they are to be married or not. If so, she says she will take a year in Europe at any rate to see whether the spell will last. She has not written home on the subject, and she would not say anything or commit herself definitely and ultimately until she had reached home."[129]

This view contradicts an earlier statement to Nellie, written in July, on the same subject. Taft surmised, "Nick and Alice are doubtless engaged, but whether in a Kentucky sense or not I do not know. They occasionally quarrel. Alice enjoys the society of some college boys in the interval, and then they make up."[130] In his letter to Nellie of August 1, 1905, Taft told his wife that Alice had admitted their engagement, but that they planned to test the relationship for a year.[131]

→ The Harbor at Honolulu.

In her memoir, Alice Roosevelt describes their arrival in Honolulu with dreamlike imagery:

> The morning we reached Honolulu, I was
> awakened by the plaintive singing voices and
> musical instruments of the natives who had

come to meet the steamer.... I had never
heard anything like it before and felt as if the
lotus eaters themselves had come to greet us.
My eyes were open and my head was out of
the porthole simultaneously to see the lively
mass of the island of Oahu lying offside in the
early dawn, mountains and valleys in cloudy
green down to the line of the white beach.[132]

In the Harbor, Honolulu.

The American authorities greeted Secretary Taft and his party with a
seventeen-gun salute, and an orchestra belted out numerous songs with "Alice"
in their titles. While part of the group visited Pearl Harbor, another contingent
inspected a sugar plantation.[133] During their day-long adventure in Hawaii,
Alice continued to steal the limelight by antics such as learning the real "pelvis
swinging" rendition of the hula dance rather than the restrained version that
the Hawaiians had prepared for the Taft party.[134] She stole the show at Waikiki
by swimming in the surf and surfboarding in a mohair bathing suit with black

silk stockings, an outfit that so closely edged into the scandalous that Taft had to plead with photographers to refrain from taking photos of the event.[135] Alice Roosevelt, Longworth, and their chaperone managed to swim for so long in the soothing Hawaii surf that they missed the ride back to the *S.S. Manchuria*, which was leaving with the outgoing tide. Sporting a lei around her neck, Alice Roosevelt, along with Nick Longworth and party, ventured forth just in time to catch the ship before it slipped too far out into the ocean. [136]

As Taft himself stated in a letter to Nellie, "After leaving Honolulu, we settled down to regular life. I walked four miles a day every day and altered my diet so as to drink but very little with my meals. I do not think it too much to say that I am in better condition than for some time." In the same letter, Taft rated the trip as the most enjoyable one that he had taken.[137]

ARRIVAL IN JAPAN[138]

On July 25th, the *S.S. Manchuria* docked at Yokohama, Japan, with every building decked out in the Taft party's honor. In the span of two generations, during the Meiji Restoration from 1868, the Japanese had mounted a campaign to Westernize in order to avoid the domination experienced by other Asian countries.[139] Upon the Taft party's arrival, the U.S. Minister to Japan, Lloyd Carpenter Griscom, greeted the passengers, and the Japanese people welcomed them as if they were royalty. They drove through streets decorated with American flags and banners and crowded with cheering citizens. As Alice Roosevelt described it, "They cheered when the American secretary of war went on the balcony to wave goodbye—they cheered the daughter of an American president when she appeared—and then they cheered us all over again."[140]

Secretary Taft and his staff stayed at the Shiba Palace and dined with the Emperor, Alice Roosevelt, Nicholas Longworth, and a small group. Alice, who stayed with Minister Griscom and his wife at the American Legation, was honored with a seat on the Emperor's right. During the trip, the delegation visited the Imperial Gardens, something that no foreigner and very few Japanese had ever done before.[141] In a letter to his brother, Griscom described their unique experience in the following way:

> After the luncheon the Emperor opened up the interior
> Palace Gardens for our inspection. This was the most

remarkable feature of the visit. This is the holy of holies, the one spot in Japan which has never been opened to foreigners before, not even to General Grant or to European Princes and potentates who have been here as the guest of the Emperor. It was the greatest compliment that could possibly have been shown a party of foreigners. The gardens certainly were beautiful and most perfect specimens of Japanese landscape gardens about three hundred and fifty years old.[142]

Japanese children greeting the Taft party.

The Japanese considered Alice to be as royal as a princess, but they were also undoubtedly hopeful of getting a better deal in the upcoming Portsmouth Peace Treaty talks. Alice noted, "No people have ever been treated with greater consideration and kindliness than we were by the Japanese, not only Mr. Taft and myself, but the entire party."[143]

In Japan, Taft conducted negotiations to prepare for the Portsmouth Peace Treaty of 1905 that Roosevelt had planned in order to end the Russo-Japanese War. Roosevelt would bring two Japanese envoys, Kogoro Takahira and Baron Komura, to meet with Russian emissaries at Portsmouth, New Hampshire. For two years, Czarist Russia and Imperial Japan had conducted the war in northeast China and Manchuria. Weakened by the Boxer Rebellion, China could not adequately protect this territory. President Roosevelt's fear of a potential major European war, presented in part by the situation in Asia, significantly contributed to his fervent interest in terminating the Russo-Japanese war.[144] In the Portsmouth peace negotiations in August, 1905, Roosevelt's role in mediating a settlement would win him the 1906 Nobel Peace Prize.[145]

→ View of five story pagoda. Kyoto. July, 1905.

→ The spectacles bridge. Kyoto.

During the now famous July 27th meeting with Count Taro Katsura, the Japanese premier, Taft would make a secret deal with the Japanese, allowing them to dominate Korea in exchange for their promise to stay away from the Philippines. Roosevelt would include the entire Liaotung Peninsula, located in what was historically known as southeast Manchuria, not simply the southern tip of Port Arthur.[146] Count Katsura promised that Japan had no interest in the Philippines. The timing of the trip to Japan indicates that President Roosevelt looked upon it as an opportunity for contributing to the success of his future Portsmouth Peace Treaty negotiations. No instructions from Roosevelt to Taft have been recovered, but the President did arrange for the meeting to take place.[147] When Roosevelt read the memo about the Secretary's conversation with Count Katsura, he cabled Taft to tell him that he agreed with "every word" that Taft had negotiated.[148] Taft believed this agreement to be a logical result of the war, a solution that would contribute to a balance of power in Asia.[149] Roosevelt gave the go-ahead for the agreement without seeking the assent of or consultation with Congress, the State Department, or his own cabinet.[150] The Taft-Katsura Agreement did not become a matter of public record for twenty years.

Traveling from Tokyo to Kyoto, the Taft party enjoyed the Cherry Blossom Festival performed out of season in their honor. When Nellie Taft subsequently became First Lady, she would play an influential role in receiving the cherry trees as a gift from the Japanese and planting them in Washington.[151] As assessed by F.W. Frost, "this week's visit to Japan was a grand fete from start to finish, the Japanese people outdoing themselves in courtesy and hospitality to such an extent, it is said that the celebrations in honor of Secretary Taft and his distinguished fellow travelers were greater even than those for General Grant or any of the heroes of the present."

THE PHILIPPINES

When the group reached Manila, they were met by Governor Luke Wright with whom they stayed at the Malacañan Palace, where Taft had previously lived with his own family when he was the first civil governor of the Philippines. The Filipinos held a huge parade in honor of the visitors, and 10,000 people went by the reviewing stand.[152] At a reception that Governor Wright hosted at the Malacañan Palace, Taft reportedly shook 3,000 hands. According to *The New York Times*, Spanish residents said "the reception surpassed any in the previous history of Manila." Filipino women had spent three months making a gown that was given to Alice Roosevelt to wear at a ball attended by the Taft party before they left Manila. *The New York Times* (August 13, 1905) described the ball as "the most elaborate affair in the city's history."[153] The same article extolled the possibilities of amending the "Cooper Bill" to provide for free trade in the Philippines in lieu of the proposed twenty-five percent reduction of the Dingley rates.[154]

After attending celebrations and tours for a week, the Taft group traveled to Jolo, where they met the Sultan of Sulu and watched games of the Moro people, a Muslim ethnic group. The festivities included a "field day of sports"—sham battles, bullfights, native dances, and a military ball attended by the Sultan.[155] A stunning crowd of twenty thousand Moros from different provinces gathered to celebrate the arrival of the Taft party.[156] The ball at the Army and Navy Club was reported to be the most brilliant in Jolo history.[157] Secretary Taft was described as light on his feet as he danced the rigadoon.[158] In Alice Roosevelt's depiction of the Moro festivities, she said the occasion resembled a "comic opera,"[159] in which she and the Taft party met the "… Sultan and the other Moro chieftains, wiry savage looking little Malays, [who] were in their best costumes."[160] Alice wore a bright red linen dress with matching parasol. She presented the Moros as a passive people and recalled receiving multiple gifts, including "a loose pearl or two," a "Moro Costume," and "a pearl ring"[161] from the Sultan. These otherwise intimidating and threatening groups of Moros were viewed by Alice Roosevelt as benign. Repelled by what she described as "long-drawn" and dull banquets, she seemed more interested in gifts of jewelry than in the event itself.[162] *The New York Times* (August 18, 1905) reported erroneously that the Sultan had asked her to marry him.[163] The same article noted that Congressman Longworth had rescued a newspaperman who was stricken by cramps and almost carried out with the tide. Risking his own life, Longworth jumped in and hauled Frederick O'Brien, editor of *The Cable News*, back from certain death by drowning.

→ The *S.S. Manchuria* at the Harbor of Manila.

In a tragic turn, during March, 1906, only seven months after these welcoming celebratory festivities, the Jolo Muslims would launch the bloody Battle of the Clouds against American soldiers. The Moros were armed with the same kind of simple swords and weapons that Woods photographed. They believed that the efforts of the United States to "civilize" them by such measures as enrolling the Moro children in schools, blazing trails, taking a census, and imposing taxes would threaten their religious and social fabric. According to David S. Woolman, a Manila-based writer in the Philippines, "Yet as they [the Americans] installed telegraph lines and introduced health programs and medicine, the Moros reacted with increased fear that their children would learn English and subtly become Christianized."[164]

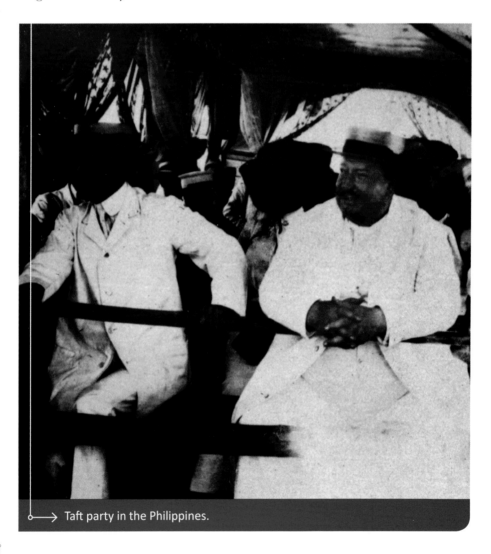

Taft party in the Philippines.

Secretary Taft shaking hands with a Moro Chieftan.

→ Jolo. Moros exhibiting their skill with native spears.

During the Battle of the Clouds, fought primarily in an extinct volcano, the U.S. military would massacre between six hundred and one thousand Moros, many of whom turned out to be women disguised as men.[165] Armed with superior weaponry such as "breech-loading, bolt-action Kraig-Jorgensen rifles," the American military bombarded and the subsequent pursued the Moros into the crater of the volcano, Bud Dajo. These actions resulted in victory with only twenty-one Americans killed. However, the news of the deadly battle roused significant criticism within the United States when the brutal descriptions of the U.S. military tactics reached home.[166] With a greater number of casualties than any other battle in the Philippines for some time, Taft contended that General Wood was there by accident. Speculating that the battle was especially interesting to members of the House who were on the 1905 mission to the Philippines the summer before, *The New York Times* (March 10, 1906) extensively quoted Representative Longworth on the battle:

> I remember the little island very well indeed. We were all over it. It was there that the Sultan of Sulu enter-tained us with an exhibition of native sports, including buffalo fights. The inhabitants of the island are en-tirely uncivilized being Mohammedans and religious

fanatics of the most pronounced types. They have no
military organization and their fights are all inspired
by religious beliefs.[167]

Although he held steadfast to his viewpoint that they were not yet prepared
for independence, Taft had promised the Filipino people that their welfare
would be one of his primary concerns as U.S. secretary of war.[168] He pressed
his case against General Douglas MacArthur to end total military rule and to
establish civilian authority. During his term as the first civil governor (1901-04),
Taft had brought notable advances to the Philippines. Early in his governorship,
he attempted to assemble an all-Filipino congress. In addition, schools were
constructed and opened, harbors and highways were expanded, sanitation was
established, fairer taxes were levied, and civil graft was reduced.[169] However,
the inability to achieve broad and lasting social and economic reforms, and the
brutal suppression of the Filipino rebellions that spanned the entirety of the first
decade of America's occupation, had an adverse impact on U.S. rule. The armed
Filipino insurgency had battled American forces for well over a year before Taft's
governorship in a bloody struggle that included the destruction of villages and
the gunning down of civilians. The insurgency continued throughout this era.[170]
Taft's 1905 stopover in the Philippines was primarily to show an increasingly
dubious American public that the McKinley-Roosevelt-Taft administrative
colonial policies were working to U.S. advantage.[171]

VIEWS ON RACE AT THE TURN OF THE TWENTIETH CENTURY

Americans generally understood the proposed economic benefits of
prolonged U.S. involvement in Asia. Many also believed in generalized concepts
of Anglo-Saxon supremacy, and in the alleged intellectual and physical deficits
of the Asians, often referred to as "Orientals," and sometimes as "the Mongolian
race."[172] Even though they were staunch believers in democracy, the governing
elites in America assumed the unconditional superiority of their Anglo-Saxon
heritage.[173] Conditions within the United States, including the arrival of large
numbers of Chinese immigrants and the ensuing Chinese Exclusion Acts, also
lent a hand in changing the American public's conception of Asian cultures.
In the decade of 1900-10, the Chinese population in the United States had
doubled—the largest increase to date—and this significant change, coupled

with the inability of Asian immigrants to easily blend into the population, also contributed to the negative reaction among many native U.S. citizens—especially on the West Coast, where large numbers of Chinese, derogatorily called "coolies," had been imported, sometimes against their will, to help build the railroads.[174]

Theodore Roosevelt, one of the greatest proponents of Anglo-Saxon virtue and superiority, served as assistant secretary of war, vice president under McKinley, and U.S. president after McKinley's assassination. Roosevelt delineated the country's "duty towards the people living in barbarism to see that they are freed from their chains, and we can free them only by destroying barbarism itself."[175] The underdeveloped countries were viewed as needing America's helping hand to create their greater receptivity for trade, industrialization, and Western views of prosperity.[176]

In the late nineteenth and early twentieth centuries, perceived inequalities between populations of different racial and ethnic backgrounds were explained by disparity in biological and cultural evolution.[177] Through the study of anthropology, academics created new pseudo-sciences to explain the uneven development of societies in underdeveloped countries. Such theories as craniometry and eugenics,[178] developed to encourage offspring from the supposed "best and the brightest," used skull shape and IQ to promulgate theories of Anglo-Saxon superiority, restrict immigration, and substantiate racist viewpoints.[179] Established in 1888 by Gardiner Greene Hubbard, the National Geographic Society provided a more positive construct for racial stereotyping by devoting a major segment of its images to third-world people and culture and the non-Western world. From 1893 to 1905, a significant proliferation of mass circulation magazines such as *Literary Digest*, *Leslie's*, *Harper's*, *Illustrated Weekly*, *The Review of Reviews*, *Cosmopolitan*, and *McClure's* mixed politics with cultural and society columns.[180] By 1905, monthly magazines had taken hold as a constant cultural experience for the U.S. population.[181]

As opposed to the negative social Darwinism of the eugenics movement, the National Geographic Society proposed a more positive picture of the triumph of rationality over primitivism and instinct. The photograph was viewed as evidence, a reality, rather than metaphor, and a view of how far the Western world had come in contrast to the images depicted in the photographs of primitive peoples. In 1905, when the *National Geographic* for the first time published eleven full pages of photographs without text, the membership shot up from 3,400 to 11,000.[182] In their book *Reading National Geographic* (1993), Catherine A. Lutz and Jane L. Collins describe the manner in which the magazine helped frame the America "civilizing" discourse:

If the sharp focus of conventional framing of *Geographic* photographs marked them as "records," it was their replication of popular understandings of the third world that made them seem neutral in their presentations and gave them the comforting feel of "commonsense" realities captured on film. In this way, the mass media's images "became mirrors, serving to reflect Americans' feelings rather than windows to the complex, dynamic realities of foreign societies" (Guimond 1988:68).[183]

Medical inspection of steerage passengers.

During the decades when the Chinese and other Asians were often unpopular in America, "Orientals" were frequently characterized by the U.S. press as decadent and spineless, dangerous, somnolent, fueled by rage, cunning, conniving, and oblivious to the freedoms permitted by democratic institutions.[184] There were also different characteristics assigned to specific groups of Asians.[185] Roosevelt considered the Chinese to be disobedient, frail, and passive, while the Filipinos were characterized as embodying "the black chaos of savagery and barbarism."[186]

In Roosevelt's eyes, the Japanese were the Asians with the most dignity; and, based on portrayal by the popular media, many Americans may have agreed. They were impressed with Japan's military prowess, specifically with that country's easy military victories over the Chinese in the 1890s and, then, over the Russians in the 1904–05 Russo-Japanese War. In essence, the United States admired the Japanese because of their intimidating and warrior-like status. This respect may have derived partly from the potential danger that Japan posed to U.S. commercial and colonial interests in Asia.[187] Although Americans had conflicting views about Asians, they sometimes felt an overall paternal obligation to protect them—which potentially included punishing them and educating them.[188]

→ F.W. Frost and Y. Okita, guide. Kyoto, Japan.

As American historian Henry Pringle summarized it, "Roosevelt and Taft were to be excessively partial to Japan in the years between 1905 and 1908. They were even to view with complacency the probable domination of China by the Nipponese."[189] In the Frost letters, elements of accepted racist attitudes of that day are sometimes evident in descriptions such as the interaction of Chinese people and Sikhs brought by the British from India to serve as guards. He admonished, "They all carry heavy canes and use them freely on over-zealous coolies with the result that a Chinaman dare not cheat or lay a hand on a white man if there is a chance of being found out." Soon afterward, Frost espoused the commonly held view of the unreliability of Chinese. "Somebody started an alarm about Chinese unreliability by saying it was a bad sign that although the Viceroy had invited the party to dine, he would not be present himself saying that he was sick. It was later found to be true that he was very ill."

Moro women and children. Note the musical instrument.

The Philippines were increasingly viewed by many American politicians and policymakers as the "insular stepping stones to the Chinese pot of gold" and as a "way station" into the greater markets of Asia.[190] While many advocates emphasized positive forecasts of the U.S. occupation of the Philippines, the arguments that propagated this myth were fatally flawed. In reality, during the first decades of the 1900s, there was little or no money to be made in China.[191] China's profitability and attractiveness had declined significantly in the second half of the nineteenth century; in fact, during the late 1890s, China absorbed a meager two percent of America's exports. Even with these known facts concerning China's actual economic significance, her large population excited U.S. economists, businessmen, and investors for the potential of what seemed like limitless trade. Fundamental problems with the notion of endless markets included China's apparent disinclination to industrialize in the near future. This insecurity was complicated by the fact that China's already weak Qing government failed to establish and foster a uniform standard of living or a middle class that could absorb large amounts of U.S. goods and capital.[192]

On the economic and commercial fronts, the Philippines, and, more specifically, Manila failed to become the hub for trade with China that many pro-expansionists predicted would result from American occupation. In 1905, this was further complicated by the Chinese embargo of American goods.[193] The new-mercantilist hope that colonies like the Philippines could create markets for America's excess raw materials and export industries went unrealized. As Emily Rosenberg explained in her book, *Spreading the American Dream* (1982), "China seemed in imminent danger of being closed off to Americans."[194] Groups of businessmen, industrialists, government officials, scholars, and even farmers sincerely believed that having the Philippines as an American possession would create a potential hub for trade with the Chinese.[195]

BOXER REBELLION

Since the 1890s, opposing the very development in China that the United States had hoped to promote, the broad-based Boxers had pitted themselves against foreigners, Christians, their missionaries, and even the Qing Dynasty. By 1894, with 2,000 foreign missionaries claiming 800,000 Christian converts, the missionary movement assisted with positive developments in areas such as women's health and education, but they also created momentous disruption by forcing Western mores on traditional Chinese society.[196] The Righteous Harmony Movement, as it was known in China, proposed that strict adherence to time-honored Chinese beliefs would invest followers with a preternatural ability to expel outsiders, and that those who wore magic shirts would be immune to foreign bullets.[197] The Boxers believed that the magnitude of their magic could be measured by the purity of their belief in traditional ways.[198]

During 1900 in the northern provinces of Shandong and Hebei, the Boxers rebelled against Christian missionaries and converts who took advantage of foreign military administrators to prevail in property disagreements, to interfere with religious practices and folk festivals, and to unfairly influence Qing officials.[199] During this period, opium, introduced by the British, caused the addiction of huge numbers of Chinese, creating significant additional social disruption. Historian Jonathan Spence has estimated that by 1900, fifteen out of the forty million Chinese users of opium were addicted. In the book *China: A New History* (2006), John King Fairbank stated: "This meant that for every Chinese converted to Christianity there were some 15 addicted to opium."[200]

Combining their forces after killing many missionaries and converts, the Boxers traveled to Peking where they surrounded the foreign legations and initiated the famous siege.[201] While some Qing government officials did not agree with the Boxers, other more reactionary members enlisted them into local government militias.[202] In a portentous move, the powerful Empress Cixi threw her lot with the Boxers when she exhorted them to help her dynasty drive away the "foreign devils." In order to ensure that the Europeans and Japanese did not take all Chinese territory as payment for the Boxer attacks, Secretary Hay published the second *Open Door Notes* (1900), confirming American interests in China.[203]

Beginning in late May, 1900, the Boxers massacred Chinese Christians and destroyed telegraph lines, churches, and railroad stations on the road to Peking.[204] When they reached Peking (Beijing), the battle lines changed. As Max Boot stated in *Savage Wars of Peace* (2002), "What had started as an internal rebellion in China now morphed into a war pitting China against the combined might of the West plus Japan."[205] The major involvement of the U.S. military in defending the American Legation in Peking was facilitated by the fortuitous presence and relatively easy diversion of a large number of U.S. military representatives already in the Philippines to fight the Filipino insurgency. Many factors also contributed to the decision-making of these U.S. military stationed overseas, including the relative isolation of U.S. military representatives, who were cut off from regular communication channels during the siege, and the distance between Washington, D.C., and North China, which prevented President McKinley and Secretary Hay from participating in some important policy decisions.[206] McKinley transferred approximately 4,000 U.S. soldiers to join troops representing other foreign powers to battle their way to Beijing.[207] Many Boxers and foreigners perished during the violence of the siege. Empress Cixi escaped with her court to Shaanxi where she resided in forced exile from the five-hundred-year Manchu home, the Forbidden City, until her return in 1902.[208]

During the Boxer siege of the foreign legations, which would last for forty-five days, the participation of the U.S. Marine Corps and Navy in defending the

American Legation in Beijing is well documented, and several of the Woods and Frost photographs show the aftermath of the conflict.[209] For instance, "Lest We Forget," is photographed on the outside wall of the British Legation, an inscription ordered by Sir Claude MacDonald after the siege. The wall is also ruptured by shot and shell. Sir Claude was the British Minister who in a desperate telegram dated June 19, 1900, to Vice Admiral Sir Edward Seymour in Tientsin, described the situation in Beijing as "extremely grave." He wrote, "Unless arrangements are made for immediate advance to Peking, it will be too late."[210] He feared an immediate assault from the Boxers.

The words and marks of shot and shell left on the Wall of English Legation tell the story of the Siege of 1900.

In his letters, Francis W. Frost describes the von Ketteler Memorial Arch, which the Qing government was forced to build in order to meet the requirements of one of the articles of the treaty that constituted the Boxer Protocols. One photograph is an image of the arch with a number of Chinese and Americans gathered in front. In the Boxer Protocol, among other provisions, the Qing government was required to construct monuments memorializing the more than two hundred Western deaths.[211] During the siege, at 10 a.m. on June 20th, to argue for more time, the impulsive Baron Clemens von Ketteler had set out smoking a cigar and reading a book in a sedan chair carried by "coolies." With no German marines along to serve as guards, he traveled only with an interpreter and servants who were transported in a different sedan chair. Von Ketteler refused to recognize the fact that he was targeted by the Boxers after he had flogged one whom he had encountered in the Legation Quarter.[212] Just minutes after his departure, von Ketteler was shot in the back of the head by Field Force imperial soldiers. His interpreter was also wounded, but managed to make it back to the Legation Quarter.

Monument in front of the English Legation.

After the Western forces took Beijing, the Germans identified the Chinese army corporal En Hai as the mastermind of von Ketteler's death and decapitated the corporal on the spot where the German had been killed. En Hai claimed to have followed orders from superiors.[213] In his letters, Frost also noted other depredations resulting from the violence associated with the siege. He remarked that the dilapidated state of "so many temples and buildings in and around Beijing is due to the occupation of the armies in 1900." During their tour of the Forbidden City, Frost also noted that after Boxer-related fires had destroyed many buildings in 1900, a number had been newly constructed.

→ The Von Ketteler Memorial Arch in Peking.

Within the relatively small area of the eighty-five-acre compound that comprised the foreign legation quarters and housed representatives from eleven countries, over 900 Europeans were crammed, with 158 women and children in addition to 3,000 Chinese Christians. Thousands of additional Chinese Catholics took shelter at the Peitang Cathedral, just outside the legation quarters.[214] During the siege, the Chinese Christians endured the harshest suffering as a result of the Europeans hoarding food. As American historian Max Boot states, "By the end of the siege, the starving Christian converts were reduced to eating tree bark and leaves while the Europeans still enjoyed free-flowing champagne."[215]

In the last days of the siege, only 408 foreign soldiers and 125 male volunteers with minimal weapons defended the foreign legations, and they faced thousands of attackers. The Chinese turned to fire as a weapon to smoke out the defendants. They set fire to the Italian, Belgian, French, Austrian, and Dutch Legations. On June 23rd they also set fire to the Hanlin Library, which held the leading collection of ancient Confucian texts. Those Chinese who attempted to save the invaluable works met with little success. Many historians have wondered why the Chinese were unable to rout out the foreigners even though they came so close, and the following are two theories for the ultimate loss: (1) the mandarins fighting for the Empress Cixi were less motivated to kill foreigners than the Boxers, who did not participate in the Peking onslaught against the legations; (2) the Chinese did not use the most advanced Krupp artillery which would have demolished the legation quarters in short order.[216] As described by Boot, "This ambivalence on the part of the attackers gave much of the siege a stilted, unreal feel, akin to a Peking opera performance. But if the Chinese soldiers were simply playing with the legations, as a cat does with a mouse, it was nevertheless a dangerous game for all concerned."[217]

While the Christians and their converts suffered mightily in Peking, some met even worse fates in the countryside of north China where the Boxers massacred in excess of two hundred people. On June 4th in Chihli, near Peking, many families were burned alive. In a horrifying account, Boot states, "When one young woman escaped from the flames, her belly was cut open with a sword by the Boxers. One could hear the sound of her skin separating from bones. Several Boxers grabbed the woman by the thighs and arms and threw her back into the flames."[218] Although some Christian missionaries and converts paid with their lives or livelihood in compensation for their disruptive influence in China, they had provided cultural incentives for expanding Chinese educational opportunities through creating schools and universities, and they assisted in advances in health and women's rights. In the 1890s, more than 500 Christian missionaries had enrolled around 17,000 students in their schools.[219]

The number of Chinese missionaries had doubled between 1890 and 1905.[220] President Roosevelt, followed by Presidents Taft and Wilson, recognized that the cultural influence of the missionaries could potentially delimit Japan's influence in China.[221] When they were joined by Chinese nationalist reformers, one of the Christian missionaries' most enduring influences was in the education of women and girls. They assisted in eliminating women's foot-binding through education and publishing articles in newsletters with graphic illustrations. [222] In 1904, the Empress Dowager issued an imperial edict against foot-binding. As Jane Hunter put it in her book *The Gospel of Gentility* (1984), "The preeminence of missionary institutions in the early education of Chinese women is claimed by friends of the mission enterprise and acknowledged by its critics."[223]

Among F.W. Frost's many observations about the Boxer Rebellion and its aftermath, which are interspersed throughout his letters, he notes that much of the construction around the foreign legations involved taking precautions so that a similar debacle could be prevented. He noted that many of the most valuable treasures were "looted" by the Allied armies during the rebellion. He attributed the desecrated state of temples and buildings in and around Beijing to the occupation of the armies of 1900. In his description of visiting the Winter Palace in the Forbidden City, he observed that many of the buildings were new, since the fires of 1900 had annihilated a large section of the palace.

BOXER PROTOCOLS AND INDEMNITY

Upon her return to the Forbidden City in 1902, in keeping with one component of the Boxer Protocols, the Empress Dowager was forced to pay an indemnity of fines in the equivalent of 450 million ounces of silver during the next forty years, an amount that turned out to be far in excess of the actual cost to repair damages incurred during the siege. In fact, the Qing annual income was thought to be around 250 million taels.[224] In his book *The Search for Modern China* (1950), Jonathan Spence estimated, "The Chinese were to pay the indemnity in gold, on an ascending scale, with 4 percent interest charges, until the debt was amortized on December 31, 1940. With all interest charges factored in, total Chinese payments over the thirty-nine-year period would amount to almost one billion taels (precisely 982,238,150),"[225] which roughly equals $30 billion 2014 U.S. dollars.

Other elements of the Boxer Protocols included the execution of Qing supporters and officials such as von Ketteler's alleged assailant, En Hai. The Protocols prohibited Confucian examinations for five years in localities that were allied with the Boxers, an act that had far-reaching consequences for Chinese society by liberating avenues to a multitude of careers as well as opportunities for study in Japan, Europe, and the United States.[226] Another part of the protocol agreement involved the forced construction of monuments such as the previously mentioned von Ketteler Arch to honor the more than two hundred Westerners who perished during the ordeal. For two years, all importation of arms into China was banned. The protection of the legation quarters with foreign guards and weaponry was required into the foreseeable future. [227]

In 1901, Secretary of State John Hay and Edwin H. Conger had demanded the Boxer Protocol remission requirement of $25,000,000.[228] Hay was concerned about balancing the remission so that it fell on the thin line between what the Chinese government could conceivably pay while also permitting the U.S. government to get its fair share of the indemnity. At the same time, the U.S. recommended that other powers scale down their demands.[229] Even though Edwin H. Conger, Minister to China, and William W. Rockhill, then Minister-designate to China, immediately questioned Hay on the wisdom of requesting almost twice the funds required to pay for American claims from the siege, Hay rejected their questions. In his article "The American Remission of the Boxer Indemnity," Michael Hunt stated, "By making his demand, which he described as 'already reasonable, twice real claims,' Hay created for himself a token to use in bargaining with the other powers over the Boxer settlement. But when he failed to effect a bargain, this avowed friend of China left the Chinese holding the debt."[230]

The truth of the matter was that President McKinley had an elephantine indemnity surplus on his hands, and the $330,000,000 total Chinese debt placed the Qing dynasty in dire straits with respect to its own needs for the country's rehabilitation and development. With over fifty percent of its income accruing to the foreigners, the already beleaguered Qing Court found itself incapable of implementing badly needed reforms and reconstruction.[231] After the United States levied the excessive indemnity remission, Roosevelt and his representatives took part in a battery of negotiations with the Chinese from 1905 to 1909 to determine the best utilization of the excess funds. The negotiations were slowed by the eruption of the 1905 Chinese boycott of American goods, the massacre of American missionaries at Liechow in Kwantung, and the Chinese government's reacquisition of the American China Development Company's contract to pay for and construct the Canton-Hankow Railway. Infuriated with each of these actions, Roosevelt, for a time, halted progress from taking place.[232] The first remission of the Boxer indemnity totaled $11,000,000, which added up to more than two-fifths of the entire amount China owed to the United States. Those funds were ultimately utilized to educate Chinese boys in America and to establish

Tsing Hua University in Beijing. When the American claims were finalized, the United States would return a second remission in 1924 to the China Foundation, a Chinese-American committee created to promote education and culture.[233]

From the first negotiation session between Liang Ch'eng, the Chinese Minister, and Minister Rockhill, the Chinese expressed their desire to receive the indemnity without American interference. While they believed that they had the right to use the funds as they saw fit without prior review by the U.S. government, Roosevelt announced that they would require a full disclosure of its use before the remission would be returned, and he affirmed U.S. interest in directing the funds for educational purposes.[234] In later discussions, Liang said that in his view the most necessary use of the indemnity would be for mining and railway development, a major portion of which would undoubtedly be devoted to Manchuria, a critical area during this time.[235] Yuan Shikai, the Commissioner of Northern Ports who served in Tientsin, attempted to satisfy American demands by suggesting that profits from such activities could be employed for educational purposes. Because foreigners such as E.H. Harriman, a railroad magnate from the United States, and many others were already vying for railroad rights in Manchuria, Liang's interest in rights-recovery met with strong resistance. Yuan Shikai also wanted to use the funds for some "self-strengthening" projects.[236]

⚬⟶ View from a city gate near the U.S. Legation.

In a memorandum to President Roosevelt dated March 23, 1905, Jeremiah Jenks of Cornell University had noted that the private claims against the Chinese indemnity added up to around $2,000,000. Jenks had been appointed to a commission, along with Hugh H. Hanna and Charles A. Conant, to draw up tentative plans for a gold-exchange standard for China. Jenks asserted that since all the U.S. claims had already been paid, the entire amount received afterward would not be subject to any monetary requirement.[237] He requested that the United States use most of the Chinese indemnity fund for the next twenty years for the establishment of a gold reserve for China, and he included a detailed study for his plan, which was never adopted.[238]

With respect to the education of promising young Chinese boys and the exchange of professors between China and the United States, Jenks argued that the indemnity could be employed to lower the cost, which had served as a preventive in facilitating those interchanges. Jenks suggested establishing as many as a thousand scholarships of $500 each, which could be paid for a period of twenty-five years. He also added that the United States should pay $2,500 toward the salary of ten American professors, who could teach history and economics in different educational institutions in China, and that the Chinese government could offer the same to their professors in the United States. [239]

According to Jenks, the principal advantage of this would be "political," and also for the implementation of a gold standard.[240] In an earlier memo, he emphasized that a number of influential Chinese had requested the use of funds for international study, and that 400 Chinese students were then currently studying in Belgium, but that Chinese students were deterred from studying in America because of undue cost. Jenks stated that he was sure that the Belgian government would have offered "special concessions" to attract the students.[241]

On July 1, 1905, Jenks had sent a letter to Secretary Taft at the Palace Hotel, just at the beginning of the 1905 mission. He reiterated to Taft his position on the use of the indemnity for the education of students and for the establishment of their monetary system, "or that at any rate such a request should be made of China." In this letter, Jenks recommended that the educational features, which he believed would be more popular than the proposals for monetary reform in China, should be pushed more to the foreground than they were in his memos and letter. He also speculated about the attitude of the Chinese toward such a plan and remarked that a few reactionaries in power were afraid of foreigners, and that some were corrupt, but he thought that "there are a number who are favorably disposed who are influential, and who can from time to time make their influence powerfully felt."[242]

F.W. Frost commented on the money changers in Guangdong and expressed frustration about the lack of standardization. One of his letters contained the following comment:

> The worst of traveling in China is the money question. The currency changes in nearly every town, and you can't use Canton money in Peking or Peking money in Shanghai, and so you lose a little every time you move, so you have to figure as nearly as possible how much you will need in each place …. There are many counterfeits about, and the Chinese when getting money at a bank test every piece spending an hour or more over a small cartload of it. As for "cash," the little brass things with holes in them, they are carried on long strings, and in Peking, I saw a whole cart full of them going through the street.

In a letter from the editor's office of *The Sun*, dated September 22, 1905, to President Roosevelt, Editor Franklin Matthews recalls discussing the indemnity with a fellow passenger, Dr. Tong, who told Matthews that all progressive Chinese privately hoped the indemnity would not be returned to Empress Cixi, whose court would simply squander the funds.[243] For his part, Rockhill took on the responsibility of selling the indemnity's funds for education, and he proceeded to obtain a formal commitment from the Chinese government. U.S. Secretary of State Elihu Root gave the proposed education plan, explicated by Jenks and presented by Rockhill, his full support. As historian Michael Hunt described the situation:

> Rockhill felt his program would benefit China and the United States. In his view, China needed nothing less than reform from the bottom up if she were to survive as an independent state. Education "on modern lines" was an instrument well suited to the task. The United States stood to gain, too. Education would promote political stability and commercial progress, thus making China a sounder and richer trading partner. At the same time the rise of American education leaders in Peking would give the United States unprecedented influence.[244]

Other groups of strong advocates for the remission for education proposals included Christian missionaries and educators. Arthur H. Smith, a China expert and dean of American missionary experts, became a strong champion of the cause and lobbied Roosevelt for funds for Chinese students to study in America and for study in American schools in China.[245]

A street scene in Peking.

The Boxer Rebellion erupted into a war of the Chinese against foreign forces on Chinese soil, and the fact that the Chinese lost the struggle added one more humiliation to a list that would become unbearable and pave the way for the new populist movement. While most Americans of the time believed that the remission segment of the indemnity for the education of Chinese boys and for Christian schools in China demonstrated altruism and the beneficence of the United States, some Chinese viewed the scheme as a way of exploiting and controlling China.[246] Michael Hunt explains the dichotomy in this way: "The final resolution of the issues, generally along the lines advocated by American leaders, reflected not so much American generosity and Chinese gratitude as this obvious disparity in bargaining strengths."[247] Rockhill, Smith, Jenks, Root, and many others espoused their belief in education as a progressive means of "civilizing" the Chinese into the modern world order and remaking them as better trading partners. This plan was actually a recycling of one originally created by S. Wells Williams a generation earlier. Just as Taft viewed the Filipinos as a people incapable of governing themselves, so Roosevelt imagined the Chinese as feeble and lacking sufficient national pride.[248]

This perspective could also describe subsequent U.S. foreign policy. For example, Woodrow Wilson explained that he was making the world safe for democracy to rationalize his brand of expansionism. According to his *New York Times* obituary (July 7, 2009), Robert S. McNamara, Secretary of Defense under President John F. Kennedy, would pose the question almost a century later: "What makes it immoral if you lose and not immoral if you win?"[249] Despite all the rationalizations that the Americans created for keeping the Boxer indemnity and only returning the ill-gotten gains under their own terms and despite all the idealistic, progressive tendencies that the education plan represented, they were able to mold the terms of the remission according to their own volition solely because they were among the dominant powers that had defeated the Boxers and the Qing Dynasty.

BACKGROUND TO 1905 CHINESE BOYCOTT OF AMERICAN GOODS

Five years after the Boxer Rebellion and during the ongoing indemnity negotiations, the Chinese were engaged in an active and powerful transnational embargo of American goods. Students, city residents, and merchants in China were horrified by the discriminatory immigration laws and appalling treatment of Chinese in the United States. Long-standing resentment erupted, with anti-American demonstrations in China.[250] The Chinese boycott movement was partly fueled by the debilitating defeats of the Sino-Japanese War, the Opium Wars, the Boxer Rebellion, and foreign occupations.[251] In the United States, the repressive modifications to the status of immigrant Chinese represented in the Exclusion Act of 1902 triggered the boycott as the laws were expanded to more fully involve the upper echelons of Chinese society, including merchants and students.[252] In his book *In Search of Justice* (2001), Guanhua Wang states, "The cause of the Chinese in the United States took on enormous significance because their fate was perceived to be related to that of millions of other Chinese abroad."[253]

Between 1850 and 1900, the need for cheap labor to lay rail lines and work in mines in the Western part of the country caused the United States to encourage the immigration of half a million Chinese. With a tremendous rate of lives lost, tens of thousands of Chinese immigrants had dynamited through the Sierra Nevada to construct the Transcontinental Railroad. Following the initial Chinese influx between 1890 and 1924, 200,000 Japanese would enter the United States. When jobs became scarce with the depressions near the end of the century, Congress had passed the first exclusion laws (1882) to stop the flow of Chinese into America.[254] According to the historian Ronald Takaki in his book *Iron Cages* (2000), "As American industry developed and as the Chinese became the main supply of labor for the 'captains of industry,' there would be intense competition and conflict between white workers and 'Chinese coolies.' Thus there would be both progress and poverty, and in the midst of both, there would be bloody conflict."[255]

Upon arrival at Angel Island, the California port of entry into the United States, Chinese were frequently mistreated by immigration officials.[256] White workers committed acts of violence against the Chinese, including numerous beatings on San Francisco streets and violent expulsions from towns such as Eureka and Truckee; the 1871 mob murder of twenty-one Chinese in Los Angeles; and 1885 mob action against Chinese mineworkers in Rock Spring, Wyoming, in which Chinese were gunned down as they attempted to flee from torched buildings.[257] The application of exclusion laws to Chinese who had freely lived and worked in the Philippines and Hawaii generated additional discontent. In Honolulu by July 13th, the local Chinese had raised $30,000, with a goal of reaching $50,000 to aid the boycott cause.[258] As assessed in one *New York Times* article (June 28, 1905), the main impediment in the settlement of the exclusion laws was the unwarranted application of those laws to the Philippines and Hawaii. Since the "coolies" were not viewed as directly competing with Americans, and since they had always enjoyed freedom of immigration to those places, this interpretation was considered particularly unjust.[259]

Discriminatory actions in the United States also included hostile entry by government officials into Chinese homes to verify registrations and unfair deportations.[260] On October 11, 1902, one Boston immigration attorney had two hundred and fifty Chinese arrested without a warrant; all except five were legal residents. A young man involved in this incident, Feng, traveled back to China, wrote a book about the disturbing event, and then committed suicide. Feng's death made him a martyr, and thousands of Chinese commemorated his tragic fate. In 1903, another young man, T'an Chin-yung, a military attaché, was mercilessly beaten, tied to a fence by his queue and then hauled to the police station. Because he was convinced that he had "lost face," he also committed suicide. In 1905, Chi You-tze, a well-known Chinese writer, documented the mistreatment that Chinese students had suffered in the United States.[261] All these violent acts of aggression combined to fuel the boycott's global energy.[262]

Significant numbers of Americans voiced concern about "the yellow peril"— that inadequately remunerated Asian workers would drastically force down American salaries.[263] During the early stages of the boycott in China, activists and intellectuals emphasized the exploitive nature of arrogant Americans who were quick to throw the Chinese out of their country after their hard labor on railroads, mines, and construction was accomplished.[264] Further antagonism was aroused by well-known American authors who contributed articles to newspapers, and by politicians who voiced the view that the Chinese had no backbone, and that they could not effectively organize a successful boycott.[265] Ex-minister to China Edwin H. Conger gave a speech in which he articulated the viewpoint that the Chinese would fail in their boycott efforts and "ridiculed the idea of Chinese organization;" this was immediately disseminated by American Chinese which generated further wrath and indignation.[266]

Articulate opposition to the exclusion laws existed among American citizens even in the West. In an eloquent letter of June 28, 1905, Edwin Gill, a lawyer from Seattle, Washington, congratulated Secretary Taft on his statements criticizing the law in the commencement speech that Taft had given at Miami (Ohio) University. According to Gill, the "Chinaphobia" advocates principally consisted of professional labor agitators, "who never did an honest day of work in their lives," and "cheap politicians," mere demagogues who wanted to win favor with the agitators. In Gill's view, most people in California wanted significant changes in the laws for Chinese merchants and students, but for the workers, they would recommend restriction of immigration for agricultural labor. He explained that all Pacific Coast states lacked workers for fruit crops, and because of substandard care, a great deal of those crops had been lost for the past several years. He also lobbied strongly against the new, restrictive law's application to the Pacific islands such as Hawaii and the Philippines—which, he contended, relied heavily on Chinese labor for development. "The greatest fault with the present law," Gill wrote, "is that it gives the immigration officials absolute power to say whether a Chinese coming here may land or not, without right of appeal to the Courts. I feel on this as Justice Harlan[267] expressed it, that such legislation by Congress is revolutionary and is a violation of constitutional rights."[268]

→ A street scene in Peking.

From 1895 to 1905, exports from the United States to China had substantially increased (from $3,844,200 to $53,384,000), but this represented less than ten percent of the total Chinese foreign imports.[269] U.S. exports included textiles, petroleum, soap, flour, candles, cosmetics, hardware, and stationery. American exports to China were less than those to Japan and Great Britain.[270] The Chinese merchants wanted to strike a blow against American interests in China.[271] Between August 1904, to January 1905, the treaty negotiations had broken down.[272] In responding to a dispatch from Rockhill, Prince Ch'ing, President of the Board of Foreign Affairs, told him that the boycott had erupted because the restrictions against Chinese entering America were too strong and the Coolie Immigration Treaty had expired, but even though the treaty was void, the exclusion laws were still enforced.[273] Historian Guanhua Wang explains, "The anti-American boycott is one of the earliest and largest urban popular movements in modern Chinese history. More notable, however, is its transnational character. Although the drama of mass protest played out in China, the movement was initiated by the Chinese in the United States and then gained support among overseas Chinese in many other parts of the world (McKee 1986; Wong 1995)."[274]

Chinese from different economic strata and geographic regions joined to orchestrate the massive social movement and provide through peaceful protest one of the first manifestations of the new Chinese nationalist movement.[275] The boycott that started in Shanghai caught on in southern Chinese seaport cities and then spread to the Philippines and Japan. [276] One unique facet of the boycott was the coming together of diverse supporting groups of Chinese, including those interested in constitutional reform, library groups, study societies, newspaper-reading societies, speech societies, women's organizations, and chambers of commerce. Many of the voluntary group members belonged to the new gentry merchant class. Their organizations would include the boycott as part of their regular business. [277]According to the American Consul Samuel Gracey, the most active society in Shanghai was the Jen Ching (Man Mirror) Literary Society of Shanghai. [278] Recently formed groups of intellectuals and professionals engaged in the new voluntary organizations were vital for the dissemination and proliferation of boycott goals and activities. They were buoyed by the participation of huge numbers engaged in the struggle around the world.

The transnational nature of the boycott movement was facilitated and molded by the development of the daily and periodic press and the telegraph, which made the breadth and reach of the boycott much greater than would otherwise have been possible. On a daily basis, Shanghai newspapers published articles on the boycott with headline status, as well as commentaries, cartoons, and photographs.[279] Only recently introduced, for the first time the telegraph was pervasively and intensively used in China during the 1905-06 boycott.[280] Wang states, "The growth of the press, the emergence of telegraph services, the rise of speech clubs, and the flourishing readership for social and political novels changed the way in which information was transmitted in urban centers."[281]

During the boycott, activists published and distributed hundreds of thousands of handbills.[282] Other modes of spreading stories of the boycott included folk songs, novels, and drama. The boycott's strength was greatest in areas with the most voluntary organizations.[283] Because of the low literacy rate in China, oratory was a critical element in relating the exclusion stories and boycott goals. To lend credibility to the cause, well-known people were frequently invited to mass rallies, especially in Shanghai.[284] In a creative campaign devised in South China, wealthy citizens of Tekhoi imported thousands of Japanese fans with images depicting the maltreatment of Chinese in America printed on one side and the slaughter of buffalo on the other. The text that accompanied the images on the widely circulated fans urged the Chinese to join the boycott against American goods.[285] Chinese merchants also capitalized on anti-foreign sentiment to increase their market share in the selling of products such as cigarettes.[286] Germans also were reported to attempt to take advantage of the boycott, by diverting trade from the United States.[287]

According to an August 11th *Washington Post* article, some attributed the boycott movement to merchants and commercial organizations from other countries, principally England and Germany, that encouraged Chinese students to organize the boycott as a front to fight the United States for the lucrative Chinese trade.[288] The Qing government at first aided the boycott movement.[289] In 1905, the recently created Qing Ministry of Foreign Relations retaliated against the Americans by opposing the renewal of the immigration treaty between the United States and China.[290] Although many Qing officials, including the Empress Dowager herself, reportedly expressed solidarity with the aggrieved overseas Chinese, Minister of Beijing Yuan Shikai was one of the few Chinese opponents.[291] According to Rockhill, even after Prince Ch'ing had agreed to take deliberate action to halt incendiary articles in the Peking press, such measures did not actually have an effect until the influential Viceroy Yuan Shikai had intervened to encourage the press to stop publishing such articles.[292]

A July 14th article in the *Atlanta Constitution* described the beginnings of a boycott against American schools. In a letter, Reverend Dr. Anderson wrote that students at Soo Chow University had received notice of a boycott of American schools and teachers, and a mass meeting was convened.[293] While at first the scope of the boycott was broad and included boycotting schools, the goals were gradually honed down to the single objective of boycotting American goods.[294] Actions taken against the Americans included a Chinese comprador's refusal to accept a good job from an American company and workers' unwillingness to unload U.S. products at ports. Consul General Thomas Sammons wrote Minister Rockhill that in Beijing the cargo of U.S. oil would not be stored by Bush Brothers, and compradors were told not to unload the oil.

The Americans were able to subvert the ban by getting the Japanese to unload Standard Oil's cargo. None of the compradors interfered with the Japanese.[295] In a letter dated August 8, 1905, to His Excellency Lo-Sang Gyal-Tsen, Viceroy of the Two Kwangs, Julius Law, American Consul General, stated that Sze Tak Shun, the representative of Standard Oil of Wuchow, had escaped to Hong Kong after he was threatened with death if he bought Standard Oil. He was also informed that a junk owned by the Standard Oil Company of Wuchow would be destroyed by the Boycott Committee.[296]

According to American Consul General James L. Rodgers, in a letter to Honorable Francis B. Loomis, Assistant Secretary of State, dated July 27, 1905, Chinese students had tried to agitate the "coolie" lighterage organizations by attacks on America through the press and books, pamphlets, posters, and placards. They reportedly wrote anonymous letters promising harassment and death to employees of American firms and their compradors.[297] Chinese newspapers refused to print American advertisements. The newspaper *Ta King Pao* rejected those advertisements, and the same newspaper told an American lawyer in Tientsin that his already placed ad would have to be removed.[298]

By July 19, 1905, according to a correspondent of the *South China Morning Post*, the boycott had spread to Amoy. The comprador of Standard Oil Company had received a harassing letter demanding that he leave his job, and several officials of the American consulate were "molested."[299] In a July 25th letter to Rockhill, Consul George Anderson copied a telegram detailing the July 19th defilement of a consular flag halyard in Amoy, which was torn down by unknown assailants who reportedly defecated around the flag area. At a meeting on July 18th, missionaries stated that they had never seen the Chinese "so worked up, not even during the troubles of 1900."[300] Ideas about burning the American Consulate and Standard Oil godowns (warehouses) were reportedly discussed. It was unclear if the flag-related action was taken by hoodlums or boycott agitators, but an effort was made to get the Taotai, officials of highest rank in the city, to disavow the event and give an international twenty-one-gun salute as an apology.

Because of the close relationship of traders in Amoy and the Philippines and the difficult recent treatment that Chinese merchants had experienced in Manila, the agitation in Amoy over the Exclusion Treaty was especially severe.[301] According to an August 23rd *Washington Post* article, it took the U.S. State Department an entire month to report the incident, which had involved throwing mud at a flagstaff. Furthermore, Chinese servants of George Anderson were threatened with death. The State Department determined that local Chinese officials had adequately punished the agitators and ended the incident. Apparently, as reported by Chinese newspapers, the American Consul, Mr. Anderson, and a British representative had asked for protection because the incident was at least for a time deemed serious. These events reportedly marked the first acts of boycott-related violence against Americans.[302]

On July 27, 1905, Shanghai bankers met to consider the idea of boycotting the International Banking Corporation, organized in June as the only American banking institution then formed to do business solely in foreign countries. The corporation, which was the agent to receive payments for the Chinese Boxer indemnity, was capitalized at $3,000,000 with a surplus of $3,000,000. Directors of the corporation included Isaac Guggenheim, E.H. Harriman, H.E. Huntington, and James S. Fearson. The local officials of the International Banking Corporation were apparently surprised at the news of the possible boycott. General Thomas Hubbard was quoted as saying, "Of course it is well known that the boycott is not in consequence to any objection to our corporation, but is due to the resentment of the Chinese against the United States, caused by the Chinese exclusion act."[303]

According to a letter from a Mr. Shaw of the Treasury Department, written to President Roosevelt on August 1, 1905, a Mr. Wilkie, chief of the Secret Service, had just returned from China to describe circulars issued that pictured a Chinese man running from "a mob armed with clubs and missiles implying that kind of treatment is commonplace." He noted that this sort of propaganda could have disastrous results for the American cause. Furthermore, he confirmed that two Americans who worked for the Consulate at Shanghai had been "molested" on the street.[304]

After the Chinese proposed a special mission to Washington to work on a settlement of the exclusion disputes, Minister Rockhill would not agree to the negotiation.[305] In an August 17th article in the *Atlanta Constitution*, Edward H. Conger, who had served as the United States Minister to China for eight years, but had recently been appointed as American Ambassador of Mexico, was to be sent on a special mission to China to help appease the boycott agitators. He had only left his job in China three months earlier, but because he was "popular among the officials of the Peking government," it was thought that he could be an effective negotiator. He was summoned by President Roosevelt to discuss the boycott and the Hankow railroad, which ran between Guangdong and Hankow. Conger advised against selling the railroad concession regardless of the amount of cash offered. His trip to China would purportedly also include negotiations on this railroad issue.[306] According to a *Washington Post* article (August 23, 1905), the suppression of the boycott by the viceroy and governor of the Shanghai province would probably cause the boycott to end before Conger arrived in Beijing.[307]

When American markets in China registered drastic losses during the boycott, President Theodore Roosevelt took action, by executive order, demanding more polite treatment of Chinese students, tourists, officials and merchants in the United

States.[308] If Immigration Bureau officials were impolite to Chinese of those classes entering the United States with correct documents, those officials would lose their jobs. If a Chinese person were to arrive with improper documentation that resulted from an incorrect action of a U.S. official, he would not be sent back.[309] Julius G. Lay, American Consul General, was also quick to point out that:

> Congress, which is the only power to make laws in the United States or confirm treaties, does not meet until December, but the vexatious treatment of Chinese at San Francisco was not due to the law, but the way the law was enforced, and this unsatisfactory state of affairs which your people have complained of, has now been remedied by the President, so why continue a boycott that can accomplish nothing whatever?[310]

Although the 1905 boycott was ineffective in causing the repeal of the U.S. exclusion laws, it demonstrated to the educated class in China that popular, grassroots actions would serve more effectively to defend the country than the Qing Dynasty. The boycott would continue for six months and lasted even longer in Guangdong. Many forces coalesced to end the boycott, including a split between the merchants who stood to lose millions of dollars and those committed to continue until the exclusion laws were repealed.[311] The Qing court walked a tightrope in trying to appease the boycott supporters and the foreign powers.[312] When Qing officials turned against the boycott movement, the Shanghai merchants had already abandoned the cause.[313] By imperial decree of August 30th, the Qing court had proclaimed its intent to halt the boycott by prohibiting the deterrence of trade in American goods.[314] Harsh penalties would be levied against those responsible for boycott-related anti-American grievances.[315] According to a *Los Angeles Times* article (September 18, 1905), after his visit to China, Taft stated that the Chinese "want American goods badly" and had already lost $15,000,000 as a result of the boycott.[316] Minister Rockhill telegraphed the State Department that the Chinese foreign office had issued an order that all viceroys and governors in the empire halt the boycott and related agitation.[317] Rockhill summarized the edict in a cable to Washington:

> Imperial edict published yesterday states that the long and deep friendship between the United States and China has

never been tried as now. The United States government has promised to revise treaty and people should peacefully await action of both governments. Boycott wrong and harming friendly relations. It [the edict] commands viceroys and governors to take effective action, making them strictly responsible. Undoubtedly will have a good effect. Shanghai reported yesterday situation improving.[318]

According to press reports, the American government threatened to assess the extent of its losses in order to make a claim against the Chinese government. Furthermore, Rockhill admonished the Qing court that it would be liable for losses unless it took action to prohibit the boycott. [319]As stated, "Precisely what it intends to do in the matter is not foretold or even hinted, but the inference is plain that its purpose now is to prepare a basis for future claims against the Chinese government which may take the form of a demand for cash."[320] Whereas the Chinese were held responsible for Boxer Rebellion-related damages to the foreign legations and foreign claims with the huge indemnity, the U.S. government asserted that local governments were responsible for damages to Chinese in America, and the federal government could not be held liable.[321]

In late 1905 and early 1906, as a result of the boycott, Roosevelt gravely considered the possibility of a major military intervention in China that would have rivaled the American response to the Boxer Rebellion.[322] When his executive order did not allay the Chinese boycotters, who had actually increased their activities, Roosevelt's anger level rose to a high pitch. Richard Challener states in his book *Admirals, General, & Foreign Policy* (1973), "Even as he was writing to Root about the need for 'speaking sharply,' he was beginning to reach for his big stick."[323]

Roosevelt considered instituting a marked increase in the number of American military vessels on Asian assignment. Furthermore, he directed Secretary of the Navy Charles Bonaparte to meet with Root and Admiral Converse to discuss direction for military intervention in China, which, it was eventually decided, would take place around Guangdong. The General Staff and General Board planned the landing of 5,000 troops from the Philippines Division to divert to Canton even though Roosevelt himself had requested 15,000 with additional reinforcements. General Leonard Wood advised Roosevelt on this plan. He promised men who would be "young and vigorous, embarked in a state of combat readiness, and well briefed about the geography of the Guangdong area."[324] Although in early 1906, Roosevelt seemed set on the attack, he never activated the mandate, and nothing resulted from all these plans.[325] Some conjectured that Roosevelt found the threat of military action to be enough to achieve his goal.[326]

Placards in San Francisco's Chinatown abounded with encouragement for the support of the Chinese boycott of U.S. goods in China and for the repeal of the exclusion laws. Meetings were regularly held and funds were raised to advance the boycott's aims.[327] Although the boycott actions had largely faded out by the end of 1905 with only scattered activities in different Chinese cities, the April, 1906, San Francisco earthquake pealed a final death knell when that city's Chinatown, the most crucial center for overseas boycott activities, was largely destroyed.[328]

THE NEW POPULIST MOVEMENT

After the defeat of the Boxers, the power base in China shifted from the more conservative government officials of the interior to the reformers of the Chinese coastal cities.[329] The 1905-06 boycott movement reflected the growing significance of the new Chinese gentry-merchant class, which inhabited the increasingly important industrializing coastal cities and was instrumental in mobilizing the boycott. Major reasons for the cessation of the boycott included the Qing edict and warning against anti-American activities; the growing conflict between Chinese reformers and revolutionaries; Minister Rockhill's active campaign against the boycott; and failure of continued coordinated leadership.[330]

Many of the Chinese boycott organizers and participants held a more comprehensive goal, which included bringing political and social change by mobilizing a grassroots effort.[331] The Qing crackdown against the boycott organizers actually assisted in defining the schism between those who opposed and those who supported the Qing regime. The boycott movement transmogrified into the railroad rights dispute; various reforms, including constitutional modifications; and, ultimately, the 1911 Revolution.[332] As Wang summarized the situation, "The real meaning of the boycott movement for Chinese city dwellers went far beyond the immigration dispute to become an expression of their concern about the more fundamental problems facing the country. From that point of view, the boycott movement was simply one link in a chain of political protests in early twentieth-century China that evidenced urban popular sentiment in favor of political reform."[333]

After Japan defeated China in 1894, efforts to modernize the Qing court that had begun in 1860 were redoubled with the establishment of Western-style factories, new schools and universities, the telegraph, artillery, steamships and other modern vessels, voluntary organizations, and chambers of commerce.[334] Inspired by the success of the Japanese in adapting Western constitutional principles in the service of modernization and transformation of its military, industrial, and general economy, the Qing officials also attempted to modify and implement constitutional structures that underlay Western governmental power. The victory of the Japanese in the Russo-Japanese War was the most startling evidence of Japan's achievement.[335]

Between the time that she and her court returned from the provinces to Beijing in 1902 and her death in 1908, as previously mentioned, the Empress Dowager instituted reforms that would lay the groundwork for social revolution. Among the many progressive reforms that she fostered were an edict to stop foot binding; the elimination of the centuries old prohibition of Han-Manchu marriage; permission for women to be seen in public; establishment of a school for upper class women and the first nursery school; the commencement of female students studying abroad; an assessment of the entire legal system with the interdiction of torture while interrogating suspects; and the cessation of the practice of death by a thousand cuts.[336] As stated Jung Chang, "Under her measured stewardship, Chinese society was fundamentally transformed, thoughtfully and bloodlessly, for the better, while its roots were carefully preserved and suffered minimum trauma." [337]

In 1905, the Empress Dowager Cixi created study groups compose d of princes and officials of differing ethnic origin who were instructed to travel and learn about the governments of Japan, Britain, France, Germany, and the United States. When Chinese radicals got wind of these efforts, they were concerned about the possibility of Qing success trumping their own revolutionary plans. One Chinese radical attempted to blow up the train in which the Qing study group traveled just as it left the Peking station. While the plan largely failed when the radical accidentally killed himself, he did manage to injure two commissioners and delay the trip for four months. Substitute commissioners were named and the study group managed to complete their mission.[338]

Among many issues during 1905 that captured the Chinese imagination such as the indemnity and the boycott, the recovery of railway rights also became an impassioned concern of the new Chinese nationalist movement. To pay off the Boxer indemnity, the Qing government turned to proffered railway development loans. To make matters worse, whether the Chinese liked it or not, foreign powers threatened to construct railways within their strongholds. The Germans in Shandong, the British in the Yangzi Valley, the French in Kunming, the Russians in Lushun, and the Japanese in Mukden—all these foreign powers completed 3,222 miles of tracks in China between 1900 and 1905.[339] According to historian Jonathan Spence, the railroad posed the greatest difficulty of all technologies that Qing officials attempted to introduce, since a great number of Chinese people considered the railroad to be a disruption of peace between humans and nature.[340]

As is often the case in transitional phases of human history, Empress Cixi and the Qing officials found themselves in a vice grip squeezed by the large numbers of people in the new voluntary organizations—women, merchants, workers—all calling for reform, and the accompanying expenses that spiraled out of control. After returning to the Forbidden City, the Empress began new efforts to modernize by hosting prominent members of the foreign diplomatic corps at her palace by the end of January, 1905, and in February she entertained ladies at a reception for the first time.[341] Inviting the 1905 U.S. diplomatic mission to visit with Empress Cixi was another example of Qing attempts to open up and reform.

Chinese revolutionary groups were inspired by the Russian Revolution of 1905 and by Marxist theories.[342] Another major 1905 development was the collaboration of Sun Yat-sen and his revolutionary group with other radical organizations to create the "Revolutionary Alliance" (Tongmeng Hui).[343] For many Chinese the ideals of Sun Yat-sen and his views on revolution were more appealing than the Kang Youwei's attempt to protect the Emperor Guangxu and to institute a constitutional monarchy similar to that of Japan.[344] An opposing group of reformers had attempted to initiate a "self-strengthening" movement in which Chinese values and learning would be primarily honored, but Western ways would be adapted for practical purposes. In order to effectuate this plan, the Chinese would employ Western advisers and learn to implement many practical Western technological developments.[345]

TAFT ARRIVES IN CHINA AND EXPERIENCES BOYCOTT

In a July 7, 1905, letter, W.W. Rockhill, Envoy Extraordinary and Minister Plenipotentiary of the United States to China, wrote to President Roosevelt from Beijing that "we will be delighted to see Miss Roosevelt here and will do all in our power to make her visit an agreeable one." He expressed his profound regret that the construction of the new American legation would not be completed by the time of her arrival and stated that they were "camping out" in old Chinese houses.[346] An August 17th *New York Times* article, titled "Miss Roosevelt May Not

Go," contended that Alice Roosevelt was undecided about whether to visit China and was waiting for her father's approval after receiving the invitation from the Empress Dowager.[347] Taft cabled Rockhill that Senator and Mrs. Newlands would serve as Miss Roosevelt's chaperone on the *Logan* from Manila to Taku; at Peking (Beijing), she would be under the chaperone of Mrs. Rockhill; and Mrs. Newlands would resume the responsibility on the trip back to Shanghai and back to San Francisco.[348]

By the time the Taft party arrived in China, the momentum of the boycott had already significantly abated. On August 31, 1905, the delegation arrived in Hong Kong where they dined with the governor at the Peak. A *New York Times* article stated that Taft had decided not to go to Canton (Guangdong) because of the strong anti-American views and "obnoxious placards" in the city.[349] Taft cabled President Roosevelt and Rockhill that he had met with Chinese merchants in Hong Kong about the boycott and had received their views on how the exclusion laws should change. In this cable to Roosevelt, he wrote, "Chinese Imperial Government seems to comply in every way with Rockhill's request." He suggested that his going to Beijing would be gratuitous, but he would do whatever the President requested.[350] On September 4th, Taft cabled Rockhill to ask whether he should go to Beijing to add additional pressure on the Imperial government to end the boycott. Secretary Taft reiterated that he was eager to return to the United States on the *Korea*.[351]

River dwellers in Canton, China.

In a telephone conversation between Assistant Secretary Francis B. Loomis and the White House, the transcription of which was wired to Secretary Taft on September 2, 1905, Loomis stated that according to the foreign adviser of the Standard Oil Company, the company had not sold anything in China whereas during the same period of the previous year, they had sold 350,000 cases of oil (one case contained ten gallons). According to Loomis, that oil market had been diverted to Russia and Germany. On the next day, a meeting would be held between American interests in Guangdong, viceroys, and other high Chinese officials. The Standard Oil Company requested that the President ask Secretary Taft to visit Guangdong from Hong Kong and to informally attend the meeting. The journey would take six hours by steamer.[352]

In another telegram signed by J. Parker and directed to Honorable F. B. Loomis at the White House on September 2nd, Parker reports receiving a cable from the London office of the British American Tobacco Company stating that the boycott had halted business. The businessmen were also "very desirous" for Taft to attend meetings with the Viceroy at Guangdong on the 4th to discuss settling the boycott.[353] After seeking counsel, Secretary Taft's final decision was to go to Guangdong with a group of forty, accompanied only by the guards provided by the Viceroy. Because of the perceived dangers, Taft banned any women from accompanying them.

While some adventurous members, including Frost and Woods, visited Guangdong, and Alice Roosevelt got as close to the city as the women were allowed, most of the members of the Taft party went on a railway trip and then up the river to the Manchu Club.[354] On September 4th, when he received a cable from Roosevelt directing him to do so, Taft and his party traveled to Guandong, where the boycott had originated, to discuss the ongoing Chinese embargo of American goods. Taft and the group of forty men first visited the American Consulate for a reception and were greeted by a battalion of the Viceroy's guards who served as their sole protectors throughout the visit. As guests of the New Canton Railroad, the Taft party traveled the length of its entire line.[355] During their visit the Viceroy was unfortunately sick in bed, but according to a September interview with the Associated Press Taft gave in San Francisco, the Viceroy had invited the entire Taft party to a luncheon with the provincial treasurer, who represented him at the Manchu Club in Guangdong. The Viceroy's representative talked about the cordial relations between the Chinese and Americans. Although Taft had worried that members of his party would be insulted, the Viceroy had issued a proclamation prohibiting indignities against Americans and requesting a peaceful visit. In a letter dated September 5, 1905, Secretary Taft greeted the Viceroy and regretted that he was too ill to attend the festivities. He also asked for the Viceroy's forgiveness for their arrival in meager "travelling costume" so that their "failure to comply with the usual costume in this respect should not be misunderstood."[356] Taft party members, who were well treated, visited the old city of Guangdong and purchased many Chinese items.

→ A page from Harry Fowler Woods' China album.

That morning, in a serious crackdown, the Viceroy had issued an order stating that the boycott should be called off, and all leaders "arrested and punished." According to the *New York Times* (September 5, 1905), "The party's trip to Guangdong has had an immediate effect, and it is believed that within two weeks the boycott will end."[357] In response, Taft also noted the countries' friendly relations and assured the Chinese that "the United States did not want one foot or one acre of the soil of China." Taft called the boycott an unjust violation of treaty rights, and he was pleased that the Viceroy had ordered the boycott halted. A front-page *Washington Post* article (September 5, 1905) also hailed the immediate positive effect of Taft's visit and repeated the view that the boycott would end within two weeks.[358] Taft would dispatch a detailed report to Roosevelt, which was written by an army officer in Manila, describing an overall diminishment of national Chinese strength, the development of the anti-foreign sentiment, and the spread of the boycott throughout the coastal cities of Beijing and Guangdong.[359]

Because the Cantonese response to the boycott had been the strongest and most organized, Taft and certain members of his party had previously expressed concern about traveling there. Throughout the city, boycott activists posted imposing red boycott posters, and people gathered in the narrow streets to attend impassioned anti-exclusion rallies.[360] The Taft party fears could also be understood in light of the many and varied spontaneous protest actions, already described, that had occurred throughout China. In Beijing and Tianjin, merchants reportedly jacked up prices when they noticed that Americans entered to purchase postcards or other items.[361]

A river scene in Canton, China.

F.W. Frost described their visit to Guangdong as "the most interesting and exciting event of our visit to Hong Kong." He mentioned that Consul General Bragg had advised them not to accept the Viceroy's invitation[362] to visit Guangdong because of the "dangerous" boycott. Frost described the city as the most "anti-foreign" of any in China. As Frost put it, "But the feeling of impending danger lent an atmosphere of mystery to the whole affair, and so ten of us decided to go on our own hook in another night boat." According to a September 13, 1905, *New York Times* article, the representatives of China urged a change in the definition of "laborer," requested that Consular certificates be recognized as valid and final proof of identification, and sought amelioration of conditions in detention sheds in America. Secretary Taft promised to present the proposals to President Roosevelt upon his arrival back in the United States.[363]

Alice Roosevelt was advised to remain in British-controlled Hong Kong; nonetheless, she expressed interest in seeing Guangdong. Because of the inherent dangers and anti-foreign sentiment in Canton, Roosevelt, her friends Mabel Boardman and Amy McMillan, her chaperone, Mrs. Newlands, Nicholas Longworth, and Consul and Mrs. Lay[364] sailed on an American gunboat to the nearby island of Shameen. They were not permitted to go onshore, but they could view the streets of Guangdong across a narrow canal.[365] In an effort to convince rickshaw drivers to refuse to carry Americans, boycott organizers created an insulting poster depicting Alice Roosevelt carried in a sedan chair by four turtles, intended to represent henpecked husbands, in place of "coolies."[366] The U.S. Consul General saw the posters in the marketplace.

Official trip photographer Burr McIntosh commented that the poster would have been insulting enough to cause a Chinese person to "fight to the death" if it were levied against him or her.[367] Alice Roosevelt reported that the visit was generally uneventful, but on one occasion, several onlookers shook their fists at her in anger.[368] Two days before their arrival, after the insistence of the United States, three members of the Guangdong Boycott Society were arrested. The Consul General claimed that they were "notorious rascals" who made constant trouble.[369] They were freed the next October. Not only was this the first such arrest, but it also heralded the stiffening of the Qing position against the boycott organizers.[370] With the unveiling of different factions within the boycott movement—the reformers and the revolutionaries—the divisions strengthened, with short-term negative results for the continuation of that particular struggle. Wang states:

> These two factions, the revolutionaries and the reform-
> ers, were now competing more intensely for influence
> within the movement and on the political inclinations of
> the public, a new dimension to the boycott struggle with
> profound implications for China's political future. The

revolutionary cause began to enjoy greater popularity both in China and overseas." (S. Wong 1955: 197)[371]

American historian Stacy Cordery affirms that it was Alice Roosevelt's seemingly whimsical and potentially dangerous adventure near the riverbanks of Guangdong that created a split in the boycott organizers between those who wanted to capitalize on the presence of the American press by strengthening the boycott and those who thought that they would sooner win their demands if they halted the boycott in honor of President Roosevelt's daughter. According to Cordery, this schism allowed Minister Rockhill to extract an edict from Prince Ching that ended the boycott. After she intervened to ensure that the artists would not be killed for creating the poster with the forbidden image making fun of the foreign visitor, Alice Roosevelt added a copy to her trove of treasures that she brought home from Asia.[372] Concerned about the effect of the boycott on U.S. trade, Alice stated in a 1905 letter to Victor Howard Metcalf that the elite Chinese should be treated no differently than visitors from other countries.[373] Hence, Taft's visit to Guangdong would have been an important element in the negotiation to reinstate a peaceful trading relationship between the United States and China.

TAFT PARTY RETURNS TO HONG KONG AND DIVIDES INTO TWO GROUPS

After returning to Hong Kong, Secretary Taft and Major General Corbin attended a luncheon with the commanding officers of the troops. During the afternoon, the racing club held gymkhana games and races in which the contestants were the leading American and English ladies, who were pulled in rickshaws by prominent Englishmen.[374] The winner was a Alice Langhorne of Washington.[375] [According to Jung Shang, in Shanghai on race days, all Chinese were prohibited from entering the grandstand. They had to access and watch the race in a segregated area. (Shang, *Empress Dowager Cixi*, 258).] In the early evening, the British and Indians participated in a parade, and that night a banquet was given by the English Governor of the Hong Kong colony, Sir Mathew Nathan, at the Government House, "which was the most gorgeous social affair in the history of this settlement." A "brilliant ball" followed the dinner and took place at the Hongkong Club.[376]

On the next day, September 6th, the Taft party split into two groups. Alice Roosevelt, Nicholas Longworth, Harry F. Woods, F.W. Frost, and about thirty others, took a transport to Taku and to Beijing.[377] Taft and the rest of his party, around sixty in all, sailed on the *Korea* to Amoy and then Shanghai. While in Shanghai, Taft received news of the riots in Tokyo, disturbances that he attributed to dissatisfaction with the Japanese ministers who had negotiated the Portsmouth Peace Treaty and unjust police interference with the protestors.[378]

Taft and his group traveled from Shanghai to Nagasaki, Kobe, and Yokohama, the normal stopping places for the Pacific Mail line. On arriving at the "seat of the disturbances," Taft found them to be "greatly exaggerated." From there, they sailed on to the United States.[379] They arrived in Washington, D.C., on October 2nd, and between Chicago and Washington, D.C., the travel time of Taft's special train, consisting of four cars, broke records.[380] In an interview with the Associated Press on his return to the United States, Taft said about the boycott in China:

> My impression is that it will fade out because of the necessity that the Chinese merchants are under of patronizing America to sell what will be in great demand in Manchuria. Chinese merchants themselves are losing money and their influence is not likely to further it. Suggestions were made of possible amendments in the exclusion laws which without in any way opening doors to the coolie class would remove the stigma which the present regulations it is insisted put upon the classes entitled to enter. I have those suggestions from merchants in Hongkong and elsewhere and shall present them to the President. The President's proclamation and assurance that justice will be done to the Chinese had an excellent effect.[381]

ROOSEVELT PARTY ARRIVES IN BEIJING WITH U.S. MARINES

Alice Roosevelt and her party arrived at Beijing in a U.S. military gunboat, the *Logan*, which also carried a group of U.S. Marines to replace a single company of the Ninth U.S. Infantry of the U.S. Army, stationed in China after the Boxer Rebellion.[382] The Woods photographs are significant because they are the only known images of the first day of the return of the U.S. Marines to Beijing on September 15, 1905. Marines had continued to visit China before 1905 onboard ships of the U.S. Asiatic Fleet, which placed them ashore on an intermittent basis during the years after the Boxer Rebellion. As U.S. ships cruised the coasts of China and the Yangtze, the visits were of limited duration. The Marines historically had a mission of protecting U.S. foreign missions. *The New York Times* (September 13, 1905) documented the arrival of Captain Harris Lee of the U.S. Marine Corps with one hundred marines and three officers. They replaced Captain Brewster and the Ninth Infantry, which had constituted the American Legation Guard after the siege. The article states, "The relations of the guard and the Chinese authorities have been uniformly pleasant.[383]

In a letter to Secretary Taft on June 7, 1905, Adjutant General Henry C. Corbin suggested that some of the Taft party would probably like to make a trip to Beijing, and he offered the *Logan* for their use. He noted that the Legation Guard had not been inspected for more than a year, and he thought that because of the extensive work that had been recently completed in the barracks and quarters, an inspection would be important. He suggested that Mrs. Corbin would happily chaperone young ladies, and he assumed that Alice Roosevelt, Amy McMillan, and Mabel Boardman "might particularly like to make the trip." In his letter, Corbin gives no indication that a change will occur in the guard, and he seems eager to conduct the inspection of the Ninth Infantry.[384]

The opportunity of the Marines to return to the Legation as guards to replace the company of the Ninth U.S. Infantry was in accordance with the Boxer Protocols of 1901. In a memorandum submitted on July 21, 1905, by Lieutenant-Commander Chief of Staff John W. Chaffee of the War Department, he proposed that the Navy could be more economically maintained in Beijing than a company of infantry because men and supplies could be delivered by its vessels, whereas the Army needed to be transported on commercial ships. It is probable that President Roosevelt deferred to Rockhill, and he chose the Marines. The memo states that "Minister Rockhill's desire for a guard of Marines in lieu of infantry was arrived at before he left the United States or had personal knowledge of the discipline of Captain Brewster's company or difficulty in maintaining the same. We have no information to the effect that the discipline of the company is not good."[385] On July 24, 1905, Charles J. Bonaparte of the Navy Department acknowledged the receipt of a letter from the Department of State in which the Minister to China, William W. Rockhill, recommended that the infantry guard be replaced by Marines.[386]

In one of F.W. Frost's accounts, Minister Rockhill visited the Legation Guard for an inspection of improvements and words of advice for the military men. Frost recounts Rockhill stating that the lack of things to do in Peking precipitated "a great deal of drunkenness, and there have been murders and robberies committed by the Legation soldiers, and he wanted to do everything to make it pleasant for the men." No one apparently told Rockhill that two men were imprisoned that day at the Guard House for drunkenness and disorderly conduct. According to this account, Lee, who was a strict disciplinarian but liked by the men, had created improvements that the Army never thought to make during their five-year stay.

On August 23rd, Henry Corbin wrote a memo to Secretary Taft in which he outlined the process of transporting the army to effectuate the change in the U.S. Legation guards. He announced his intent to return afterward with his staff on the *Logan* to Manila.[387] Along with the company of Marines from the Philippines, two officers were selected to go: Captain Harry Lee and Lieutenant Thomas Holcombe. Both officers left China in 1906. Captain Lee went on to become a general. Thomas Holcombe returned in 1908 and remained through 1914 as a language officer. In 1928, he resumed his residence in Beijing as the commander of the Legation Guard and in the 1930s went on to become commandant of the Marine Corps.

Captain Harry Lee's horse.

ROOSEVELT PARTY VISITS DOWAGER EMPRESS

Minister and Mrs. Rockhill, Major General Corbin, Rear Admiral Train, Alice Roosevelt, and other members of the party arrived in Peking (Beijing) in the evening. Sent by President Roosevelt to visit the Empress Dowager Cixi as an important emissary, Alice spent her first night at the American Legation with the Rockhills. Wu Ting Fang, Vice-President of the Chinese Board of Foreign Affairs, Liang Fang, and other important emissaries met them.[388] In her autobiography, *Crowded Hours*, Alice Roosevelt wrote that after dinner a Chinese magician demonstrated a delightful array of tricks by the light of lanterns swinging from trees. She also mentioned that when he was younger, Rockhill had disguised himself as a Chinese person and visited Tibet, and that "he was a great Chinese student and lover of China."[389]

On Wednesday Alice visited the Temple of Heaven, and she set off the next day with Mrs. Rockhill, Mrs. Newlands, and other women of the Roosevelt party to spend the night at the Summer Palace.[390] The rest of the party remained in Beijing, about fourteen miles from the palace.[391] A number of historians have thought that only the most important members of the Roosevelt party were allowed call on the Empress Dowager,[392] but according to F.W. Frost, anyone could have visited if he or she had put in a request early enough. He lamented, "The rest of us were disappointed afterwards to find that we could have gone also if our names had been sent in from Hong Kong, but even Vice Governor Ide, whose name was omitted, could not go and under no conditions could be included after the list was once made up. It was the largest party presented at one time, and in many ways, it was an unprecedented occurrence." Frost describes it as a "great event" that was "known all over China." Alice Roosevelt was carried in a sedan chair by four bearers. The Rockhills, Newlands, Mabel, Amy, and Alice Roosevelt spent the night in Prince Ching's palace, and Miss Roosevelt resided in an entire hall. For dinner, they had alternating courses of European and Chinese food. That night, Miss Roosevelt found herself almost drunk on rose wine.[393]

The much-anticipated visit with the Empress Dowager occurred at eight o'clock the next morning. The remaining party, which had stayed in Beijing, had to travel to the palace early in their best attire.[394] During the visit with the Empress Cixi, Alice was introduced first by Mrs. Rockhill, while the others entered in order of importance.[395] According to Stuyvesant Fish, a member of the Taft party, in his privately printed book, *1600-1914*, Alice Roosevelt penned the following description of the Empress Cixi:

Our first sight of her was through the doorway of the Hall of Audience. She was seated on a throne several steps higher than the floor, very erect, one slim hand with its golden nail sheathes on the chair arm, the other in her lap. She wore a long loose Chinese coat covered with embroidery, strings of pearls and jade around her neck, her smooth black hair arranged in a high Manchu head-dress decorated with pearls and jade and artificial flowers.[396]

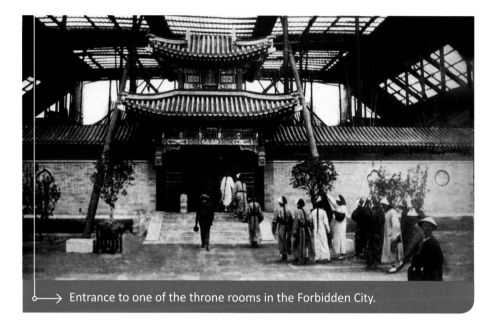
→ Entrance to one of the throne rooms in the Forbidden City.

Wu Ting Fang, former Minister to America (1897-1902), international attorney, and scholar, acted as interpreter. Alice and the women of the party enjoyed their luncheon with the Empress of the East and the Empress of the West. The luncheon highlight was "Snow-flake Shark's Fins." In a famous incident, at the command of the Empress Dowager, Wu Fang reportedly fell to the floor, with his forehead touching the ground. He was impelled to continue to interpret in this forced bow and was only permitted to lift his head to emit the sounds of his speech.[397] Miss Roosevelt described the impressive and cruel power of the tyrannical Empress Dowager—contrasted with the young Emperor, who huddled in the corner, destroyed by the opium addiction that had ravaged the country since the arrival of the drug through trade with the British. In Alice Roosevelt's own words, "On the lowest step of the throne sat the Emperor, a man in his early thirties; limp and huddled, his mouth a little open, his eyes dull and wandering, no expression in his face. We were not presented to him. No attention was paid to him. He just sat there, looking vacantly about."[398] The Empress Dowager walked among the group of Westerners, talked informally, and adorned Alice and her party with gifts, including rings and gold bracelets, presented individually by the Empress herself.[399]

The gifts that the Empress Dowager bestowed on Alice Roosevelt included two rings, a pair of earrings, some white jade, and a white fox and ermine coat.[400] *The New York Times* and *New York Herald* (September 24, 1905) noted the startlingly uncharacteristic lack of formality in the visit.[401] In her autobiography, Alice ranks the Empress "with Catherine of Russia and Elizabeth of England, with Egyptian Queens Hatshepsut and Cleopatra, as one of the great woman rulers in history."[402] Alice was later carried on a tour through the Imperial Gardens in a yellow chair "tasseled and cushioned," by eight bearers.[403] Many of the most important delegation members, decked out in their best attire, were invited to attend the audience.[404]

In her evocative description of the scenery, Alice Roosevelt wrote:

> There are few things lovelier than the sweep of a Chinese roof, the eaves painted in brilliant greens, blues, and vermilions, and often the eaves and roof ridge decorated with grotesque figures of dragons, phoenixes, and lion dogs.[405]

The next morning, the Empress Dowager had a special messenger bring a Pekinese dog to Roosevelt. Later, the Empress sent another present, a portrait of herself in a gilt frame in a box, which was carried by itself on an imperial yellow chair and surrounded by a troop of cavalry.[406] After dining at the German Legation and meeting "most of the foreigners in Beijing," Alice saw the Llama Temple and the Forbidden City the next day. She spoke of her intense desire to stay longer in Beijing since she wanted to see the Great Wall and the Ming Tombs. Even at the end of her life, Alice Roosevelt reportedly wore the dresses fabricated from silk bestowed on her by the Empress Cixi.[407] She yearned "to take a temple for the summer in the western hills" and made an unfulfilled vow to return to China.[408]

ROOSEVELT PARTY DEPARTS FOR TIENTSIN AND KOREA; WOODS AND FROST TRAVEL TO GREAT WALL

After visiting the Forbidden City, Alice and all but six of her group departed for Tientsin to meet and dine with Yuan Shikai, Viceroy of Chi-li, and his wife, who was apparently permitted to meet with foreigners for the first time.[409] At this point, H.F. Woods and F.W. Frost broke from the official party. They could not afford to sacrifice two days to attend the Viceroy's glamorous dinner but instead stayed to visit the Winter Palace in the Forbidden City. According to Frost, such a large group of foreigners—about twenty to thirty by Frost's estimate—had never before received an invitation to explore the Forbidden City. Many of the visitors were foreigners living in Peking who wanted to take advantage of a once in a lifetime opportunity.

As described by Francis Frost:

> We were first escorted to barges and poled across the Lotus Pond and taken through court after court and many palace buildings full of the most beautiful work of art—carvings, wonderful specimens of jade and coral, and no end of clocks. In nearly all the rooms was a most delightful odor which came from piles of apples set about in large dishes everywhere.

In the afternoon after a light luncheon, they viewed the more ancient parts of palace, which were hundreds of years old. As the entire palace was open, they were able to view objects—bronzes, woodwork, paper, cloisonné, porcelains, silk—that were one-of-a-kind and could not be seen anywhere else. Except for the few whom they would soon meet, Frost and Woods would not see most of the Roosevelt party again. Despite his glowing descriptions of Alice Roosevelt at the beginning of his letters in which he says she is "always ready for a frolic" and has "won the hearts of all," Frost at this time mentions that it was not a hardship to leave "Princess Alice," because "she has no attractive qualities" that he could discern. He does not give details to support this negative description.

On the same Saturday that the Roosevelt party left for Tientsin to visit Yuan Shikai's "magnificent" estate, Woods and Frost started their four-day ride on thirty-six miles of difficult roads to the Great Wall. They hired a local guide and assembled supplies, two horses, a Peking cart, and a few more ponies and horse boys. The following accounts of the camel trains passing, farmers harrowing and planting, and dynamically changing Chinese countryside are among Frost's most colorful descriptions. They visited the town Sha-Ho for only a few hours, and they stayed for the night at Nankow, where they met Warren, Mr. and Mrs. Godchaux from New Orleans, and Hobart. During this part of the trip, they encountered "long trains of pack mules and little donkeys hardly more than waist high, but all bearing heavy loads."

After reaching the Great Wall, where hundreds of camels grazed and slept under its shadow, Woods and Frost engaged in a celebratory picnic lunch with a tablecloth draped over bricks and stones for seats. They returned to Nankow for the night. The next day, with some of the most treacherous riding, they set out for the Ming Tombs, a fifteen-mile distance. Frost includes a description of the tombs and their subsequent visit to Tong Shan, where they stayed at an inn that was also a Lama temple, housing one of the Buddhist sects.

When they returned to Peking, they had completed a journey of 125 miles. They stayed at the officer's quarters of the Legation Guard for several days in Beijing because they could not locate a steamer that was traveling to their desired destination. Frost and Woods disembarked from Tientsin and booked on the *Shenking* for Chefoo. During their later travels, upstaged by the magnate E.H. Harriman who had commandeered the *Ohio* for his personal party, Woods and Frost found themselves stuck at Chefoo. Because of this fateful occurrence, they took the *Chin Hua* from Chefoo to Shanghai. After encountering the wreck of the *Hsei-Ho*, which had exploded after striking a mine just south of the Shau tung Peninsula, they rescued a number of seriously injured passengers. On their arrival, Frost dubbed Shanghai as "the most cosmopolitan city in the world." He includes colorful descriptions of streets "brimming full of life," "soldiers of all nations," "signs and newspapers printed in every language," and "fine stone and brick buildings." Since they planned to spend more time in Japan, after their stay in Shanghai, Frost and Woods traveled to Nagasaki before beginning their journey to Burma, India, Egypt, and Greece, where they would take four hundreds more photographs, and Frost would document their travels with many more letters.

On the battleship *Ohio*, the Roosevelt party sailed from Tientsin to Chemulpo, where they met a number of Korean officials, who took them on a special train to Seoul. They were responding to an invitation from the Korean king. On September 19, the remaining Roosevelt party paraded through streets thronged with white-robed Koreans and the imperial bodyguard. The roads had been recently paved and draped with American flags.[410] The women attended a luncheon at the palace hosted by the Emperor's consort. This was the first time in Korean history that women of the court entertained foreigners. On the way to the American legation, Alice Roosevelt was once again carried on an imperial yellow palanquin, "escorted by men carrying lanterns on long poles."[411] The party remained in Korea for ten days. Ironically, while Roosevelt and Taft traded Korea to Japan with the Philippines as the U.S. prize, Alice Roosevelt described the general state of the Korean people:

> Korea, reluctant and helpless, was sliding into the grasp of Japan. The whole people looked sad and de-jected, all strength seemed to have been drained from them. Everywhere there were Japanese officers and troops, militant and workmanlike; a contrast to the poor abject Koreans.[412]

A page from Harry Fowler Woods' China photo album.

From there, the group traveled back to Japan and then took a steamer across the Atlantic to the United States.

ROOSEVELT PARTY RETURNS TO JAPAN

On a Canadian Mail steamer, Alice Roosevelt, Nick Longworth, and most of the others traveled through the inland sea to Yokohama and stayed again with the Griscoms in Tokyo. According to Alice, they saw much more of Japan on this leg of their trip. They went to Kamakura to see the great Buddha, to Chuizenji, and to Nikko where they viewed the temples and mausoleums of the Shoguns and visited the "innermost sacred shrines."[413]

Following the signing of the peace treaty on September 5th in Portsmouth, New Hampshire, the mood of the Japanese people had changed overnight. Alice was advised to pretend that she hailed from England, to avoid the ire of the populace. The Japanese had expected to receive a large indemnity from Russia, and the failure of this to occur was blamed on Roosevelt.[414] In a September 12, 1905, memorandum to Secretary of State Elihu Root, Lloyd Carpenter Griscom wrote:

> The news of the important concessions made by Japan spread like wild-fire throughout the Empire and was received with amazement and disappointment. The unparalleled series of naval and military victories had encouraged the Japanese public to believe that Japan would surely be able to conclude peace on very advantageous terms. A large section of the press demanded, and confidently expected, the cession of Vladivostok and the Russian maritime provinces, as well as the island of Saghalien, and the payment of a thousand million dollars indemnity.[415]

Rioting was quelled only through severe military control. Griscom concluded that yellow journalism and overzealous politicians coalesced to ignite the imagination of the public and create impossible expectations about the gains that Japan's dominance over Russia would create.[416]

CONCLUSION OF THE DIPLOMATIC MISSION

With the E.H. Harriman party led by Harriman himself, who was in Asia investigating his railroad interests in Japan, China, and Korea, the Roosevelt party sailed from Yokohama for San Francisco on October 13, 1905.[417] They achieved a speed record, arriving in New York after just thirteen days. Alice Roosevelt may have brought home more gifts from a foreign trip than were ever before acquired by anyone. Her twenty-seven boxes of presents set off a contentious debate over whether she should pay or be spared the duty reported by the *New York Times* (October 18, 1905) as $25,000.[418] Some rumors inflated the price to $60,000. The gifts were ultimately stored in the White House basement. The question arose as to whether she or the federal government owned the items, which included artwork, her dog, Manchu, expensive fabric, and clothing. She ended up paying only $1,026.[419]

Despite the constant haranguing from the American press, Alice sported no ring from Longworth, but since mid-August their engagement had been recognized by the Congressional travelers. The couple announced their wedding plans a month after their return home.[420] Disembarking in October from the French liner *La Lorraine* and hearing about the engagement, Mrs. Longworth of Cincinnati, mother of Nicholas Longworth, quipped that it was the first that she had heard of her son's good fortune.[421]

A page from Harry Fowler Woods' China album.

To the Chinese people, the imperialists, adventurers, photographers, missionaries, and businessmen from Britain, the United States, France, and even Japan must have sometimes seemed like aliens from another world, rife with insatiable expansionist appetites, violent ways, inscrutable laws, and treaty rights.[422] While America was catapulted to far-flung places in a blaze of imperialistic zeal, China was engulfed in the throes of foreign expansionism, poverty, and rebellion.

The Woods images reproduced in this book derive from an early use of the hand-held camera; they thus provide for a more spontaneous record of human experience within the documentary format. They include snapshots from places such as San Francisco, Tokyo, Nagasaki, Manila, Guangdong, Beijing, Shanghai, and Hong Kong that were thereafter substantially altered or destroyed by earthquakes, wars, other manmade or natural disasters, and urban development. While these photographs often depict the awkward collision and delicate interweaving of disparate cultures, the Philippines images additionally provide documentation of America's only overseas administrative colonial experiment. They depict a groundbreaking but, until recently, largely forgotten U.S. foreign policy trip, major political figures on the international scene, and a life and times that have disappeared.

ANALYSIS OF SELECTED PHOTOGRAPHS

→ Outside the Hotel du Nord in Peking.

Some of the most impressive Woods photographs indirectly document the East-West dichotomy and the encroachment of the industrialized foreign powers on traditional Chinese ways. In "Hotel du Nord," the harmonious line of rickshaws contrasts with a traditional-looking Chinese building which disjointedly sports a French name. The Chinese men gathered outside the hotel are dressed in Chinese clothing that differs markedly from Western dress at that time.

Chinese band holding a "post mortem" over the "Star-Spangled Banner."

Troops awaiting the arrival of the U.S. Delegation at Tongku.

In "Chinese Band Holding a 'Post Mortem' over the 'Star-Spangled Banner,'" the palpable steel of the train is lined up against the backdrop of a Chinese military band playing the American national anthem, with the U.S. flag flying from a nearby building. A Westerner faces the camera with a cigarette in his mouth. Both hands on his hips, he exudes an appearance of confidence and control. Another Westerner, dressed in a white style of clothing worn by the upper classes, walks the other way. The only Chinese element of the photograph is the group of band players, who are not visible as individuals; they are pressed into the service of Westerners.

View of parade ground of the American Legation Guard from the city wall, Peking.

New buildings in the U.S. Legation, Peking.

The Woods photograph shows the entire U.S. Marine guard shortly after they had arrived with the Alice Roosevelt party. Wearing their summer uniforms, they are featured in the guard portion of the American Legation compound. The officers' quarters comprised four separate two-story apartments, with the senior commanders' quarters to the left. As Corbin noted, they were still under construction during this time. One image was taken from the city wall (Tartar Wall) and shows the officers' quarters to the right and a piece of the sickbay building on the left. The long building to the right side of the photograph is one of two barracks. Company offices and support buildings are in the lower center. In 1914 the whole complex was landscaped with grass and trees. The image at the bottom right is the US diplomatic portion of the compound, which was completed in 1906. In another, a slightly blurry photograph, the Marines are in their compound facing the west barracks. In the background are the Tartar Wall and the company offices. The armory is on the far left. The cannon just visible in the picture was probably a Boxer War prize and remained in the compound until 1941. From the muster rolls, it is evident that the trumpeter was named Dwight Davis and the drummer was Milton Ober. Lieutenant Holcomb was probably the officer in the front.

U.S. Legation Guard. Marine Corps on parade.

Officers' quarters of the U.S. Legation Guard, Peking.

Sitting room in residence of Captain Harry Lee, of U.S. Legation Guards.

An image above shows the officers' quarters with scaffolding. In 1910 the wall in front of the officers' quarters was extended to include the commander's apartment. The "upping blocks," with potted plants on top, were removed by 1910, and the wall was straightened. In another photograph, the compound tennis court was in place in that location (until 1941). The Army must have used the courts before the Marines did. The photographer also documents the inside of Captain Lee's quarters, complete with antlers and Lee's bell crown hat, with white and blue hanging from it. The sparse nature of the room reflects the fact that Lee was a bachelor with no family. The spears and cloth wall hanging above the fireplace probably came from his time in the Philippines. He has a map case on the table and a brass shell casing on the fireplace. Holcomb is pictured with a swagger stick and Dr. Taylor with a silver-topped cane. Swagger sticks were popular with the Marines through the 1930s. The shot of Captain Lee on a horse shows him mounted in front of the west barracks.

Capt. Lee, Lieutenant Holcombe, Dr. Taylor of the U.S. Legation Guard.

Captain Harry Lee on his horse.

ENDNOTES

1   All of the photographs in this book were taken from the private albums of Harry Fowler Woods, who was an accomplished photographer. Some of the photographs also appear in the papers of F.W. Frost, who was part of the delegation and subsequently traveled with Woods to what was then called Burma (now Myanmar), India, Egypt, and Greece.

2   Walter Isaacson, *Einstein: His Life and Universe* (New York: Simon & Schuster, 2007), 140.

3   Ishbel Ross, *An American Family: The Tafts - 1678 to 1964* (Cleveland and New York: The World Publishing Company, 1964), 167.

4   Stacy A. Cordery, *Alice: Alice Roosevelt Longworth from White House Princess to Washington Power Broker* (New York: Viking, 2007), 162-178.

5   William Howard Taft Papers, Library of Congress Manuscripts Division: Series Two, letter titled "Landing of Secretary of War and Party" August 5, 1905.

6   Henry F. Pringle, *The Life and Times of William Howard Taft* (New York and Toronto: Farrar and Rinehart, Inc, 1993), 291.

7   *Ibid.*, 293.

8   Frank Ninkovich, *The Wilsonian Century* (Chicago and London: The University of Chicago Press, 1999), 25.

9   Pringle, *Life and Times of William Howard Taft*, 311.

10   *Cincinnati Times-Star*, "Just One Ship Sighted by Taft Pary in Voyage from Honolulu to Yokahama, Japan," Ohio Historical Society, N110, Volume 145, August 19, 1905, 2.

11   *Ibid.*

12   Charles Cist, *Sketches and Statistics of Cincinnati in 1851* (Cincinnati: William H. Moore & Co., 1851), 4.

13   Carl Sferrazza Anthony, *Nellie Taft: The Unconventional First Lady of the Ragtime Era* (New York: William Morrow, 2005), 5.

14   Charles Dickens, *American Notes* (New York: St. Martin's Press, 1985), 147. In his *American Notes*, the great English novelist described Cincinnati in 1885 as follows: "Cincinnati is a beautiful city; cheerful, thriving, and animated. I have not seen a place that commends itself so favourably and pleasantly to a stranger at the first glance as this does: with its clean houses of red and white, its well-paved roads, and foot-ways of bright tile. Nor does it become less prepossessing on a closer acquaintance. The streets are broad and airy, the shops extremely good, the private residences remarkable for their elegance and neatness." (*American Notes*, 147).

15   All H.F. Woods and F.W. Frost photography albums were donated in April, 2009 to the Beinecke Rare Book and Manuscript Library, Yale University, New Haven, Conn.

16   *Cincinnati Times Star*, "Retired Firm Head—Funeral Services Set for Harry F. Woods, 95," February 21, 1955, 14, cols. 2 & 3.

17   Rose Angela Boehle, O.S.U., *Maria: A Biography of Maria Longworth* (Dayton, Ohio: Landfall Press, Inc., 1990), 17.

18   *Ibid.*, 16-19.

19   *Cincinnati Enquirer*, "Harry F. Woods Dies at 95; Formerly Active Paper Executive, Active in Art, Philanthropy," February 21, 1955, 26, cols. 7 & 8.

20   Interview, Eric Besch, collateral descendant of F.W. Frost, April 22, 2009.

21   *Ibid.*

22   Frost's China letters begin with the declaration, "At the end of a history making trip, the important stage of which has just been concluded …" At the conclusion of the trip, Frost states, "On the whole, I am glad to get away from China as it is a depressing country unless one is pursuing a particular line of study, but I am glad I have been here …" These statements suggest that Frost didn't believe the China part of the trip was as important as the others.

23   Letter of Henry C. Corbin to William Howard Taft, June 7, 1905, William H. Taft Papers, Library of Congress, Manuscript Division, Reel 51, Series 3, 1.

24   Henry C. Corbin to S. Fish, Sr., Manila, September, 25, 1905, included in *1600-1914*, by S. Fish (New York: Privately Printed by J.J. Little & Ives Company, 1942), Desmond-Fish Library, Garrison, N.Y, 235.

25   Frances Trollope, *Domestic Manners of the Americans* (New York: Alfred A. Knopf, 1949), 88, 89. In her own humorous descriptions and a footnote by a Dartmouth College student, Cyrus P. Bradley, who visited Cincinnati in 1835, Trollope chronicles the drama of pigs roaming through the streets of "porkopolis." Bradley wrote, "There is a good deal, far too much, of mud and dirt and stagnant water about the streets; if the cholera approaches, it will set them a scrubbing. Swine are here in abundance— to be expected in this vast pork market." He continued, "… for the beasts are impudent. They know enough to give way to a carriage, but as to a foot passenger, he must always turn out; they won't budge an inch for a whole regiment, and no one wishes to come in contact with their filthiness" (*Domestic Manners of the Americans*, 88).

26   Mark P. Painter, *William Howard Taft: President and Chief Justice* (Cincinnati: Jarndyce & Jarndyce Press, 2004), 8.

27   Joseph Needham, *Science and Civilization in China*, 24 vols. (Cambridge: Cambridge University Press, 1954-2004).

28   Simon Winchester, *The Man Who Loved China: The Fantastic Story of the Eccentrist Scientist Who Unlocked the Mysteries of the Middle Kingdom* (New York: HarperCollins, 2008).

29   Jeffrey Simpson, "Cultural Reflections: Period Photography Richly Documented the Complexity of Chinese Life in the 19th Century," *Architectural Digest*, August, 2008, 147.

30   Mary M. Ison, "Uriah Hunt Painter and the 'Marvelous Kodak Camera,'" *Washington History*, Fall/Winter, 1990-1991, 32-33.

31   *Ibid.*, 164.

32   Michael Hunt, *The American Ascendancy: How the United States Gained & Wielded Global Dominance* (Chapel Hill: University of North Carolina Press, 2007), 4.

33   Whitney Griswold, *The Far Eastern Policy of the United States* (New York: Harcourt, Brace and Company, 1938), 89; Ralph Minger, *William Howard Taft and United States Foreign Policy* (Chicago and London: University of Illinois Press, 1975), 139-140.

34   David H. Burton, *William Howard Taft: Confident Peacemaker* (Philadelphia: St Joseph's University Press and New York: Fordham University Press, 2004), 29.

35   Hunt, *Ascendancy*, 2.

36   *Ibid*, 4.

37   Paul Kennedy, *The Rise and Fall of the Great Powers* (New York: Random House, 1987), 242.

38   *Ibid*, 198.

39   Hunt, *Ascendancy*, 6.

40   *Ibid*.

41   Carol Felsenthal, *Princess Alice: The Life and Times of Alice Roosevelt Longworth* (New York: St. Martin's Press, 1988), 81.

42   Hunt, *Ascendancy*, 18.

43   Kennedy, *Great Powers*, 198.

44   *Ibid.*, 243.

45   Hunt, *Ascendancy*, 48.

46   Kathleen Dalton, *Theodore Roosevelt: A Strenuous Life* (New York: Random House, 2002), 128-129.

47   Kennedy, *Great Powers*, 242.

48   Robert Whitaker, *Mad in America: Bad Science, Bad Medicine, and the Mistreatment of the Mentally Ill* (New York: Basic Books, 2002), 46.

49   *Ibid*.

50   George M. Rosen, *Madness in Society: Chapters in the Historical Sociology of Mental Illness* (New York: Harper and Row, 1969), 282.

51   Ronald Takaki, *Iron Cages: Race and Culture in 19th-Century America* (New York: Knopf, 1979; Seattle, University of Washington Press, 1985), 260.

52   Lynn Gamwell and Nancy Tomes, *Madness in America* (New York: Cornell University Press, 1995), 134-135.

53   *Record of the Yale Class of 1867* (New York: J.G.C. Bonney, 1867), 277, 278.

54   Doris Kearns Goodwin, *The Bully Pulpit: Theodore Roosevelt, William Howard Taft, and the Golden Age of Journalism* (New York: Simon and Schuster, 2013), 27, 28.

55   William Howard Taft Papers, Series I, Reel II.

56   William Howard Taft Papers, Series I, Reel II.

57   *The Obituary Record of Graduates of Yale University: Deceased during the Academic Year Ending in June 1890*, (Presented at the Meeting of the Alumni, June 24th, 1890, No. 10 of the Third Printed Series, and No. 49 of the whole Record), 615,616.

58   *The Report of the Trigintennial Meeting with a Biographical and Statistical Record of the Class of 1867, Yale University* (New York: John G. C. Bonney, Printer), 277, 278.

59   Ross, *An American Family*, 104

60   Mark Bartlett, *The President's Wife and the Librarian, Letters at an Exhibition* (New York: The New York Society Library, 2009), 8.

61   Dalton, *Theodore Roosevelt*, 36, 37.

62   *Ibid.*, 37.

63   *Ibid*.

64   *Ibid*.

65   *Ibid*.

66   *Ibid.*, 6.

67   *Ibid*.

68   Takaki, *Iron Cages*, 278, 279.

69   *Ibid.*, 278.

70   Michael Lind, *The American Way of Strategy* (New York: Oxford University Press, 2006), 87.

71   Emily S. Rosenberg, *Financial Missionaries to the World: The Politics and Culture of Dollar*

Diplomacy 1900-1930 (Durham, N.C., and London: Duke University Press, 2003), 19-20.

72 Hunt, *Ascendancy*, 51.

73 William Appleman Williams, *The Tragedy of American Diplomacy* (New York: W.W. Norton & Co., 1959), 29.

74 *Ibid.*

75 *Ibid.*

76 *Ibid.*, 38-40.

77 *Ibid.*, 60.

78 Williams, *Tragedy*, 40

79 Hunt, *Ascendancy*, 47.

80 Shaller, *The United States and China*, 30-33.

81 Williams, *Tragedy*, 59.

82 Barbara W. Tuchman, *Sand against the Winds: Sitwell and the American Experience in China, 1911-1945* (London: Macdonald Future Publishers, 1981), 34.

83 Rosenberg, *Financial Missionaries to the World*, 19-20.

84 Hunt, *Ascendancy*, 49.

85 Christopher Endy, "Travel and World Power, Americans in Europe, 1890-1917," *Diplomatic History* (Malden, Mass. and Oxford: Blackwell Publishers), SHAFR, Vol. 22, No. 4, Fall, 1998, 567.

86 *Ibid.*

87 *Ibid.*, 569.

88 Stephen Kinzer, *Overthrow: America's Century of Regime Change from Hawaii to Iraq* (New York: Henry Holt and Company, 2006), 78.

89 John D. Alden (Commander, U.S. Navy), *The American Steel Navy: A Photographic History of the U.S. Navy from the Introduction of the Steel Hull in 1833 to the Cruise of the Great White Fleet, 1907 to 1909* (New York: American Heritage Press, 1971), 93-127.

90 Lind, *The American Way of Strategy*, 86.

91 Takaki, *Iron Cages*, 265-270.

92 George W. Baer, *The U.S. Navy, 1890-1990: One Hundred Years of Sea Power* (Stanford, Calif.: Stanford University Press, 1944), 10.

93 *Ibid.*, 10, 11.

94 *Ibid.*, 11; Williams, *Tragedy*, 35

95 Baer, *One Hundred Years of Sea Power*, 10, 11.

96 *Ibid.*, 12.

97 *Ibid.*, 25.

98 Takaki, *Iron Cages*, 266-268.

99 Baer, *One Hundred Years of Sea Power*, 24, 25.

100 *Ibid.*, 19.

101 *Ibid.*, 24.

102 *Ibid.*, 24-26.

103 Takaki, *Iron Cages*, 266.

104 *Ibid.*

105 Felsenthal, *Life and Times of Alice Roosevelt Longworth*, 78-79.

106 Interview with Taft by Associated Press, September, 1905, San Francisco, William

Howard Taft Papers, Manuscript Division, Library of Congress, Reel 52, Series 3, 1.

107 James Brough, *Princess Alice: A Biography of Alice Roosevelt Longworth* (Boston and Toronto: Little, Brown and Company, 1975), 170.

108 Cordery, *Alice*, 79.

109 Felsenthal, *Life and Times of Alice Roosevelt Longworth*, 80.

110 *Ibid.*, 115.

111 Brough, *Princess Alice*, 171.

112 Alice Roosevelt Longworth, *Crowded Hours* (New York and London: Charles Scribner's Sons, 1933), 72, 73.

113 *Washington Post*, "Taft on Exclusion," July 9, 1905, 1. It should be noted that Taft and others benefited from the work of Chinese laborers who worked as deckhands on the *S.S. Manchuria*.

114 *Ibid.*

115 Commencement speech at Miami University, Oxford, Ohio, June 15, 1905, William Howard Taft Papers, Library of Congress, Manuscript Division, Reel 51, Series 3.

116 Longworth, *Crowded Hours*, 75-80; Cordery, *Alice*, 81.

117 http://www.archives.gov/education/lessons/hawaii-petition.

118 Brough, *Princess Alice*, 170. "The special train pulled out of Washington bound for San Francisco in a reek of smoke and magnesium flaring up from the photographers' flash pans ... Singly or in groups of every size, ladies protected from the sun by outsized hats, gentlemen sporting white bucks and tweed caps, they posed from morning until nightfall" (Brough 170).

119 Stacey A. Rozik, "The First Daughter of the Land: Alice Roosevelt as Presidential Celebrity, 1902-1906," *Presidential Studies Quarterly*, Winter 1989. Vol.19, No. 1, 51.

120 Cordery, *Alice*, 116.

121 Letter, William H. Taft to Nellie Taft, Tokyo, July 25, 1905, William Howard Taft Papers, Library of Congress Manuscript Division, Reel 25, Series 2, 1.

122 Lewis E. Gleeck, Jr., *Nine Years to Make a Difference: The Tragically Short Career of James A. LeRoy in the Philippines* (Manila: Loyal Printing, 1996), 54.

123 Longworth, *Crowded Hours*, 78.

124 Pringle, *Life and Times of William Howard Taft*, 293.

125 Stacey A. Rozik, "The First Daughter of the Land," 53, 54.

126 Longworth, *Crowded Hours*, 75.

127 *Cincinnati Times-Star*, "Just One Ship Sighted," August 19, 1905, 2.

128 Cordery, *Alice*, 113.

129 Letter, William H. Taft to Nellie Taft, *S.S. Manchuria*, September 24, 1905, William Howard Taft Papers, Library of Congress, Manuscript Division, Series 2, Reel 25,16,17.

130 Letter, William H. Taft to Nellie Taft, Tokyo, July 25, 1905, Library of Congress, Manuscript Division, William Howard Taft Papers, Reel 25, Series 2.

131 Letter, William H. Taft to Nellie Taft, August 1, 1905, Library of Congress, Manuscript Division, William Howard Taft Papers, Reel 25, Series 2.

132 Longworth, *Crowded Hours*, 76.

133 Gleeck, *Nine Years to Make a Difference*, 53.

134 Brough, *Princess Alice*, 171, 173.

135 *Ibid.*, 173.

136 *Ibid.*,175.

137 Letter, William H. Taft to Nellie Taft, Tokyo, July 25, 1905, Library of Congress, Manuscript Division, William Howard Taft Papers, Reel 25, Series 2.

138 It appears that Doris Kearns Goodwin makes a significant error related to the chronology of the 1905 mission. Goodwin implies that the Taft party began the trip in Manila, Philippines, and arrived in Japan around the time of the Portsmouth Peace Treaty to a rousing welcome. She gives the impression that they received such a welcome because of the peace negotiations. In fact, as described on these pages, the Taft party disembarked in Japan on July 25th to great fanfare. In September, only Alice Roosevelt's part of the Taft party, including many of the younger members, who had split with Taft and his group in Hong Kong, traveled on to Peking (Beijing) and then returned to Japan in September after the treaty was signed. Taft had traveled back with his part of the party to the United States and did not return to Japan in September. Goodwin, *The Bully Pulpit*, 429-433.

139 Kennedy, *Tragedy*, 206, 207.

140 Cordery, *Alice*, 119.

141 Letter, Lloyd Carpenter Griscom to Brother Rodman E. Griscom, American Legation, Tokyo, Japan, August 9, 1905, Lloyd Carpenter Griscom Papers, Library of Congress, Manuscript Division, 4.

142 *Ibid.*

143 Longworth, *Crowded Hours*, 86.

144 Pringle, *Life and Times of William Howard Taft*, 297.

145 Michael Shaller, *The United States and China: Into the Twenty-First Century* (New York and Oxford: Oxford University Press, 2002), 34.

146 Pringle, *Life and Times of William Howard Taft*, 297.

147 Ralph Eldin Minger, *William Howard Taft and United States Foreign Policy: The Apprenticeship Years, 1900-1908* (Urbana and London and Chicago: University of Illinois Press, 1975), 143.

148 *Ibid.*, 148.

149 Pringle, *Life and Times of William Howard Taft*, 293.

150 Dalton, *Theodore Roosevelt*, 282

151 Anthony, *Nellie Taft*, 245-246.

152 Longworth, *Crowded Hours*, 86, 87.

153 *The New York Times*, "Miss Roosevelt's Ball Closes Manila Visit: Taft Guests at Most Elaborate Affair in City's History," August 13, 1905, 4.

154 *Ibid.*

155 William Howard Taft Papers, Section 2; Longworth, *Crowded Hours*, 90-91.

156 *New York Herald*, "20,000 Moros in Parade for Taft," August 21, 1905, 9.

157 *New York Herald*, "Tribes Gather to Greet Taft Party, August 24, 1905, 9.

158 Ross, *An American Family*, 171.

159 Longworth, *Crowded Hours*, 89.

160 *Ibid.*, 90.

161 *Ibid.*

162 *Ibid.*, 89-92.

163 *The New York Times*, "Sultan of Sulu Offers to Wed Miss Roosevelt: Says His Filipino People Wish Her to Remain Among Them," August 22, 1905, 7.

164 David S. Woolman, et al., "Fighting Islam's Moro Warriors – P," *Military History Magazine*, April 2002, 1.Dec.2006<http://www.freepublic.com/^http:/freerepublic. com/focus/news/654540/posts.

165 *Ibid.*

166 *Ibid.*

167 *The New York Times*, "War Department Gets News," March 10, 1906, 4.

168 Pringle, *Life and Times of William Howard Taft*, 295.

169 Minger, *William Howard Taft and United States Foreign Policy*, 65.

170 Burton, *William Howard Taft*, 31.

171 Herbert S. Duffy, *William Howard Taft: Life of a President* (New York: Minton, Balch & Co., 1930), 273; Max Boot, *The Savage Wars of Peace: Small Wars and the Rise of American Power* (New York: Basic Books, 2002), 69; Ninkovich, *The Wilsonian Rise of American Power* (New York: Basic Books, 2002), 69; Ninkovich, *The Wilsonian Century* (Chicago and London: The University of Chicago Press, 1999), 25.

172 Michael Hunt, *Ideology and U.S. Foreign Policy* (New Haven, Conn., and London: Yale University Press, 1987), 69.

173 Hunt, *Ascendency*, 5, 40.

174 Shaller, *The United States and China*, 18.

175 Williams, *Tragedy*, 63

176 *Ibid.*, 64.

177 Catherine A. Lutz and Jane L. Collins, *Reading National Geographic* (Chicago: University of Chicago Press, 1993), 18.

178 One of William Howard Taft's brothers, Horace Taft, founded the prestigious Taft School, which has long been considered one of the best boarding schools on the east coast of the United States. Toward the end of his life and shortly after the outbreak of World War II, Horace Taft authored a conceptualization of a super-community in a thesis that he presented to Margaret Sanger, an advocate of planned parenthood. In this utopian eugenics-based community, Horace Taft suggested the selection of women who would be artificially inseminated by the sperm of a group of the supposed "best and the brightest" white, Christian men including Oliver Wendell Holmes, William Howard Taft, Elihu Root, then Harvard President Charles William Eliot, and more. The wives would live with their own husbands even though they wouldn't be true biological fathers. Birth control would be employed to prohibit offspring from less desirable genetic matches with the overall purpose to increase measurable intelligence. Horace Taft wanted to place his experiment outside a major city in a peaceful spot and included more description of how to form his utopia. The original draft of this plan resides in the Taft papers in the Taft School archives, but it will not be open to researchers until 2016. Another transcription is located in the Sanger Papers in the Library of Congress. Letter, Horace Taft to Margaret Sanger, May 27, 1941, Taft, "Plan," 15, and Sanger to Taft, May 27, 1941, Library of Congress, Manuscript Division 10:719-722.

179 Lutz and Collins, *Reading National Geographic*, 19.

180 *Ibid.*, 16.

181 *Ibid.*, 17.

182 *Ibid.*, 28.

183 *Ibid.*, 30.

184 Hunt, *Ideology and U.S. Foreign Policy*, 69-77; As Hunt states, "The Chinese were the first East Asians to appear on the American horizon. Initially, the Chinese had been seen secondhand, through the writings of European observers who filtered imperial China though the soft haze of their Enlightenment preconceptions. From a distance China appeared an ancient civilization whose cultured people and achievements in the fine arts and benevolently despotic government gave much to admire. But alongside this positive view prevalent among the American elite, there developed another strain of thought that was critically condescending toward a people who did not embrace free trade, who suspiciously held foreigners under control, and who followed pagan rites and such immoral practices as infanticide and polygamy." (Hunt, 69).

185 *Ibid.*, 127.

186 *Ibid.*

187 *Ibid.*, 126-128.

188 *Ibid.*, 58-79.

189 Pringle, *Life and Times of William Howard Taft*, 297.

190 *Ibid.*, 43, 69; Emily S. Rosenberg, *Spreading the American Dream: American Cultural and Economic Expansion,1890-1945* (New York: Hill and Wang, 1982), 43; Ninkovich, *The United States and Imperialism* (Malden, Mass.: Blackwell, 2001), 38.

191 *Ibid.*, 38.

192 *Ibid.*, 30-40.

193 David F. Musto, *The American Disease: Origins of Narcotics Control* (New York and Oxford: Oxford University Press, 1999), 30.

194 Rosenberg, *Spreading the American Dream*, 43.

195 *Ibid*, 43-45.

196 Boot, *Savage Wars of Peace*, 71.

197 Walter Russell Mead, *God and Gold: Britain, America, and the Making of the Modern World* (New York: Alfred A. Knopf, 2007), 375.

198 *Ibid.*

199 Jonathan Spence and Annping Chin, *The Chinese Century: A Photographic History* (London: HarperCollins, 1996), 27.

200 John King Fairbank and Merle Goldman, *China: A New History* (Cambridge, Mass.: Harvard University Press, 1992), 234.

201 *Ibid.*

202 Boot, *Savage Wars of Peace*, 74.

203 Shaller, *United States and China in the Twentieth Century*, 34.

204 Boot, *Savage Wars of Peace*, 74.

205 *Ibid.*, 78.

206 Richard D. Challener, *Admirals, Generals, & Foreign Policy: 1898-1914* (Princeton, N.J.: Princeton University Press, 1973), 198.

207 Hunt, *Ascendancy*, 48.

208 Spence, Chin, *Chinese Century*, 30.

209 Boot, *Savage Wars of Peace*, 69-98.

210 Shaller, *The United States and China in the Twentieth Century*, 75.

211 Jonathan Spence, *The Search for Modern China*, (New York: W.W. Norton & Co., 1990), 235.

212 *Ibid.*, 79.

213 *Ibid.*, 78-80.

214 Boot, *Savage Wars of Peace*, 80.

215 *Ibid.*

216 *Ibid.*, 82.

217 *Ibid.*

218 *Ibid.*, 85.

219 Williams, *Tragedy*, 62.

220 Jane Hunter, *The Gospel of Gentility: American Women Missionaries in Turn-of-the-Century China*, (New Haven, Conn.: Yale University Press, 1984), 5.

221 Hunter, *Gospel of Gentility*, 18.

222 *Ibid.*, 18-21.

223 *Ibid.*, 25.

224 "Any of various Chinese units of value based on the value of a tael weight of silver." from *Merriam Webster's Collegiate Dictionary*, Tenth Edition, (Springfield, Mass.: Merriam-Webster, 1996).

225 Spence, *Search for Modern China*, 233.

226 Spence, Chin, *Chinese Century*, 30.

227 Spence, *Search for Modern China*, 233.

228 Michael Hunt, "The American Remission of the Boxer Indemnity: A Reappraisal," *The Journal of Asian Studies*, Vol. 31, No. 3 (May, 1972), 541, 542.

229 *Ibid.*, 542.

230 *Ibid.*

231 *Ibid.*

232 *Ibid.*, 544.

233 *Ibid.*, 539.

234 *Ibid.*, 547-548.

235 *Ibid.*, 548. According to Jenks, "On the average for the next twenty years there will be received in the average of about $1,200,000 per annum, thereafter an average of about $1,600,000. In my judgment it would be peculiarly fitting to have this money so expended by the United States as to bring about closer relations politically and industrially with China."

236 *Ibid.* Jenks assessed that the United States had already employed $50,000 to aid China in formulating a plan for their monetary system

237 *Ibid.*, 2.

238 *Ibid.* In an additional memorandum to Roosevelt, dated March 23, 1904, Professor Jenks noted that the indemnity should not be considered a "conscience fund," but rather should promote the interests of the Chinese and Americans; nor should recommendations for use of the returned remission suggest that the indemnity demanded by the "Powers" was unfair. He reiterated that the Chinese requested the return of the funds with as few conditions as possible, but that the "United States, of course, would need to be assured beyond question that the right use would be made

of the money." Since Jenks was appointed to create a gold standard for China, and all the great powers had declared that they were in favor of a new monetary system on a gold basis for China, one of his major recommendations for the indemnity lay in that area

239 *Ibid.*, 2. About establishing such a system, Jenks stated: This action should be taken now as promptly as possible. China is now considering a new monetary plan. Her government has within a few months committed itself to the desirability of this plan but they are still drifting on in the old way, coining their old moneys steadily. The longer China delays, the more expensive and difficult it will be for her to change. Such a gift would possibly tend also to allay the present irritation against the United States.

240 *Ibid.*, 1.

241 *Ibid.*, 3.

242 Letter, Jenks to William H. Taft, July 1, 1905, San Francisco, William Howard Taft Papers, Manuscript Division, Library of Congress, Reel 51, Series 3, 1-3.

243 Franklin Matthews, *The Sun*, Editor's Office, New York, September 22, 1905, Theodore Roosevelt Papers, Reel 59, Series 1, 1. According to the Editor, His (Tong's) plan was that the United States should retain the money and use its income for the education of Chinese boys to be sent here by the government. He said that fully fifty boys a year could be educated in that way, and he pointed out what a boon to China that would be and also what a bond of perpetual friendship such a course might create.

244 Hunt, *Reappraisal*, 549.

245 *Ibid.*

246 Hunt, *Reappraisal*, 539-541.

247 *Ibid.*, 541.

248 *Ibid.*, 550.

249 *The New York Times*, "Robert S. McNamara, the Architect of a Futile War, is Dead at 93." July 7, 2009, A20. It was a question he was incapable of answering. After playing a supporting position in fire-bombing cities and killing 100,000 men, women, and children in Tokyo alone during World War II, McNamara was plagued by guilt in his later years. General Curtis E. LeMay of the U.S. Army's Armed Forces, who was also involved in the bombings, said that they would have been prosecuted as war criminals if they had lost the war. LeMay said about McNamara and himself, "And I think he's right. He – and I'd say I – were behaving as war criminals.

250 William Nimmo, *The United States, Japan, and the Asia/Pacific Region*, 1895-1945 (Westport, Connecticut: Praeger Publishers, 2001), 71.

251 Guanhua Wang, *In Search of Justice: The 1905-1906 Chinese Anti-American Boycott* (Cambridge, Mass. and London: Harvard University Asia Center and distributed by Harvard University Press, 2001), 3-5.

252 *Ibid.*, 6.

253 *Ibid.*, 11.

254 Hunt, *Ascendancy*, 39.

255 Takaki, *Iron Cages*, 248.

256 Dalton, *Theodore Roosevelt*, 284.

257 Takaki, *Iron Cages*, 248.

258 *New York Times*, "Chinese in Hawaii Aid the Boycott," July 14, 1905, 6.

259 *New York Times*, "Chinese Very Bitter Against This Country," June 28, 1905, 4.

260 Spence, *Search for Modern China*, 235.

261 Shih-shan Henry Tsai, *China and the Overseas Chinese in the United States, 1868-1911* (Fayetteville: University of Arkansas Press, 1983), 106.

262 The U.S. Congress issued a proclamation of 'regret' about the Chinese Exclusion Act on June 12, 2012. Jung Chang, *Empress Dowager Cixi: The Concubine Who Launched Modern China* (New York: Alfred A. Knopf, 2013), 258.

263 Kristin Hoganson, *Consumers' Imperium: The Global Production of American Domesticity, 1865-1920* (Chapel Hill: The University of North Carolina Press, 2007), 20, 21.

264 Wang, *In Search of Justice*, 138.

265 Letter, Henry B. Miller, U.S. Consul General to Francis B. Loomis, Assistant Secretary of State, August 8, 1905, Theodore Roosevelt Papers, Library of Congress, Manuscript Division, Reel 57, Series 1, 2.

266 *Atlanta Constitution*, "American Boycott Forerunner of Cry by the Chinese of Death to Foreigners," September 14, 1905, 1.

267 John Marshall Harlan was a respected Justice of the United States Supreme Court from 1877 to 1911.

268 Letter, Edwin Gill to William H. Taft, June 28, 1905, William Howard Taft Papers, Manuscript Division, Library of Congress, Reel 51, Series 3, 1,2.

269 Wang, *In Search of Justice*, 89.

270 *Ibid.*, 89.

271 Tsai, *China and the Overseas Chinese*, 104.

272 Ibid.

273 Enclosure No. 3 in Dispatch No. 23, H.I.H. Prince of Ch'ing, President of the Board of Foreign Affairs to Honorable W.W. Rockhill, July 6, 1905, P. 1, 2, Theodore Roosevelt Papers, Manuscript Division, Library of Congress, Reel 56, Series 1.

274 Wang, *In Search of Justice*, 2.

275 *Ibid.*, 2, 3.

276 Dalton, *Theodore Roosevelt*, 284.

277 Wang, *In Search of Justice*, 166.

278 *Atlanta Constitution*, "All Americans Are Under Ban," July 21, 1905, 4.

279 Tsai, *China and the Overseas Chinese*, 110.

280 Wang, *In Search of Justice*, 8, 9.

281 *Ibid.*, 39.

282 *Ibid.*, 112 .

283 *Ibid.*, 9.

284 *Ibid.*, 113.

285 *Los Angeles Times*, "That Chinese Boycott," July 13, 1905, 14.

286 Spence, Chin, *Chinese Century*, 35.

287 Consul General Thomas Sammons to Honorable W.W. Rockhill, American Consulate General, August 2, 1905, Niuchwang, China, Theodore Roosevelt Papers, Manuscript Division, Library of Congress, Reel 57, Series 1.

288 *Washington Post*, "Extends the Boycott: Anti-American Movement Has Spread to Siam," August 11, 1905, 4.

289 Wang, *In Search of Justice*, 10.

290 Spence, *Search for Modern China*, 236.

291 Wang, *In Search of Justice*, 127.

292 Memo, W.W. Rockhill, to the Secretary of State, Washington, D.C., No. 23, American Legation, Peking, China,, July 6, 1905, Theodore Roosevelt Papers, Reel 56, Series 1, 5.

293 *Atlanta Constitution*, "American Schools Menaced By Boycott," July 14, 1905, 14.

294 Wang, *In Search of Justice*, 115-117.

295 Thomas Sammons, Counsul General, American Consulate General, Niuchwang, China, to Honorable W.W. Rockhill, August 2, 1905, Peking, China, Theodore Roosevelt Papers, No. 41, Manuscript Division, Library of Congress , Reel 57, Series 1.

296 Letter, Sd. Julius Lay, American Consul General to His Excellency Tsen, Viceroy of the Two Kwangs, Canton, China, August 8, 1905, No. 117, Enclosure No. 3., P. 2, Theodore Roosevelt Papers, Manuscript Division, Library of Congress, Reel 57, Series 1.

297 James L. Rodgers, American Consul-General, Shanghai, China, to Honorable Francis B. Loomis, Assistant Secretary of State, Washington, D.C., July 27, 1905, No. 27, Theodore Roosevelt Papers, Manuscript Division, Library of Congress, Reel 57, Series 1.

298 No. 2 in Dispatch No. 23, W.W. Rockhill, Envoy Extraordinary and Minister Plenipotentiary of the United States, American Legation, Peking, China, June 17, 1905, Enclosure 12, Theodore Roosevelt Papers, Manuscript Division, Library of Congress, Reel 57, Series 1.

299 *Los Angeles Times*, "Chinese Going for Americans," July 20, 1905, 11.

300 George Anderson, Consul, to Honorable W.W. Rockhill, American Envoy and Minister Plenipotentiary, Peking, China, July 25, 1905, Theodore Roosevelt Papers, Manuscript Division, Library of Congress, Reel 57, Series 1.

301 *Ibid.*, 2-4.

302 *Washington Post*, "Chinese Attack Flag," August 23, 1905, 4.

303 *Los Angeles Times*, "Chinese Forcing the Boycott Fight," July 28, 1905, 12.

304 Mr. Shaw, Treasury Department, Washington, D.C., to President Roosevelt, Oyster Bay, New York, August 1, 1905, Theodore Roosevelt Papers, Manuscript Division, Library of Congress, 57, 1.

305 *New York Times*, "Chinese Very Bitter Against This Country," June 28, 1905, 4.

306 *Atlanta Constitution*, "Conger to Go to Orient to Fight Chink Boycott," August 19, 1905, 5.

307 *Washington Post*, "Chinese Attack Flag," August 23, 1905, 4.

308 Wang, *In Search of Justice*, 15, 131.

309 Tsai, *China and the Overseas Chinese*, 121, 122.

310 Sd. Julius G. Lay, American Consul General, Canton, China, August 4, 1905, Enclosure No. 1, No. 268 to The President of the Opposing Exclusion Treaty Society, Kwong Chai Hospital, Theodore Roosevelt Papers, Manuscript Division, Library of Congress, Reel 57, Series 1, 2.

311 Wang, *In Search of Justice*, 161.

312 Tsai, *China and the Overseas Chinese*, 115.

313 Wang, *In Search of Justice*, 180.

314 *Ibid.*, 181.

315 Tsai, *China and the Overseas Chinese*, 121.

316 *Los Angeles Times*, "Taft Leaves for America, Found No Hostile Feeling Among Japanese, Chinese Lost Fifteen Millions by the Boycott," September 18, 1905, 12.

317 *Washington Post*, "Boycott Forbidden," July 2, 1905, 5.

318 *Atlanta Constitution*, "Imperial Ban Put on Boycott," September 2, 1905, 2.

319 Tsai, *China and the Overseas Chinese*, 121.

320 *New York Herald*, "Seeking to Learn Losses in Boycott," August 23, 1905, 20.

321 Wang, *In Search of Justice*, 27.

322 Challener, *Admirals, Generals*, 215.

323 *Ibid.*, 216.

324 *Ibid.*

325 *Ibid.*, 217.

326 *Ibid.*

327 *Washington Post*, "Boycott Forbidden," July 2, 1905, 5.

328 Wang, *In Search of Justice*, 190.

329 Hunter, *Gospel of Gentility*, 3.

330 Tsai, *China and the Overseas Chinese*, 121, 122.

331 Wang, *In Search of Justice*, 188.

332 *Ibid.*, 190.

333 *Ibid.*, 194, 195.

334 Spence, *Search for Modern China*, 243.

335 *Ibid.*, 244.

336 Chang, *Empress Dowager Cixi*, 325-329

337 Chang, *Dowager Cixi*, 325.

338 *Ibid.*, 247, 249.

339 *Ibid.*, 250-252.

340 *Ibid.*, 247, 248.

341 *Ibid.*, 234.

342 *Ibid.*, 256.

343 *Ibid.*, 238.

344 *Ibid.*, 234.

345 *Ibid.*, 240.

346 W.W. Rockhill, Minister of China, from American Legation, Peking, to President Roosevelt, July 7, 1905, Theodore Roosevelt Papers, Manuscript Division, Library of Congress, Reel 56, Series 1.

347 *New York Times*, "Miss Roosevelt May Not Go," August 17, 1905, 1.

348 Cablegram, Secretary of War to Minister Rockhill, August 28, 1905, William Howard Taft Papers, Manuscript Division, Library of Congress, Reel 52, Series 3.

349 *New York Times*, "Taft Party at Hong Kong," September 3, 1905, 1.

350 Cable, Taft to Roosevelt, Theodore Roosevelt Papers, Manuscript Division, Library of Congress, Reel 59, Series 1.

351 Telegram, Taft to Roosevelt, Canton, September 4, 1905, Theodore Roosevelt Papers, Manuscript Division, Library of Congress, Reel 59, Series 1.

352 Telegram to Secretary Taft, Telephone conversation transcription between Assistant Secretary Loomis and White House, Oyster Bay, N.Y., September 2, 1905, Theodore

Roosevelt Papers, Manuscript Division, Library of Congress, Reel 59, Series, 1.

353 Telegram, J. Parker to Hon. F.B. Loomis with request that it be given to the President, White House, New York, September 2, Theodore Roosevelt Papers, Manuscript Division, Library of Congress, Reel 59, Series 1.

354 Interview, William H. Taft by Associated Press, September, 1905, San Francisco, William Howard Taft Papers, Manuscript Division, Library of Congress, Reel 52, Series 3, 12-13.

355 *Washington Post*, "Canton Boycott Checked: Visit of Secretary Taft and Party Has Immediate Effect," September 5, 1905, 1.

356 Letter, Secretary William H. Taft to Viceroy, Canton, China, September 5, 1905, William Howard Taft Papers, Manuscript Division, Library of Congress, Reel 52, Series 3.

357 *New York Times*, "Canton Cordial to Taft," September 5, 1905, 6.

358 *Washington Post*, "Canton Boycott Checked: Visit of Secretary Taft and Party Has Immediate Effect," September 5, 1905, 1.

359 Challener, *Admirals, Generals*, 216.

360 Tsai, *China and the Overseas Chinese*, 112.

361 Wang, *In Search of Justice*, 114.

362 *Washington Post*, "Miss Roosevelt's Pluck in Face of Peril in the Orient," February 9, 1905, 6.

363 *New York Times*, September 13, 1905, 1.

364 *Washington Post*, "Miss Roosevelt's Pluck," 6.

365 Longworth, *Crowded Hours*, 91.

366 Cordery, *Alice*, 123.

367 *Washington Post*, "Miss Roosevelt's Pluck," 6.

368 Longworth, *Crowded Hours*, 91.

369 Wang, *In Search of Justice*, 190.

370 *Ibid.*

371 *Ibid.*

372 Cordery, *Alice*, 123, 124.

373 H.W. Brands (ed.), *The Selected Letters of Theodore Roosevelt* (New York: Cooper Square Press, 2001), 1235.

374 *Washington Post*, "Washington Girl Won," September 6, 1905, 5.

375 Shang, *Empress Dowager Cixi*, 258

376 Interview with the Associated Press, September, 1905, San Francisco, William Howard Taft Papers, Manuscript Division, Library of Congress, Reel 52, Series 3, 13.

377 *Ibid.*

378 Letter, Taft to Nellie Taft, September 24, 1905, William H. Taft Papers, Manuscript Division, Library of Congress, Reel 25, Series 2.

379 Taft's interview with Associated Press, September, 1905, San Francisco, William Howard Taft Papers, Reel 52, Series, 3, 14.

380 *New York Times*, "Taft Arrives at Capital," October 2, 1905, 6.

381 Taft's Interview with Associated Press, September 1905, San Francisco, 17.

382 *Washington Post*, "Taft Party's Itinerary," August 29, 1905, 1. As recorded by *The Washington Post*: Governor Wright cabled the War Department from Manila that "the

following members of the Philippine party will go to Pekin, and thereafter travel independently: Senator and Francis G. Newlands, of Nevada; Senator Francis E. Warren, of Wyoming; Representative Bourke Cockran, of New York; Representative Frederick H. Gillett, of Massachusetts; Representative Nicholas Longworth, of Ohio; Miss Alice Roosevelt; Miss Mabel Boardman, of Washington, D.C.; Miss Amy McMillan, of Washington, D.C., William S. Reyburn, of Washington, D.C.; Rogers K. Wetmore, of Newport, R.I; Arthur H. Woods, of Groton, Mass.; Fred E. Warren, of Cheyenne, Wyo.; Mr. and Mrs. Emile Godchaux, of New Orleans, La.; Mr. Lafe Young, of Des Moines, Iowa, editor of the Capital; J.G. Schmidlapp, of Cincinnati, Ohio, president Union Savings Bank and Trust Company; Stuyvesant Fish, Jr., of Washington, D.C.

383 *New York Times*, "Legation Guard Changed, Marine Officer Displaces Infantry Captain at Peking," September 13, 1905, 4.

384 Letter, Henry C. Corbin to Secretary William H. Taft, William Howard Taft Papers, Manuscript Division, Library of Congress, Reel 51, Series 3, 2.

385 Memorandum, John W. Chaffee, War Department, July 21, 1905, Theodore Roosevelt Papers, Library of Congress, Manuscript Division, Reel 57, Series 1.

386 Letter, Charles J. Bonaparte, July 24, 1905, Theodore Roosevelt Papers, Library of Congress, Manuscript Division, Reel 57, Series 1.

387 Memorandum, Henry Corbin to William H. Taft, August 23, 1905, William Howard Taft Papers, Manuscript Division, Library of Congress, Reel 52, Series 3, 2.

388 *Los Angeles Times*, "Corbin at Peking," September 13, 1905, 11.

389 Longworth, *Crowded Hours*, 93.

390 *Ibid.*

391 Felsenthal, *Life and Times of Alice Roosevelt Longworth*, 84.

392 Cordery, *Alice*, 124.

393 Longworth, *Crowded Hours*, 94, 95.

394 *Ibid.*, 95.

395 *New York Times*, "Chinese Empress Cordial: Chats Informally with Miss Roosevelt and Other Americans," September 16, 1905, 7.

396 S. Fish, *1600-1914*, 236.

397 *New York Times*, "Chinese Empress Cordial, September 16," 1905, 7.

398 S. Fish, *1600-1914*, 236.

399 *Ibid.*, 99.

400 Felsenthal, *Life and Times of Alice Roosevelt Longworth*, 83.

401 *New York Times*, "Miss Roosevelt at Peking," September 13, 1905, 4; New York Herald, "Empress Dowager and President's Daughter," September 24, 1905, magazine, 1.

402 Longworth, *Crowded Hours*, 95.

403 *Ibid.*, 100-103.

404 Cordery, *Alice*, 124.

405 Longworth, *Crowded Hours*, 100-101

406 *Ibid.*

407 Felsenthal, *Life and Times of Alice Roosevelt Longworth*, 83.

408 Longworth, *Crowded Hours*, 101-102.

409 *Ibid.*, 102.

410 *New York Times*, "Rides on Palanquin," September 20, 1905.

411 Longworth, *Crowded Hours*, 100-101.

412 *Ibid.*, 103.

413 *Ibid.*, 105.

414 Ross, *An American Family*, 170.

415 Lloyd Carpenter Griscom Papers, Memorandum to Elihu Root, September 15, 1905, No. 306, General Correspondence, 1905-1911, Library of Congress, Manuscript Division.

416 *Ibid.*, 9.

417 Longworth, *Crowded Hours*, 107.

418 *New York Times*, "Miss Roosevelt to Pay $25,000 Duty on Gifts," October 18, 1905, 9.

419 Cordery, *Alice*, 136-137.

420 *Ibid.*, 139-161.

421 *New York Times*, "Luck, Says Mrs. Longworth," October 1, 1905, 14.

422 John K. Fairbanks, *China Reinvented: Images and Policies in Chinese-American Relations* (New York: Vintage Books, 1976), 94.

CHAPTER 2   FRANCIS W. FROST →

Letters to His Father from China

→ Sunday dinner on the Great Wall.

On Board *Logan*
China Sea
En Route, Hong Kong
September, 1905

My Dear Father,

At the end of a history making trip, the important stage of which has just been concluded, it is difficult to form a clear impression of the ground covered, so kaleidoscopic and rapid have been the changes of events since we reached Manila, almost four weeks ago; suffice it to say, taking the trip as a whole, that it has been without doubt the best managed and most satisfactory personally conducted party that ever crossed the sea. From San Francisco to Japan, to Manila, and the week's visit there, and then the triumphal progress from island to island in the wonderful Philippine archipelago, back to Manila, and thence to Hong Kong. All has been accomplished without hitch or accident of any nature which can be traced to those in whose hands the conduct of the party had been placed. To Colonel Clarence R. Edwards, Chief of the Bureau of Insular Affairs, belongs the credit for the handling so efficiently this large party of some eighty persons representing as they do every section of the United States and so many different tastes and inclinations.

Only a man with tact and a military training and such efficient Aides as Captains J.K. Thompson and William Kelly could carry out successfully a plan covering so wide a range of possibilities. In every way has the party been

→ On deck of the transport *Logan*.

favored with the best. The Pacific Mail Steamship Company went to large expense said to be $11,000, by changing its schedule so that the magnificent "Manchuria," one of the largest vessels afloat, could carry the party to Manila—not in her regular route—and the "Korea" bringing back from Hong Kong those whose plans are to return at once. Speaking only for the trip over, the meals, service, and general management of the "Manchuria" left nothing to be desired, and a testimonial to that effect complimenting Capt. Saunders and his officers has been drawn up and signed by the entire official party—and will be presented to Mr.

Schwerin, President of the Pacific Mail, upon the return of the party to San Francisco. As to the Transport "Logan" which safely carried its precious cargo through the islands and reefs of the Archipelago, too much praise cannot be given to the Quartermaster Captain Simpson for his thoughtful consideration of the comfort and welfare of his passengers. In the matter of food the quantity and quality—the latter especially has been without precedent on a Transport, and this with other attentions has won for Captain Simpson the well-merited esteem of all on board.

The ship's master, also Captain Simpson, deserves praise for the way he has handled his vessel in waters known to be treacherous, and for being on schedule timed to a minute at every stop. Fair weather has prevailed since July 8th until the last few days when we got into the outer edge of a typhoon. This is not unusual in the tropics at this time of year as typhoons and deluges of rain are the regular thing. Calm seas have also been the order until recently and on the "Manchuria," the decks were in continual use for games, lounging, or dancing. If anyone aboard was under the impression when starting that those who make our national laws cannot unbend, he was very soon undeceived for a jollier and more unconventional family party would be hard to find. From the secretary of war down to the humblest unofficial guest, the best of spirits prevailed, and all entered healthily into whatever was afoot, whether a lecture on the Burnham plans for beautifying Manila or a sheet and pillow case party. Thus, the time was passed crossing the broad Pacific except for one delightful day at Honolulu (See photo. Party at Nu'uanu Pali, Hawaii). The week's visit to Japan was a grand fete from start to finish, the Japanese people outdoing themselves in courtesy and hospitality to such an extent, it is said that the celebrations in honor of Secretary Taft and his distinguished fellow travelers were greater even than those for General Grant or any of the heroes of the present. But the spirit of the party, and quite the liveliest member of it, was Miss Alice, the charming daughter of President Roosevelt, known on board as "The Princess," who lived up to, and perhaps at times surpassed in unconventionality—her democratic Republican father. Always ready for a frolic, she was the center and leading spirit of many a jolly party, and with her offhand, girlish manner, won the hearts of all. One week was allowed for Manila, and probably a week so full of events social and official seldom occurs. Besides functions planned ahead for several evenings and some for the afternoon, conferences were held daily at the "Palace" for the purpose of discussing affairs of state. The tariff in all its ramifications was overhauled. Arguments on free trade, sugar, tobacco, etc., were heard; visits were made to factories and plantations, and the last two days before leaving for Hong Kong, complaints were received from anyone who was "agin the Government." These last were mostly from agitators and chronic hecklers who were quickly dispatched, their arguments for the most part being childish and demonstrating their utter incompetency to conduct a government in modern civilized times. However, the tour has been a wonderful eye-opener for many members of Congress and some who heretofore had most pronounced views on Philippine's questions have modified them considerably, and all express themselves as being much benefited by the observation they have made. There is one point on which they are almost unanimous, and that is the question of independence. It has been clearly demonstrated that the Filipino of the present generation is utterly unfit for that high estate, and that it depends entirely on the results of the system of education now in force to decide what future generations will be capable of doing. Some of the commissioners have tried to defend their old opinions on this burning question, but while all have not been converted to the views of the majority, some have, and the rest have modified theirs. On other matters there seems to be the unanimous opinion that if prosperity is to be a fact in these islands, the tariff and stringent laws governing the holding of lands or mining claims by corporations or even private individuals must be abolished or considerably modified. Under present conditions it would be the maximum of folly for any capitalist to invest any large sum of money in the Philippines.

There are plenty of opportunities for investment here provided proper legislation is enacted, and in such a case, lots of American money, the only solution for the Islands, will be brought here. There are immense tracts of sugar, tobacco, and hemp lands uncultivated and grazing lands capable of supporting over a million head of cattle. The mining proposition has scarcely been scratched, and, so far, coal, though not containing as high efficiency as some of our steaming coals or Japanese coal, has been located in large quantities. Gold, silver, iron, and copper are also here, but in what quantities have not yet been determined. Another line which is ripe for development is the establishment of small water-works, sewer systems, and light and power plants. There are many towns of fair size lacking these essentials entirely, and others where the methods used are vague or absurdly inadequate. On the other hand, it is said that the wants of the Filipino are so small that he will not take kindly to what we consider necessities. He takes his water from the nearest river or well and goes to bed at dark or sits up by the light of an oil lamp, but as about 98 % of the inhabitants are uneducated, this luxury is unnecessary as they do not read. The better classes use oil lamps and in Manila and Iloilo electric lights. Thus, it would seem that the whole problem hinges on education, and this is welcomed everywhere, and the schools are taxed to the utmost. The one fault, if such it can be called, with education is that instead of applying his knowledge along lines of usefulness, the one idea of the Filipino who has learned to read and write is to get a government position when actual labor, as it is generally understood, is not called for. I believe that the curriculum as carried out in many schools will be reorganized and instead of teaching higher mathematics, geometry, algebra, etc., manual training will be brought more to the front. In the early days of the American regime, it was claimed that we could not get the Filipino "tao" (laborer) to work steadily but Mr. Krusi of the Atlantic, Gulf and Pacific Company, who has the contacts for the great harbor improvements at Manila, killed this theory by taking the native in hand and training him and giving him a square deal as a man, something which he was not used to, with American overseers, and paying living wages. The result has been that more Filipinos handle their machinery, lay concrete masonry, and, in fact, perform all the labor in their works. J.G. Whittles have had the same experience and the trolley line in Manila, as fine a system as can be found in the U.S., was built with Filipino's labor, and the cars are now run by native motormen and conductors. It is education, then, and the next generation of Filipinos that we may look to for results, and I believe they will justify the government of the U.S. for holding the Islands. As the Honorable W. Bourke Cochran (sic) said in a speech in Manila a few nights ago that it is from philanthropy, and that is the first case on record where conquest was conducted for any other purpose than plunder, but in this instance it will be to the everlasting glory of the United States.

After a week in Manila full of banquets, receptions, and dances, a tired but grateful party sailed out by Corregidor Island for the southern trip. Briefly, I've touched on the following places: Iloilo and Bacolod in the sugar district, then Zamboanga, the capital of Mindanao and Jolo where lives the Sultan of Sulu, and where we were entertained with the sight of thousands of picturesque Moros; thence to Malabang where we dropped a small party who crossed the peninsula of southwestern Mindanao by way of Lake Lanao to Camp Overton where we picked them up the next day. Cebu, the great hemp port on the populous island of the same name was the next stop followed by Tacloban in the province of Leyte and reached by small vessels through the beautiful straits of Juanico. Legaspi, with splendid smoking volcano, Mayon, Albay, and Sorsogon, were the next places in order which with Tacloban are situated in the richest hemp country in the world. In all the towns at which we touched, Secretary Taft was welcomed by processions and banquets and most laudatory speeches. If there is any discontent on the Islands, it is in Luzon and generally close to Manila and fomented by a few agitators and soreheads.

We are now at Hong Kong and are to spend one day at Canton, and then our party will be scattered to the four parts of the Campos. A little party of about 30, including Miss Roosevelt, Senator and Mrs. Newlands, Representatives Gillette, Cochran, and Longworth, and general and Mrs. Corbin, are going to Peking to pay our respects to Tsi An, the Dowager Empress (sic). I remarked yesterday that we will have seen two picturesque personages—the Sultan of Sulu and the Dowager Empress, and my friend said, "and the Dowager is the better man of the two."

Am trying to write a more detailed letter.

Your loving son,
Francis

With Miss Roosevelt in China
On Board *Logan*
Yellow Sea
Friday, September 8, 1905

○—→ Landing from the tugs at Taku.

Dear Father,

We are now sailing north with beautiful weather bound for Pekin. At this moment—numbers are 28 degrees 58' N to 122 degrees 56' E, just about opposite Shanghai but out of sight of land. The "Logan" will not stop at Shanghai but go straight to Taku where we expect to be on Monday. Then there is a day's trip to Pekin with a stop at Tientsin. Traveling as we are now is superb. I have the sensation of touring on a private yacht. We have a ship of nearly 500 feet, exceptionally well provisioned with only about forty passengers and a most congenial party at that, and our band of four officers. The main object of the trip is to take 150 marines to Peking to relieve the present Legation Guard. Every evening at five o'clock, the bugle blows and the marines form for inspection on the forward deck and mount guard, and at 10 p.m. the bugle blows "taps" and the lights go out in the men's quarters. At nine a.m., there is another guard mount. Some of the passengers are the following: Miss Roosevelt, Misses Boardman, McMillan, Critten, Schmidlapp, Langhorn, Vice Governor Ide of Manila and two daughters, General and Mrs. Corbin, Senator and Mrs. Newlands, Senator Warren and son and daughter, Mrs. Pershing, Col. Knight, Capt. Cosby, Moss, Penn, Horton and Lee, Lt. Holcombe and Capt. and Mrs. Hocum, (Moss, Penn and Horton are General Corbin's aides and Lee and Holcombe are in charge of the marines), Reps. Cochran, Gillette and Longworth, Colonel and Mrs. Coleman, Chief J.M. in the Philippines, Mr. and Mrs. Godchaux, New Orleans, Messrs. A. Woods, H. Woods, Cary, Hobart, Coolidge, Wilson, Eveland, Young and Reed, Associated Press Agent. At my table are Col. And Mrs. Glenn, the Misses Ide, Capts. Cosby, Moss, and Lt. Holcombe. There is not much doing. We sit about and talk and sometime play games and for a couple of hours after tiffin (lunch), the decks are almost deserted while everyone takes a nap. The band plays on the forward deck under the awning for almost an hour and a half in the morning and from one and a half and two hours in the after deck in front of two great ventilators under the stairs in the evening. In the morning they usually play popular music, but run to the classical in the evening.

General Corbin is a quiet taciturn sort of a man and keeps pretty much to himself reading all day while his wife who was a Miss Patten of Washington and quite a society woman, and Bourke Cochran entertain each other. Miss Roosevelt improves our acquaintance, and now that our party is so small, there is plenty of opportunity to know her.

Since leaving Manila, we have had the Misses Ide who are very nice. They are tall handsome girls and very intelligent having had a great deal of travel and experience. Their father, Judge Ide of Vermont, was Governor of Samoa for four years, and they have lived in Manila where he is Vice-Governor, for five years. They are going home where they have not been for two years.

We have the best of the young fellows in the party here, a good many having left at Hong Kong. Bourke Cochran is a very pleasant man and was telling me yesterday about the trip he expects to make in China. He is going to leave us at Peking and go north by caravan and take the Trans-Siberian Railroad somewhere near Lake Baikal and will then visit Constantinople and other cities and countries in that section. His object is to learn conditions throughout the Orient as he predicts that China will be the great bone of diplomatic contention within a few years, and that things are only beginning there. I like my friend Woods very much and am sure that we will get along well together. We have no inbound plans but at present propose to go to Peking, the Great Wall—a three or four days round trip on horseback—if steamer time will allow. The "Logan" will have left by the time we return from the Wall, and we will either take a local boat plying between Taku and Kobe, Japan, and touching two or three Korean ports or the railroad from Pekin to Hanchow and thence by boat to Shanghai and then to Japan for two or three weeks. Then, we will take a steamer at Kobe (either German or French) and stopping at Shanghai, Hong Kong, and Saigon (if French) will get off at Singapore. We want to go back to Japan, and if it is possible to do so, go around the world without covering same ground twice. We have been advised to go from Singapore to Malacca by local boat and from Malacca to Panang by rail so as to see some of the Confederated Malay States, and then to Rangoon by boat. Then we will see Burma going "from Rangoon to Mandalay" either by rail or by boat on the Irrawaddy River reversing the operation on the return. Then, by boat to Calcutta as we feel that we will not have time to go to Ceylon and southern India so will only try to see the places across the northern route to Bombay from which place we will go direct to Egypt.

The party is allowed only three days in Peking and before we can arrange for our trip to the Wall, we must figure on the steamers for Japan both from Taku and Shanghai as we would not care to be stranded in either of those places for ten or twelve days.

Hong Kong, September 1905.

Hong Kong.

A street scene in Hong Kong.

Victoria Monument, Hong Kong.

Queen's road, Hong Kong.

We had an uneventful trip from Manila to Hong Kong except the first two days when we had rough seas which drove many to the rail and their berths, but those who live in these parts say it was nothing at all for the China Sea. The last day was delightful and everybody forgot his or her troubles, and we sailed into Hong Kong bright and early Sunday morning. Hong Kong was a surprise to me. I had formed no opinion of the place, but knew it was an island, not so small. It is only twenty-seven miles around. The name of the island is Hong Kong and the city, Victoria, but it is all known as Hong Kong. The sight as you approach on a bright morning is beautiful. The mountain, Victoria Peak (1800 feet), rises almost from the sea, and the city is built up the side on terraces and the buildings, three or four or five stories in height and built of stone with arcades and porticos, from the ground up, look like pictures of ancient Athens and Rome. They have gone in for a uniform style of architecture, and the city proper is full of handsome stone buildings, especially the large hotels and banks. The streets are broad and there is a fine sea wall supporting the Praya, or waterfront street. The streets are well macadammed and are not worn out by horse as there are scarcely any used for hauling or driving in Hong Kong, both light and heavy loads being moved by man or woman power. I saw an ice wagon with twenty men, some pushing, others pulling, and all the bricks used on the addition of the Peake Hotel almost 1600 feet up are carried by men and women in baskets suspended from a bamboo strip on their shoulders, all the way from the water level. You move about either in rickshaws or chairs although there is a new trolley with Chinese motormen and conductors. I prefer the rickshaws as the chairs are too springy. The rickshaw rate is twenty cents (ten cents American) an hour and fifteen cents for the chairs, but there was a great shout and haggling if any of us strangers gave only the legal rate. However, if you have any trouble, we have only to call a Sikh policeman for whom the coolies have a wonderful fear and things are quickly straightened out. The policemen are tall, handsome, turbaned Sikhs from India, and a prouder lot of men you never saw. They are about the street everywhere, some of them six feet, six inches tall and of most dignified presence. They all carry heavy canes and use them freely on overzealous coolies with the result that a Chinaman dares not cheat or lay a hand on a white man if there is a chance of being found out.

Hong Kong. The peak in background.

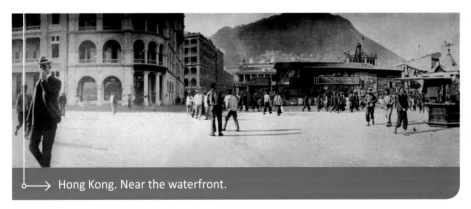
Hong Kong. Near the waterfront.

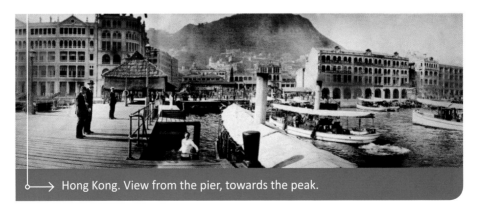
Hong Kong. View from the pier, towards the peak.

→ Hong Kong. View from the peak.

Besides the English and Chinese, we see all other nations represented in Hong Kong—Americans, French, Germans, Russians, Malays, Japanese, and East Indians—in a multitude of costumes. There are fine shops and prices are low, this being the great free port of the world. The English treated us beautifully, of course. As soon as we arrived, one of the Governor's aides came on board, and he was followed by aides from the naval and military commanders. The principal members of our party were invited to luncheons and dinners, but only on the last day, Tuesday, was a general invitation extended. That was to the gymkhana games and races in the afternoon and to a torchlight tattoo and dance and supper at the Hong Kong Club in the evening. There was also a dinner at the Government House by Sir Matthew Nathan, the Governor General, to the official party. By some fluke, the invitations were delivered at the "Korea," so that the few who remained on the "Logan" did not get ours at all and only learned of the affairs at the last moment. We had no difficulty, however, in getting into the grounds both at the races and the Hong Kong Club. Most of us remained in the steamer although some went to the Peake Hotel, while the Ides were entertained at the Governor General's palace. The tattoo was in a large open field and scheduled for 9:00, but it did not commence until 10:00 o'clock. It consisted of five bands, one from some West Kent regiment, two of pipers, and two Indian bands, and several companies of Sikhs with torches. We all had reserved seats and enjoyed the music and marching very much. After the tattoo, we all adjourned to the Hong Kong Club, about five minutes' walk. All of us walked except the Ides who were provided with chairs by the government, and it was a picturesque sight to see them carried by four men each, down the long land, followed by the double row of Sikhs, each holding a torch, and the chairmen wearing the scarlet livery of the Government with a gold crown on the sleeve. These chairmen are Chinese and wear white trousers gathered at the ankle, a small red cap, and loosened coats or capes with sleeves bearing the gold crown. The Hong Kong Club is a large stone building, and we had a dinner there about eleven o'clock. Woods, Eveland, and I were the guests of a Dr. Jordan and his wife. There were two other ladies, but I can't remember their names. We had a good dinner, and then there was dancing, but the English dance with such a rush that the Americans were all exhausted when we left at about 1:30.

A Chinese funeral in Hong Kong.

Chinese boats near Hong Kong.

A rickshaw in Hong Kong.

Hong Kong. Halfway up the peak.

The trip to Canton was really the most interesting and exciting event of our visit to Hong Kong. On Sunday morning, Consul General Bragg came on board and advised the Secretary on account of the boycott not to accept the invitation of the Viceroy to visit Canton, or if he did so, to take a bodyguard of marines with him. A long argument followed in the smoking room in which the General stated that it was dangerous for Americans to go unprotected to Canton as that city is the most anti-foreign of any in China and is now especially anti-American. The Secretary finally decided to go and invited a party of forty to accompany him without a guard of any kind except such as was promised by the Viceroy. He said the women should not go and could not be responsible for those not invited and requested that they remain in Hong Kong. This was a disappointment to the greater portion of our party as Old Canton was one of the chief objects of our long journey. But the feeling of impending danger lent an atmosphere of mystery to the whole affair, and so ten of us decided to go on our own hook in another night boat. Somebody started an alarm about Chinese unreliability by saying it was a bad sign that although the Viceroy had invited the party to dine, he would not be present himself saying that he was sick. It was afterwards found to be true that he was very ill. Woods had a letter of introduction to Ah Kum, the best guide in Canton and sent him a telegram on Sunday and received an answer in the evening that he would meet us at the boat. Our river boat, the Hankow, left Hong Kong at 10:30 p.m. and just before going to, we heard that word had been received from Consul Lay that the boycott had been raised, so that those who got cold feet and remained behind were mad enough.

Inside the five-story pagoda in Canton.

> Steps near the five-story pagoda, Canton.

> A Chinese junk.

It was a beautiful cold night, and Hong Kong lighted was wonderful to behold; along the river front were myriads of lights, both from paper lanterns and oil and electric lamps, and these could be followed up the mountain showing the lines of the terraces clear to the signal station at the top. We wound about through the river boats, junks, and sampans on which a large portion of the population spend almost their entire lives, up behind the island of Hong Kong and into the Pearl River. The Hankow is a large side wheeler built thirty years ago in Glasgow and was packed below and forward with Chinese until it seemed as though not another one could come on board. In the cabin, however, we were very comfortable. There was a good-sized dining saloon with a long table in the center, and around this were the staterooms, the largest I ever saw except the best rooms on ocean liners, and arranged for three to a room. They were all taken as some of the Secretary's party had to go on our boat. I slept very well and on waking in the morning, the first sight to greet my eyes was a row of large wooden buildings and oil tanks on shore bearing the legend in great painted letters, "Standard Oil Company of New York," showing the similarity of that infant industry with the British Empire, on which the sun, it is said, never sets.

We dressed and had breakfast on board—a breakfast of so many courses that I lost count—and when engaged in this pursuit, Ah Kum was announced. He is quite a good-looking Chinaman, sixty-one years old he told us later, but doesn't look it and wore a little skull cap, a short grey silk jacket and dark-colored silk trousers, and the usual Chinese shoes. He has lived in Canton most of his life and has been a professional guide for twenty years and enjoys the reputation of being the best and most honest of his kind. He has two sons who are following his footsteps, and all speak good English. While guiding a tourist about, he pays for all purchases, tips, etc., and you square up at the end of the day. It is absolutely necessary to have a guide in Canton for without one, the foreigner would be lost in the labyrinth of narrow streets before he had gone one hundred yards from the river, and as the city is built without any pretense of regularity; a stranger is in much the same plight as one lost in a forest. We left our boat at eight o'clock and found that Ah Kum had provided chairs for each of the four in our party, consisting of Woods, Cary, Chapin and myself, and one for himself much better than ours, and which I believe was his own. Each chair had three bearers dressed in nothing but a bit of cheese cloth and a circular hat two feet in diameter and coming to a point at the middle. The steamer had provided us with a lunch as there is no place in the native city where a foreigner can eat, and this was stored in the guide's chair.

When all was ready, we started off and before I could realize it, it seemed as if we had gotten into another world. The narrow streets with their hundreds of signs hanging overhead, the bright garish colors everywhere, and the shouting chairmen, and those bearing boxes, packages, refuse, everything— all shouting incessantly to clear the way. The crowd was with us always, not following but right there wherever we happened to be, and everywhere we were pointed to and stood out. The only exceptions were occasionally when we passed in his chair some man of the better class. These paid little or no attention whatever to us, but gazed ahead expressionless through their great heavy rimmed spectacles. We saw no women of the better classes and few who were not of the coolie class bearing heavy burdens the same as the men. Everywhere in the streets, shops, and even the money changers, the men wore nothing above the waist. The entire city seems to be given over to trading, the rich living in the suburbs, but we saw only shops everywhere, all small but generally clean. There were rows upon rows of shops selling shoes, fans, jade, silks, linen, or what-not, and we stopped at several. There is another street for money changers, and on all sides you could hear the clink as coins were shoveled into bags or sifted through sieves with holes cut just large enough for pieces of a certain amount to fall through.

We went into the money changer as Cary wanted some more Canton money. This money is good only in Canton and Hong Kong and will not be accepted for the same value in Shanghai or Peking. The houses in Canton are three or four-storied brick structures, each with its little notch by the ground where incense sticks are kept burning to the god of good fortune, and every shop has its alter with candlesticks inside, the rest of the decorations being the gaudy Chinese style of silks, paper, tinsel, and painted wood. The pawn shops—and there are many of them—are seven or eight-storied square buildings, and here you may pawn anything of any value from a cent up. The streets, or more properly lanes, are narrow, the two widest in the city being only eight feet across and in some instances at a corner, the chair man in front would go into a shop to give the men in the rear room enough to turn, and at other times, we had to stop crowded against a wall to let another chair pass. Above everywhere are the long signs and in some cases lamps dripping with glass prisms of all colors so that it is only rarely that any sunlight is seen causing the stone-flagged streets to be continually damp and slimy.

But the worst feature of Canton is the stench that constantly assaults you, especially when passing one of the many cook shops, but everywhere the same smell or smells prevail. The blocks are built solid in most cases from street to street so that the houses do not get aired, and you can imagine the result is a city of four million or more packed solidly in an area no larger than an American city of thirty-five or forty thousand. Besides the foul smells of the place, you have a particular loathing for the people who everywhere crowd about, and when the day was over, I felt as if I had every disease in the calendar. The mortality must be appalling, if known, for everywhere were children especially and older people in all stages of physical disintegration most sickening to behold.

About noon we worked over toward the edge of the city where there is a five- storied pagoda by the Wall, and where there is open country. The pagoda is on a hill, and we walked up a long flight of stone steps while the men followed with the chairs. At the pagoda, we climbed to the top floor and ate our lunch on a balcony overlooking the city. From there we were carried along the wall where there are still some old cannons to the City of the Dead where fine lacquered coffins of the rich are left in little alcoves until the time for burial. There is one coffin said to have cost $3000 Gold. In the rooms are also the jewelry and a few other belongings of the deceased, and food and tea are set on the table every day and incense kept burning. The whole place is nicely kept up—cement floors and neat white, one-storied houses and outside are quantities of flowers giving the effect of a garden.

From this place we returned to the city passing through the Tartar City where the soldiers live in small one-storied barracks, and here we saw women with their feet bound so that they stumbled about in a most ungainly fashion. Another stop was the law courts, but they were closed. We looked into the prison to where a crowd of malefactors were clanking about in chains behind wooden bars. There did not appear to be much restraint, and we were invited to go behind the bars. One of the fellows did, but the rest forfeited not to take the chances of catching some disease. From here we went back through the town by devious ways, making few stops, to the steamer where we paid Ah Kum for the purchases and his time and agreed that the whole thing was not real, but a hideous nightmare, but at no time was cause given by word or look to show that there was any ill feeling towards the United States. Ah Kum's charge for the whole day including chairs with three men each, all tips and his fee was $4.50 a piece or $2.25 gold.

Some of the places we visited were feather, linen, silk, and other shops, and some temples, particularly that of the "500 Genii" with its 500 gilt carved wood Buddha's. We passed through the Shameen, or European concession, and I tried to find Charles R. Paget, a friend, but it was too early as people do not come to their offices here until about 10 o'clock, and I did not have time to make another attempt. The official party saw scarcely anything of the city, and the ladies nothing. When we were through with our guide, Cochran took him to see some of the city for an hour before the boat left.

The river population of Canton is estimated at half a million people, most of whom are born and brought up on boats and know nothing of the shore, but swarm about the river. I tried to get some pictures in Canton, but it was hard to take them in the streets as the light was bad, and the people crowded right up against you when you stop; and, besides, they do not like to have their pictures taken. At the pagoda, I wanted a picture of our party in the chairs, but the coolies dropped the chairs and fled when I pointed my camera, so I did not press the matter. On the return trip we passed many junks and small boats with some old fashioned iron cannons for protection against the pirates who still infest these waters and prey upon the small sailing vessels. There were also three nine-storied octagonal pagodas, very old, one with a large tree growing from the tip. On our arrival at Hong Kong we had breakfast and returned to the "Logan" on a sampan, and all hands made a break for a much needed bath.

Sunday, September 10, 1905

Our trip from Hong Kong has been uneventful except our one incident which commenced with all the symptoms of one of the mysteries of the deep. Last night just at sunset, a small boat was sighted rolling and plunging without mast or spar, and a lantern and small flag at the stern. I was in my room dressing for dinner when a boy knocked and said we had overhauled a shipwrecked crew so I pulled on a coat and rushed to the deck above and on the starboard side saw a small Chinese fishing boat bobbing on the waves. Our searchlight was brought to bear on the boat, and we could see about a dozen men in the after part in what we imagined to be the last stages of exhaustion clinging to anything they could hold onto. Our ship slowed down and circled about them, and a boat was manned and lowered, and we all quivered with excitement on the deck as we watched the two boats in the ring made by the searchlight. Presently, our boat turned and was pulled back, and when she came alongside, the officers in charge said there was nothing the matter but that the fisherman had only stored everything away for the night. One of the men who went out told me that when they arrived at the junk, the men all laughed, and one of them asked our people if they had any cigarettes. So our rescue at sea was a complete fiasco.

This morning when I appeared on deck, we were passing the Shantung peninsula, and there are four steamers and several sailing vessels and a lighthouse in sight. Yesterday afternoon we passed a large English steamer quite close. We are now just about west of Wei-Hei-Wei and heading straight for Dalny and will pass about twenty-five miles north of Port Arthur. There is some talk of stopping at Port Arthur on the way to Japan, but this is still uncertain. That we are out of the tropics is very evident as it is too cool for white clothes, and yesterday I dug up my blue suit which I have not worn since the first few days out of Frisco and find it very comfortable.

Monday, September 11, 1905

Yesterday, almost an hour before sundown, we passed Port Arthur and everyone tried to pick out the opening, but nobody knew exactly where it was. This morning we have been met by the whole Asiatic Squadron in Chinese waters and the "Ohio" which left Manila after us, but arrived here first. They saluted as we dropped anchor. We are still out of sight of land, and it is said that the Viceroy will send a steamer about to take us to Tientsin. This ship cannot go to Taku as the harbor is bad. It is also rumored that we will not go ashore today as we were not expected until tomorrow. I will mail this letter as soon as I can and write another about Pekin, the Wall, etc.

12:30—We're still here at anchor and cannot leave until the Viceroy sends a boat for us so we are making the most of it. Everything is packed to go ashore, but we have settled back to the routine of the day. This afternoon we will take tea on the different battleships. The squadron consists of three battleships, the "Ohio" (flagship—Admiral Train), "Oregon," and "Wisconsin," two cruisers, the "Raleigh," and "Cincinnati," and two gunboats, the "Alava" and "Quiros" and five destroyers. The Admiral and the Captains have all made their calls, and the boys on board have been gossiping with wig wags, and the bands have played on the "Logan" and on the battleships. I am going to take tea on the "Wisconsin," but have not heard yet who else is going on that ship. I have just paid my bill for the entire time since coming on board for the southern cruise on the 13th of August, and it was only $30.00. I think that is the cheapest traveling I will ever do. Besides this there are numerous trips, and I gave $5.00 to a fundraiser for the band to take the trip to Peking. They are allowed to go only by permission of General Corbin, but the Government cannot pay their way.

A lighter and two tugs have just come alongside with the most piratical-looking crew one ever saw. The coolies, burned as dark as some of our negroes, are stripped to the waist and have their hair tied up in red, yellow, blue, or dirty white cloths and are busy unloading the marines' stores under the direction of Lt. Holcombe. The prospect for tonight is not pleasant to contemplate. The understanding now is that we leave the ship at twelve midnight arriving at Taku about three or four in the A.M. where we will cool our heels until 8 a.m. when a special train will convey what promises to be the most disgruntled and ugly-tempered party of Americans that ever arrived in China, to Peking. I am afraid that I will not have the pleasure of meeting the Dowager as only a small and selected party will enjoy the privilege, but no doubt there will be some rare opportunities offered for seeing things. Accommodations are scarce in Peking, and it is reported that there are but fifty-four available rooms in the city for transients, but Holcombe has offered me a cot in the Marine barracks if all else fails.

11:30 p.m.—We have had one of the pleasantest afternoons of our trip. At 3:30 a naval launch and several boats came alongside to take our party to the "Wisconsin." It was a pretty sight, the white battleship and cruisers in one row and the black destroyers in another, and the launch and gigs with their crews of twelve oarsmen, and helmsman, and an officer in each in the foreground. Each of the small boats had a flag at the stern and the seat reaching about six feet forward from the stern on either side was covered with cushions and a silk bunting cover, and as the boats came and left the steps, the sailors "tossed" the oars. Twelve of us went in the Captain's barge from the "Wisconsin," and we had twelve husky seamen to row us over a distance of about half a mile. The big battleship was decorated and the crew and marines and officers, in all about 750 men wore their best white uniforms, and a band was playing on deck. We were received and introduced all around and there was some dancing, but none of our fellows took part as there are not many ladies and thought the uniforms ought to have the floor. One of the young officers named Holmes invited a few of us to go over the ship, and he showed us everything. We crowded into the turret containing the two thirteen inch guns, and he had one of the guns manned and explained the entire mechanism and set the whole machinery going from the ammunition hoist three decks below to turning the turret around. They have the record for big gun practice, and this gun has fired twelve shots in one minute and twenty seconds and this means hoisting each shell from the bottom of the ship. It takes twelve men to man the gun and each has his specific duty to perform. We went to other parts, and I climbed up the outside of the mast to the crow's nest where the range finder is. Then, we came back and cleaned up and had a pleasant tea.

Just after dinner our company of marines left amid cheers and the waving of handkerchiefs to commence their three years as the legation guard. The guard which will be returned has been there since the Boxer troubles five years ago. We had at table with us this evening Capt. Leonard, Military Attaché in Peking who lost one arm in the fight at Tientsin. He went back with Capt. Lee and Lt. Holcombe and the Marines. Mr. Carey of our party went with them, and they asked Woods and me to go, too, but as the best sleeping accommodations they could offer was a blanket on the iron floor of an open lighter, we declined as the nights are getting cool.

Tuesday, September 12, 1905

We did not go ashore last night but are still here. Some legation officers from Pekin came down last night and seem to have a long program proposed extending through the week, but Gen. Corbin says he is going to pull out Thursday. This will not affect us, however, as I am leaving the "Logan" here.

Your loving son,
Francis

→ Launches on the way from *Logan* to Taku.

September 13, 1905

We got away this a.m. and are now 11:30 in Pekin. We had to go almost 20 miles in tugs and launches sent by the Viceroy. We passed Taku and at Tongku; the Empress's own cars were in waiting, and after some kowtowing by Mandarins present, we pulled out for Peking. The train was a magnificent one, the furniture upholstered, and the heavy curtains of the finest silk and tapestry. We had the best lunch I have eaten for months, and everything was done on an excellent scale. Three or four high class Chinese went along and at Tientsin, there was a very unsoldier-like company of Chinese soldiers drawn up on the platform with a good band. We arrived at Peking a few minutes after five, the whole trip from the boat having occupied seven hours. We had to wait at the bar while the water rose high enough to pass over. At Pekin we had been assigned to the two hotels in the foreign city. I am at the Hotel du Nord with most of the men and the wives of some of them. They are mostly officers. This hotel has a very unpretentious front, but inside it rambles all over the country, and it requires an expert guide to go to and from one's room. It must have been an ancient temple almost a thousand years ago. It is all on the ground floor and is run by a Frenchman. If a stranger from Mars dropped in here, he would wonder if the country was German, French, Russian, English, American, or something else—the foreign flags and soldiers are so much in evidence. Only a very small party is going to see the Empress, about ten I think.

Francis

→ Inside the Hotel du Nord.

→ A courtyard in the Hotel du Nord.

→ A courtyard in the Hotel du Nord.

→ A courtyard in Hotel du Nord.

September 24 (Tuesday), 1905

My Dear Father,

I arrived here this a.m. on my way back to Japan from Peking. We thought that our five or six days flying visit to Japan was not enough, and so are returning for a two or three week's stay. Peking is a hard place to get away from as steamers are very irregular and the channel at Taku bad. Woods and I returned from the Wall last Tuesday, but no boat left Tientsin until Sunday morning, and as we had seen all we wanted of Peking, we had the unpleasant prospect of waiting three or four days in a hotel when our friends, the officers at the Legation Guard, came to our rescue and carried us off to their quarters, and when time came to go, we hated to leave. The present Guard is a company of Marines who came from Manila with us on the Logan to relieve a company of the 9th Infantry who had been stationed at Peking since the Legation were relieved in 1900. The present Guard is a picked company, and they are all fine-looking men; in fact, a much better- looking set in every respect than any of the other guards. They are tall, slim, well set up fellows, young and intelligent and in their clean, close-fitting khaki uniforms, make a fashionable contrast against the sloppy, wooden-headed Germans, Russians, Austrians, and others. The officers in charge are Capt. Lee, Lt. Holcombe, and Dr. Taylor of the Navy, and another lieutenant named Larned, brother of the well known tennis player, is expected out shortly. The American Legation Guard is the last on the west end of Legation Street and runs through to the Wall which is under American control from the Chien Men to the Water Gate. The Wall is fortified at the west end of the concessions with a concrete wall about eight feet high, apparently solid, but built so that loopholes can be knocked out in certain spots by removing a few inches of cement and a brick or two, and a stone blockhouse with loopholes. Field pieces can also be mounted here so as to sweep the wall in either direction. These defenses are in charge of the Americans, and the magazine is in the Wall directly below the blockhouse which can be approached from the ground by a perpendicular iron ladder in the Wall reaching from the magazine to the blockhouse so that in case of trouble, it would not be necessary to ascend the Wall from the outside. These defenses as well as others around the legations have been built since the Boxer Rebellion in the 1900s. At the east end of the concession, the Wall is defended by a blockhouse in charge of the Germans. On two sides of the concessions (north and east) not touched by the Wall, all ground is cleared to a distance of one hundred to two hundred yards where were previously low, wooden Chinese houses. There are still many houses on the west side, but these are to be removed. Every precaution is being taken to prevent another such recurrence as took place in 1900. Some of the ministers, among whom is Mr. Rockhill, do not approve of making a display of force, but others, principally the Germans, do and have frequent parades through the streets with several companies of men, cannons, wagons, etc. Mr. Rockhill would not even have sentries posted at the gates of the compound, but apparently this is required by the regulations and is kept up. Captain Lee is making many improvements in the territory under his command which seems to have allowed to run down badly by the army, and in the short time he has been there, he has introduced running water where it has always been carried before, and the grounds generally look cleaner and better kept than when we arrived. At present the American Legation is in the small quarters nearly a mile from the barracks, but the handsome new stone buildings next door are nearing completion. We went through them the other day with the architect and in my opinion the United States may well be proud of its new quarters. They are plain dignified buildings of granite taken from quarries almost thirty miles from Peking and are five in number and are built on three sides of a rectangular court. The minister's residence is at the end nearest the street, but facing the city wall. On its left are the houses built from the same general design, but much smaller, for the first and second secretaries, and on the other side, the office building and the residence of the Chinese secretary. The compound enclosing these is four hundred feet square, and next door is the Dutch Legation while to the west is the Legation Guard. This compound is a little larger than that containing the Legation buildings and contains the officers' quarters, a solid block of five two-storied houses, with separate buildings for a small office and the hospital to the north. On the west are the men's quarters; on the south, separated from the Wall by the street, are the lavatories, kitchens, and mess rooms for the men and guard house, and on the east side are the quartermaster's office and store houses. In the court is the parade ground, and to one side, a distilling plant through which all the drinking water passes, and a *small* house containing ten field pieces including two Gatlings, two to three inches, three Vickers-Maxim, and three Colts quick-firing guns, so that there is quite a formidable battery besides the troops. There is also a tennis court on the ground. On the other side of the Dutch Legation is the corral where the horses and wagons are kept.

⟶ Near the railway train in Taku.

3rd class accommodations on the train.

A special train for the U.S. Delegation, Taku.

Miss Alice Roosevelt on the train.

→ At the railway station of Tientsin.

But I have got off the regular course of event. As stated in my last letter, we arrived at Taku on Sunday night, the 11th, and through some fluke had to spend all day Monday down the bay. We were cheered, however, by taking tea on board the "Wisconsin" and early Tuesday morning left for Tongku on small steamers. At Tongku, a representative of the Viceroy met the party with more Chinese soldiers, and the private train made up principally of the Empress's own cars was at the dock waiting for us and started almost immediately. On the way up we stopped at Tientsin where there was a crowd, a very good Chinese band, and two companies of Chinese soldiers. We were given a splendid lunch and arrived at Pekin a few minutes after 5 o'clock. The ride to Peking is a tiresome one. The country is flat and much resembles

→ Crowds at a railway station on the way to Peking.

Nebraska with its acres of sorghum, a kind of sugar cane which looks like corn. There are also other acres of uncultivated ground covered with large and small mounds—the graves of ancestors. Even the fields are full of these, but the farmer is careful to plow around them and not disturb the mounds themselves.

There were quite a lot of people at the station when we arrived in Peking, and one of General Corbin's aides, who had gone up the day before to make arrangements, gave each of the party a card with the name of the hotel to which he or she had been assigned. Some were sent to the Hotel Wagon Lits, a new hotel near the Water Gate, while the rest including myself went to the Hotel du Nord just across from the eastern end of the concession and on the Hatamen Road. Our hotel is the older, and until the Wagon Lits was completed, was the best in Peking, but neither would be even second class at home. The Wagon Lits is a poor attempt at an up-to-date house and is kept by a German, and the advantage of the Hotel du Nord was that is nothing more than it pretends to be, and you get lost every time you step out of your room. It is all on the ground floor and is composed of a lot of old Chinese buildings mixed up in a regular maze so that to go from the office to my room, I went through two narrow winding passages and crossed three courts. The place was patronized by all kinds of Europeans and is kept by a Swiss who doubles in trying to do his best under very unfavorable conditions. When we struck the place, we filled every available corner, and other arrivals had to be turned away. The other hotel had the advantage as an evening resort, and while the party was in town, we would jump into rickshaws after dinner (which commences at 8 o'clock out here) and visit for an hour or two at the Wagon Lits.

→ A street scene in Peking.

→ Arch on Main Street of Tartar City, Peking.

→ An arch at a city gate in Peking.

On Wednesday morning we started on a sight-seeing trip. Our party consisted of four—Cary, Woods, and myself, of the original party, and Eveland of the Geological Department in Manila, who came up on a vacation. We got a useless Chinese guide and took rickshaws and bumped over vile roads along the Hatamen Street to the Lama Temple. On the way we passed under the Von Ketteler Arch built by the Chinese on the spot where the German minister was killed by the Boxers on his way to call on the Yamen or Chinese consul. It is a granite structure after the Chinese style, and its being built by the Chinese was one of the articles of the treaty after the Boxers were suppressed. The Lama Temple, only a few years open to the public, was very interesting. There was a solid stone tablet about eight feet high by three feet wide, and on each of the four sides was the history of Lamaism in a different language— Chinese, Manchu, Mongol, Tibetan. There were prayer wheels and ancient maps. In the large temple hall is a Buddha seventy feet high, all lacquered, fine old cloisonné, and carvings. Like other temples and palaces in Peking, many of the finest treasures were looted by the Allied Armies in 1900. From the Lama Temple, we went to the Confucian Temple with its marble terraces and teak wood columns forty feet high and which contains tablets to Confucius, Mencius, and other ancient Chinese teachers. There are some five Cyprus trees here said to have been planted over a thousand years ago during the Sung Dynasty. But the principal objects of interest are the Stone Drums dating from the Zhou Dynasty—about 1170 B.C. There are ten of these solid masses of hard stone with Chinese characters engraved upon them, and it is said that they commemorate great hunting and fishing expeditions of ancient rulers and are very much revered today.

→ Hall of Classics, Peking.

→ Hall of Classics, Peking.

Pi Yung Kung in the Hall of Classics.

Pi Yung Kung in the Hall of Classics.

Pi Yung Kung in the Hall of Classics.

→ Pi Yung Kung in the Hall of Classics.

The next place was the Hall of Classics with two hundred texts of the Nine Classics. This was done so that if the books were destroyed (which happened later), the works of the great writers of antiquity could be preserved. We went to the Drum Tower next, built in characteristic Chinese style, but like everything else, rapidly going to decay. It is one hundred feet high, and you get a splendid view of the city. After lunch we went to the Temple of Heaven and the Temple of Agriculture. They are great tracts of land with some forlorn buildings in them which would be beautiful if kept up. There is fine marble work with intricate carving and the buildings have tiled roofs of wonderful shades of blue, green, and yellow. But everywhere you find the same neglect, rank weeds, and long grass overgrowing what must once have been magnificent stone-flagged drives and delightful gardens. When the Allied Armies entered Peking, the British occupied the grounds of the Temple of Heaven and the Americans the Temple of Agriculture. The Emperor visits these places only three times a year, and then the weeds in the immediate vicinity of the temples are cleared up, and the place put in condition, but at other times somebody pockets the money appropriated to keep the places in order.

A city gate in Peking.

View of Peking from the Great Drum Tower.

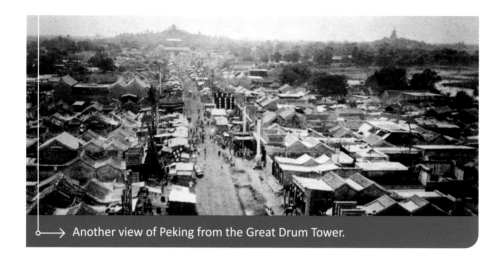

→ Another view of Peking from the Great Drum Tower.

→ The Bell Tower of Peking.

This finished our first day except for stopping on the way back at a place where a lot of mountebanks were doing stunts. Then, we wandered back through the throngs looking into the shops and through the Chien Men Gate where the gate is being repaired of the damage done during the siege. The scaffolding is much like that used in building England of a multitude of sticks tied together but here the scaffolding is put up, and the actual work commences at the top, and at present on the Chien Men about one hundred feet up is a most ornately painted beam which will be the highest point of the gate when the work is completed.

→ Yellow Temple, outside the Wall of Peking.

> Base of a tomb in the Yellow Temple.

The next day the same party took rickshaws, but no guide except a little book which Eveland had and visited the Yellow Temple about a mile north of the city.

> Tomb in the Yellow Temple.

This place that was once very beautiful is now in a most dilapidated state, and in this respect the Chinese temples differ mostly from the Japanese. But the attraction at the Yellow Temple are the beautiful and magnificently carved white marble monuments erected over the clothes of Tishu Lama, a religious figure who died of small pox when on a visit to Peking. His body was carried home, but his clothes were buried at the Yellow Temple. This temple was once famous for images of gilded bronze which were made there and sold mostly for the Mongols and various ethnic groups. There are only a few Chinese living there now, and as in all other temples, they all hold out their hands for something and are never satisfied with what they get. The marble monument is certainly a thing of beauty being covered with rich carving, but unfortunately nearly every face has been chipped by the Japanese. The fallen down state of so many temples and buildings in and around Peking is due to the occupation of the armies in 1900.

Curious monument near five pagoda temple, North of Peking.

From the Yellow Temple we worked our way across fields and bad roads to the Great Bell Temple. The temple was built in 1734, but the bell dates back to 1403. It is thirty-four feet in circumference, eight inches thick, and weighs 87,000 pounds and is engraved in small Chinese characters, both inside and out over its whole surface. At this place the Lama priests gave us tea, and we were apparently a great source of amusement to them. The rickshaw men had some "chow" outside, and then all hands proceeded to the Five Pagoda Temple. To reach this, we wander through famous and small hamlets quite off the track inquiring of everybody. It was along toward the middle of the afternoon, and the rickshaw men showed signs of a strike, but we pushed forward on foot most of the time as the paths were narrow and finally reached our destination and were repaid for the journey for the Pagoda Temple is one of the rare sights of Peking and quite unlike anything else there. Its style is not Chinese but East Indian as we all recognized at once from the images carved all over it. It was built almost five hundred years ago by a Hindu who came to Peking on a visit. It is a square mass of masonry fifty feet high covered all over with images of animals and gods, and on the flat top are five small pagodas each eleven stories high.

→ Five pagoda temple outside the Wall of Peking.

The Italian soldiers were quartered here, and the adjoining temple has been almost completely demolished, and the whole place is a picture of ruin and rubbish. We next put for the hotel, and much of the route was along the road which leads from the Winter Palace in Peking to the Summer Palace about fifteen miles to the north. This road outside the city walls is paved or flagged with large stones and must be a very old road as the edges of the stones are quite round and smooth and there are spaces of two or three inches between most of them, but as the nobility usually are carried in chairs or in litters supported by horses or donkeys, they do not get the jolting which made me black and blue in many spots.

Five pagoda temple outside the Wall of Peking.

At the Great Bell Temple in Peking.

Before going on with my own travels, I should say that this was the day on which Miss Roosevelt was received at the Summer Palace by the Emperor and the Dowager. The party consisted of Miss R.; Senator and Mrs. Newlands; Senator Warren; and General and Mrs. Pershing; his daughters; Representatives Gillette, Cochran, and Longworth; Mr. and Mrs. Rockhill; and Legation Secretaries and wives; Mr. Morgan, Minister to Corsica; General Corbin and staff; Admiral Train and staff; Mrs. Corbin; the Miss Ides; and a few others in official positions; or who were wives or daughters of officials. The rest of us were disappointed afterwards to find that we could have gone also if our names had been sent in from Hong Kong, but even Vice Governor Ide, whose name was omitted, could not go, and under no conditions could he be included after the list was once made up. As it was the largest party ever presented at one time, and in many ways, it was an unprecedented occurrence. It was, in fact, the reason we came to Peking as the Empress had sent an invitation to Miss R. to visit her, and it was thought a good time to bring the Marines up. The trip with the "Logan" cost the government almost $25,000, and there were some people in Manila who were very outspoken about using the transport for a picnic of such expense. A single company of troops would usually be sent on a collier or by some cheap boat. At any rate, grafters like myself were not finding fault. We had an ocean steamer with about forty cabin passengers, a good band, and fine food, all for $1.50 a day. Miss R. and someone else, I don't remember who, were invited to spend the previous night at the Palace—an unheard of thing—and the rest started from Pekin in chairs and carriages at five o'clock the next morning. It was a very dirty, dusty ride, and they carried their dress clothes and uniforms with them and dressed at the Palace.

Temple of Heaven in Peking.

Temple of Heaven in Peking.

Temple of Heaven in Peking.

The Ch'I Nien Tien in Temple of Heaven.

Huang Ch'iung Yu at Temple of Heaven.

→ Chai Kung at Temple of Heaven.

It was a great event and was known all over China. As it was told to me, the men and women were sent to different parts of the Palace upon their arrival to dress and did not meet again until they returned to Peking. Everybody wore full dress and civilian dress suits; the ladies wore dresses such as might be worn to a tea. It was quite amusing to hear the fellows tell about the presentation of the men—they did not see the ladies presented. They entered in order of precedence and were introduced by Mr. Wu Ting Fang, former minister to America, who acted as an interpreter. There were a few steps and a bow, then a few more steps and another bow, and finally they were all lined up on both sides of the throne where the Empress was the whole show, and the Emperor sat on one side and frowned like an amused child. The Empress, they say, is a strong featured business-like woman, and like nearly all the Chinese, has very long fingernails, but in addition to this, she wears on the fourth and fifth finger of each hand a gold spike about four inches long, slightly curved and very sharp, and the general effect is like the gaff put over the spur on a fighting cock. She was loaded with jewels and wore some especially large pearls. She made a few remarks which Mr. Wu translated, and Mr. Rockhill replied, and then they all backed out bowing and side-stepping as they went. They were taken to the gardens and shown about and given a good luncheon and were taken back to town as far as possible on the private canal—always, of course, being kept from the ladies. While they were in the gardens, the Empress passed through and made a few remarks, but was much more impressed with the ladies spending considerable time with them and, best of all, placed on the fingers of each a beautifully worked heavy gold ring set with a large pearl. People at the hotel said the rings could not be worth less than $200 or $300 each. To Miss R., she gave a ring with several precious stones and a heavy bracelet set with rubies, emeralds, and diamonds—so that it really paid for her going. The men received no presents. Altogether, it was a notable occasion.

→ The "Great Lofty Shrine" at Temple of Heaven.

In Lama Temple, Peking.

In Lama Temple, Peking.

In Lama Temple, Peking.

That evening we all received an invitation to a reception to Miss R. given by His Excellency Viceroy Yuan Shikai at his magnificent residence in Tientsin on Saturday night. The invitation came in a long red and gold envelope enclosing a large piece of red paper bearing his name which was his card, and the invite on another piece written in Chinese with a gilt border. I was unable to go to this affair, unfortunately, as we started for the Great Wall Saturday morning, and we could not lose the two days. On Friday, several of our party left on the 8:30 train to get the "Logan" which was to sail Saturday morning. The rest of us stayed to visit the Winter Palace in the Forbidden City. This was a noteworthy event as heretofore so large a party of foreigners has never been admitted to the Forbidden City on invitation. There must have been twenty or thirty, but many of these were foreigners living in Peking who were availing themselves of the only chance they would ever have to see the place.

Corner tower on the city wall of Peking, partly destroyed during the War of 1900.

Lama Temple, Peking.

Lama Temple, Peking.

→ Outside the city wall of Peking.

We started from the Wagon Lits Hotel at ten o'clock, headed by a squad of cavalry, and the party rode in two army wagons from the Legation Guard

→ Gate to one of the walls in the Forbidden City.

and rickshaws, and it was a wild ride over unspeakable roads for which Peking is famous, and another squad of cavalry brought up the rear. At the gate we were met by some troops and scores of mandarins whose grade could be determined by the color of the button on top of their hats. Mr. Wu was there and took the leading part although there were members of the nobility present ranking higher than he. We were first escorted to barges and poled across the Lotus Pond and taken through court after court and many palace buildings full of the most beautiful works of art—carvings, wonderful specimens of jade and coral, and no end of clocks. In nearly all the rooms was a most delightful odor which came from piles of apples set about in large dishes everywhere. The Chinese use apples a great deal for decorative purposes and enjoy the odor as well. Many of the buildings we passed through are new as a fire in 1900 destroyed a large portion of the palace.

> Entering the Forbidden City in Peking, Mrs. Godchaux is in the chair.

> A courtyard in the Forbidden City.

One of Empress Dowager's thrones in the Forbidden City.

After a light luncheon, we were conducted to the older part which dates back several hundred years, and the bright gaudy colors are more pleasing than the new having been toned by time. Here were bronzes, woodwork, paper, cloisonné, porcelains, and silks, etc., such as cannot be seen anywhere else, and it is doubtful if Vautine could find such anywhere for sale. Everything was opened, and we went through palace after palace, through the private apartments and gardens of the Empress, until I was dizzy. Mr. Wu was very talkative, and I had several minutes conversation with him. He is about the most broad-minded man in China and some think too free with his opinions. I asked him about the Empress, and he said that she was a very clever woman, but both she and Prince Ching, the Prime Minister, are unfortunate in not having traveled outside their own country and so don't know what is best although they think they know it all. Wu is not so influential in China as a great many in America think, but nevertheless, they say over here that he is a thorn in the flesh and would like to make some changes if he had the power. On the other hand, many Americans here hold him responsible for the boycott. Our party broke up after leaving the Winter Palace, and that is the last I saw of all but three besides Woods.

On Saturday morning all but six left for Tientsin where they would attend the Viceroy's reception and then go on one of the gunboats to Korea in response to an invitation from the King after which I believe they were going to Japan to return on the "Korea" to America. On Saturday morning at six o'clock, Woods and I started on our four days tour to the great Wall, and as a result, we missed a boat for Japan and are now languishing in Chefoo with small prospect of getting away for two or three more days. We had given up all idea of going to the Wall on account of the trouble and hardship and the aforesaid uncertainty of ships sailing from Tientsin. Those sailing on the "Logan" could have only two days in Peking, and only a very small party was going to Seoul, but if we went on the "Logan," we would have missed the Winter Palace, and then we concluded that we don't come here every summer and so decided to take our chances to see things, so we stated our determination to go to the Wall, and the hotel people made the arrangements. They found a good guide and supplied us with bedding and provisions. Then we got two horses and a Peking cart for the stuff and when we started, we had two horses or ponies for ourselves, the guide, and a horse boy on donkeys, and a cart with two more boys drawn by two ponies, one in front of the other.

→ The courtyard of an inn at Sha-Ho on way to the Great Wall.

→ The courtyard of an inn at Sha-Ho on way to the Great Wall.

→ A room in the inn at Sha-Ho on the way to the Great Wall.

It was a beautiful cold morning when we started, and that day we rode thirty-six miles over roads that it would be difficult to describe. In some places it was a broad sandy plain with the road anywhere you chose, and then it would be a donkey trail, or the road would be down in a chasm, or there would be two or three roads all on different levels full of deep ruts or big rocks or water nearly waist deep. We passed several villages and any amount of people on foot, donkey, or horseback, and long strings of camels within a few miles of Peking. After twenty miles or so, there was little besides farm life and much of this was picturesque. There were open, earthen threshing floors with men and women working flails or "separating the wheat from the chaff" by tossing it in the air so that the wind would blow the chaff away while the good grain fell to the ground. Men were plowing and harrowing and working the fields with the most primitive implements in grinding corn or other grains by scattering it on a circular stone while a blindfolded donkey walked demurely round and round, pulling a stone roller. It was like a different race from those in the cities—more cheerful and better fed—and the villages were not unlike some English hamlets that I have seen with their square one-storied mud and thatch houses. The larger towns had high stone walls and massive gates, and here as well as in Peking were the earmarks of what was once a magnificent highway. We crossed several long bridges with carved marble railings partly fallen off, and supported by substantial arches was the stone flagging, many of the stones eight feet long by three or four wide and six or eight inches thick.

→ In an inn at Nankow.

A group of "grangers" on the road to the Great Wall.

Geese and herder, on the road to the Great Wall.

It was a wonderful trip, if hard, and there was always something worth looking at. The ponies we had were poor specimens with a hard trot and no canter or gallop to speak of, and owing to the roads as much as the horses, we went at a walk most of the time. Our friends, the Marines, had fitted us out with riding togs and lent us two army cots which fold up. Otherwise, we would have been very uncomfortable. But the weather was charming. Four more delightful cloudless September days never happened. We always turned in soon after dinner by the light of the full moon and were up early in the morning, and it was great to crawl out from under three blankets into the cold mountain air just about sunrise with the moon looking like a big silver dollar. It made you forget that you were sore or stiff. The first day we stopped at a town named Sha-Ho at a Chinese inn and were given the best room while Kuan, the guide, prepared lunch. We had to put up at Chinese inns everywhere, and the guide and two boys made up the beds and got the meals while the other man looked after the horses. A Chinese inn at best is not a desirable place as a summer hotel. They are all ground floor affairs, and the kitchens, vile smelling places, are in front with the other rooms and horse sheds around the side of an inner court. The windows are lattice covered with tissue paper, and this is generally pretty well perforated; the floors are stone, and there is usually a square table with a chair on two opposite sides, and a sort of shelf place with a mirror against the wall. There are also several vases, a few paper lanterns, a couple of pewter candlesticks, and a nitch in the wall for your favorite god, and some Chinese pictures stuck about. The bed is a built-in platform across one end of the room about seven feet wide and three feet above the floor and covered with matting. No clothing is supplied as travelers are expected to carry that with them. In winter the rooms are heated by a charcoal fire under the bed or floor.

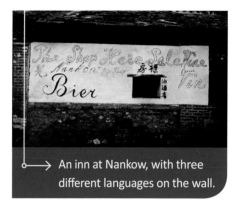

An inn at Nankow, with three different languages on the wall.

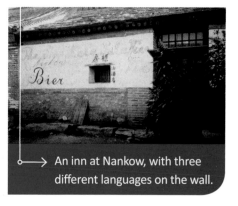

An inn at Nankow, with three different languages on the wall.

→ Courtyard of Chinese inn at Nankow, on the road to the Great Wall.

→ A bedroom in the Chinese inn. In winter, a fire is built in the opening seen in the floor.

After resting about two hours at the Sha-Ho, we remounted out steeds and walked or trotted on finding the country more desolate and barren as we got nearer the mountains. Sometimes for a change, we could get off and walk for a mile or so. At one time, we passed a great herd of sheep from Manchuria, and Kuan said they had started for Peking over two months ago. All the mutton, which is very good, comes from Manchuria. There were also droves of big black pigs and large flocks of geese and ducks. The mountain roads were so strong that I don't see how the cart, which followed at some distance, ever pulled through. In the spring the water rushes from the hills and fields up many of the roads to a depth of four or five feet, and there are deep gorges and gullies where the earth has been washed out. Our day's journey ended at the village of Nankow, an old walled town with streets full of boulders and situated in a pass in the mountains and a very important place in the old days when the Chinese and Mongolians were separate nations. Mongolia is on the other side of the Wall about fifteen miles further, but we put up at the best inn at Nankow for the night. It was a more pretentious place than the inn at Sha-Ho and just before arriving there, we were overtaken by four of our friends who were making the same trip. They were young Warren, Mr. and Mrs. Godchaux, and Hobart. The final three are with us now. The interior court was a large square, and the Chinaman who kept the place showed evidence of his contact with foreigners, for painted on the wall in a labored attempt at English was a legend, "The Shop Here Sale Wine." The entrance from the street was through an arch and on the street side and part of one other side were kitchens and servants' quarters. On the side facing the entrance in back of the square were five guest rooms, and we took them all; on the other side was a sort of open stable, and there was another stable back of our rooms made very evident by the smells and the sonorous voices of the donkeys. The whole place was thoroughly oriental, however, with the exception of the aforesaid sign and harmonized well with the ancient agricultural methods and the total ensemble might just as well have been in ancient Judea as in China as far as it was affected by modern civilization.

→ A camel train passing through Nankow.

→ On the way to the Great Wall.

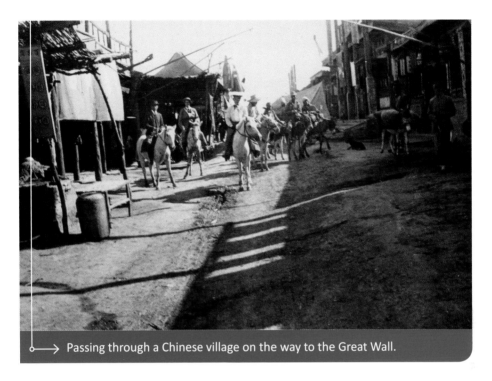

Passing through a Chinese village on the way to the Great Wall.

Entrance to the inn at Nankow on the road to the Great Wall.

Gambling in court, at Nankow Inn.

Warren, Hobart, and Godchaux, on their way to the Great Wall.

→ A caravan in front of the inn at Nankow.

→ Gateway of a Chinese inn at Nankow on the road to the Wall.

→ A Chinese inn at Nankow, on the road to the Wall.

To add to the illusion when I stepped out in the morning, a caravan of camels loaded with boxes and sacks of stuff from away up in the interior was passing the inn slowly winding its way up the crooked, stony street. Several more caravans passed before we had finished breakfast, but we did not meet any moving during the day, although we saw hundreds of camels grazing on the hills or asleep at the roadside inns. The reason for this is that the caravans move by night and rest all day, and this became very evident towards evening. The deep sound of the leaders' bells could be heard all night as train after train moved through town on their way to or from Peking. We started for the Wall—a fifteen mile ride—shortly after breakfast. The carts did not go, but we took provisions and water in baskets on a donkey as we were to take only "tiffin" there and return in time for dinner. The road to the Wall is through the Nankow Pass and is very old and one of the most important from

Pekin to the north. Instead of meeting camel caravans, we overtook or met many long trains of pack mules and little donkeys hardly more than waist high, but all bearing heavy loads. The road itself was sandy and full of rocks, but well defined and in places supported by a retaining wall. At other places when the solid rock was the road bed, some idea of the age of the road could be obtained from the way the rock was worn away to a depth of one and a half to two feet on either side, just as water wears a rock away from constant running over it.

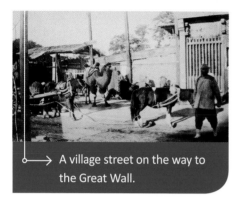

A village street on the way to the Great Wall.

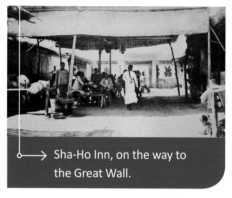

Sha-Ho Inn, on the way to the Great Wall.

Warren and Frost on the road to the Great Wall. Camel train passing.

On the road to the Great Wall.

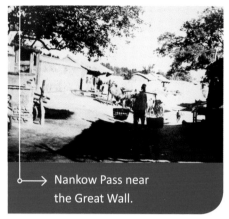

Nankow Pass near the Great Wall.

Threshing floor at a farm on road to the Great Wall.

On the road to the Great Wall.

In Nankow Pass, near the Great Wall.

On the way to the Great Wall.

⊶⟶ At Nankow.

⊶⟶ A Chinese tea-house seen at crossroad on the way to the Great Wall.

We passed through two walled towns, and some small walls stretched across the valley by the Emperors of the Ming Dynasty, but about eleven o'clock, we arrived at the Great Wall itself just as it is pictured in the books stretching over hill and valley in different directions for miles like a monster serpent. It is an impressive sight and picturesque in the extreme, and this was added to when we arrived by a hundred or more camels grazing or sleeping on the hillsides under the shadow of the Wall. We set out at once to climb to the highest nearby point, about half a mile distant, and this was no easy matter as the incline on the top is very steep in places, and the steps where there are any are broken and overgrown. The Great Wall is about 2,200 years old and 1,500 miles long. It is from fifty to sixty feet high and almost twenty-five feet wide at the top. The inside seems to be built of large and small stones mixed with cement, and the whole is faced with large and very hard bricks of a grayish composition. The Wall was repaired from time to time before China was conquered by the Mongols and Manchus, but for several centuries nothing has been done. The view from the square tower to which we climbed was magnificent. On one side you look for miles into Mongolia and from the other, over the hills into China. On the Mongolia side we could count five walled towns a few miles apart on what appeared to be a fertile plain. We could not have had a finer day—the air was clear and chilly and not a cloud in the sky. Unfortunately, my camera was out of commission as I ran out of films in Peking and bought some French ones which were the right size, but not marked the same on the back so I had to return them when I got back to Peking, but will have the use of some of the three other cameras which were taken along. Woods and I took tiffin on the Wall, but the other four went back to a village where their guide had prepaid lunch for them at an inn. I think it was much more appropriate to eat on the Wall with all its romantic surroundings with a few old bricks for a table and stones for a seat placed where you could enjoy the view through a parapet.

A view of the Great Wall.

The Great Wall.

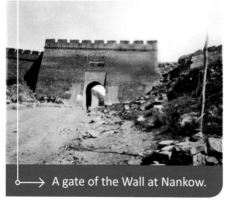

A gate of the Wall at Nankow.

Beacon towers on the Wall.

→ A magnificent view of the Great Wall.

→ An American on the Great Wall.

→ Mrs. Godchaux on the Great Wall.

The arches of a Beacon Tower on the Great Wall.

The serpentine walls on the ridge of the mountains.

Another view of the Great Wall.

F. E. Warren on the Great Wall.

An arch over roadway through the Great Wall.

Mr. and Mrs. Godchaux, F. E. Warren, F. W. Frost, and Richard B. Hobart on the Great Wall, September 1905.

→ View of the Great Wall.

We returned to Nankow over the same road, and Kuan's supper and the Army cot felt pretty good and left at seven for the Ming Tombs fifteen miles away and had some of the roughest riding we had yet encountered. The cart took a round- about way to the village of Chang Ping Chow where we were to take tiffin while our guide led us across country to the Tombs. At times we had to dismount and lead the ponies, and at others they climbed up steep paths or came down almost sliding on their haunches, and it was quite a trick to stay on board; but they never missed or slipped once. The Ming Tombs are thirteen in number when the Emperors of that Dynasty are buried and are situated in different parts of a beautiful valley. They are splendid monuments of ancient Chinese architecture, and each is surrounded by five groves and orchards, great temples and pagodas. We went to only the largest as they are all more or less alike and at some distance apart. But I was impressed here more than anywhere else with the evidences of departed glory. Five broad roads flagged with huge stones are overgrown, and unkempt and handsome marble bridges have fallen down and been washed away leaving only an arch here and there. The most impressive sight, however, is a long stone-flagged avenue, slightly curved and lined on each side with ancient generals and priests and animals, real and fabulous, each carved from a single stone and in a most wondrous state of preservation, the climate here being very dry and the stone hard. There were elephants, I should think, twenty feet high, camels, lions, donkeys, and other animals whose names I don't know.

The ride the rest of the way to Chang Ping Chow was through barren sandy country, and we were glad to get inside the walls of the town and wash off the dust and have lunch. The inn here was much the same as the others, and we had a long afternoon crossing a hot, dusty plain and interminable cornfields until we reached Tong Shan in the evening and dismounted at a place that seemed to be a combination of Buddhist temple and inn. The principal attraction at Tong Shan is a natural hot spring and some emperor a few hundred years ago built a palace there and marble basins with carved railings for the hot and cold springs which are only a few feet apart, and you can see the water come bubbling up on either side. Woods and I each took a hot bath and felt much refreshed and returned to our temple-hotel for dinner.

→ Room in an inn at Chang Ping Chow, North of Peking.

→ Gate to a Ming tomb.

→ Entrance to the Ming Tombs.

→ Three marble gates to the Ming Tombs.

→ A marble monument on Holy Way to the Ming Tombs.

→ Marble figure of a eunuch on Holy Way to the Ming Tombs.

→ Marble figure of a minister on Holy Way to the Ming Tombs.

→ Marble figure of a general on Holy Way to the Ming Tombs.

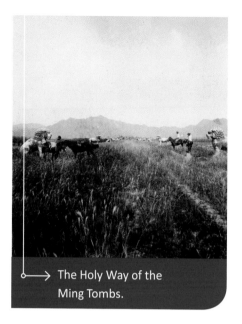

The Holy Way of the Ming Tombs.

Marble figure of a horse on Holy Way to the Ming Tombs.

Marble figure of an elephant on Holy Way to the Ming Tombs.

Interior of the temple at hot springs, near Peking.

Temple at hot springs, near Peking.

On way to Peking from the Ming Tombs.

Temple at hot springs, near Peking.

Saturday, September 30
On Board *S.S. Chin Hua*,
Chefoo to Shanghai

I have to make a slight digression here to keep up with current events. We sailed yesterday noon on this ship of 1,200 tons as we got tired of waiting at Chefoo where the agents don't seem to know anything about their own ships. We came down from Tientsin on the Shen King intending to take a steamer for Japan, touching at Korean ports, but although one was scheduled to sail last Thursday, it had not arrived yesterday, and it was only through unofficial sources that we found that it had been chartered in Japan by Harriman and his party and was then at Taku, and the office in Kobe had not taken the trouble to notify their Chefoo agents. At eleven o'clock yesterday morning we were told of this boat to

Shanghai and packed up and took passage. She is a good boat for these parts as far as accommodation goes, but rolls terribly. Another steamer somewhat smaller of the Chinese Merchants Co. named the "Hsie Ho" sailed about three hours ahead of us, hence the break in my narrative. I was awakened from my second nap about seven this morning by the ringing of bells and blowing of our whistle and looked out of the port and saw a lifeboat approaching and another following at some distance surrounded by a lot of wreckage. Woods and I pulled on our overcoats and sandals and put for the deck just as the first boat drew alongside. We had stopped by this time, and the boat had two white men in their pajamas and a lot of howling, groaning Chinese. They clamored onboard up the ladder and one of the white men, a German, speaking very good English, came up on deck, and I asked him what was the matter? He said that the "Hsie Ho" had been blown up by a floating mine about two hours before and sank in seven minutes. The other white man was the first mate. The other boat soon came up and this had the captain in his underclothing, and the chief engineer, another passenger (English), and a lot more Chinese.

We then drew up closer to the wreckage and on every log and overturned boat were a lot of Chinese clinging for dear life. The boats went out again and gathered them in and picked up also the second mate. They were all quite exhausted, and most had to be hauled up with ropes and flopped down as soon as they reached the deck. The only white men lost were the second and third engineers. There were no white women on board, but seventeen Chinese including some women were drowned. Some of the Chinese were badly hurt from the explosion and lay groaning about the decks, and the rest were acting like chickens with their heads cut off running almost squealing and frothing at the mouth. Everybody lost all they had except the chief engineer who was on duty and had twenty- five dollars in his pocket. The Englishman, a very nice fellow almost thirty-five, who has been traveling in the East for over a year, is most put out about his notes and papers and says the whole thing "is a great nuisance." The first mate is a Scotchman and is bemoaning the loss of a silver watch with a gold chain and eight dollars were in a drawer in his room, but the German says he is lucky to be on board with such good company and lots of eat and drink. The Englishman and German were the only passengers in the "Hsei Ho," and the officers were five white men, and the crew all Chinese. The two passengers say the whole thing was mismanaged. There were only a few minutes, and it was pretty much every man for himself, but the officers with exception of the chief engineer lost their heads and had no control over the crew who went wild. The Germans hands are badly torn from letting down one of the boats, and then the first mate jumped in and pushed off, and he had to jump and swim for it. The Englishman also had to jump and swim and would have been lost but for the engineer who had to do some clubbing to make the men stop and take him aboard. We immediately fixed the two passengers up with clothes, and they sat down with us to breakfast.

The place where the explosion occurred is about ninety miles out and a night's run south of the Shan Tung Peninsula. There are lots of boats plying between Shanghai and Chefoo though, so they would have been picked up soon if we had not happened along. As it was a German boat met us soon after, and we hailed them, and they will report the wreck at Chefoo this evening. Our boat is a much finer one belonging to Butterfield & Swire, a large London house, who has trading steamers all through the East, and is better manned, and the passengers of the "Hsei Ho" say it is every way superior. We expect to be in Shanghai at one o'clock tomorrow afternoon—if we don't strike any mines. The German is in charge of some department of the Arsenal at Shanghai and lost some important papers. He says that the last time he made this trip a few weeks ago, his ship nearly went to pieces in a typhoon and now he thinks that he will wait for a railroad to be built to take him back to Peking. The passengers on our ship are a French officer and an American woman who speaks terrible English, Mr. and Mrs. Godchaux, Warren, Woods, and myself.

To continue with the original story, we put up at the Llama temple and were quite a curiosity to two priests with shaven heads and very sad countenances who watched us eat our chow with the most absorbing interest. They had been two months coming to the hot springs from somewhere up in Mongolia, the people said, but our guide could not speak their language so that the conversation was chiefly on our side. At sundown an old fellow rang a gong three times in one of the little temples and repeated the process in the other across the yard and then left a cup of tea, a piece of dirty bread, and an apple before each god. Kuan, who is a good Confucian, was full of contempt for the Buddhists, but said the ringing of the gongs was to call the gods to chow. In the morning, I prowled about while breakfast was being made ready and found the old man and woman who kept the temples at breakfast with one of the sad-faced Lamas. They invited me in, and the old man held out his cup to me. As it would have been impolite to refuse, I took a sip of the greasy liquid but declined the other things except some lumpy cakes which I gave to our boys later. The old man was tall and quite patriarchal with a long, thin white beard, and the woman was better looking than most Chinese women and wore the most wonderful headdress—a sort of close-fitting cone-shaped thing with a lot of fine, large red jade stones. I wish I could have bought it. They good naturedly refused to be photographed.

We started soon after breakfast and were in Peking shortly after one o'clock, thus completing a horseback trip of nearly 125 miles. On our return to Peking, we went direct to the officers' quarters of the Legation Guard, and it was fortunate we did as we had to remain in town from Tuesday afternoon until Saturday morning, and as we had seen all we wanted to of Peking, we would have had a dull time at the hotel. The quarters were very bare and unfurnished as the present guard has not had time to get their stuff in yet. Woods put up with Capt. Lee, and I stayed with Lieutenant Holcombe. Dr. Taylor lived next door, and we took our meals in his house. He expects his wife and children out in October. It was exceedingly pleasant there—lots of first class servants and elegant food. The bugle blew every morning at 5:30 for the men, and Captain Lee was out to drill them at seven o'clock for one hour, and then we had breakfast. Holcombe was very busy as he is Quartermaster, but the rest of us usually went riding in the morning or for a walk on the Wall in the afternoon or calling. One afternoon Mr. Rockhill came over and made a short address of welcome and advice to the men, inspected the improvements that Lee had already made and stayed about one hour talking with us. He says the Peking post is a hard one for soldiers as there is nothing to do, and the temptations are many, and he hopes to hold the American Guard up as an example to the other nations. He says that there is a great deal of drunkenness, and there have been murders and robberies committed by the Legation soldiers, and he wanted to do everything to make it pleasant for the men. The captain did not tell him that he had there two men in the Guard House for drunkenness and disorderly conduct. These men were returned to the fleet a few days later, and two others sent back in their place. Lee is said to be a good officer, and although a strict disciplinarian, is liked by the men of the Marine Corps, and in the short time he has been in charge has made improvements which the Army never seemed to have thought of during their five year's stay. The officers are all young—Lee about thirty-five, Holcombe, twenty-five, and Taylor between thirty and thirty-five.

On another afternoon, we called on Captain Weinards, the Dutch Attaché next door, and at another time took tea with the Rockhills, so that the time passed very pleasantly. The reason we stayed so long in Peking is because there was no steamer scheduled to leave for Japan until September 28 from Chefoo, but in order to get this, we had to leave on the 23rd for Tientsin and take a ship there. We left Peking Saturday a.m. arriving at Tientsin at noon and there booked on the *Shen-king* leaving Saturday night. It is a twenty-four hours run from Tientsin to Chefoo, but there is a bar off Taku which the Chinese have been talking for fifty years about dredging, and if you get caught on the bar on the wrong side of it at low tide, there you will sit and wait for the proper wind and tide to float over.

Tientsin Settlement is a large well built and well paved city, and the principal hotel as in Shanghai is the Astor House—why Astor I don't know—and there we found the Godchauxs and Warren who had been there trying every possible means to get away while we had been visiting in Peking. We went on board the *Shen-king* Saturday night, and she started at eight o'clock Sunday a.m. going very slowly down the muddy, shallow and winding Pei Ho river with a man taking soundings all day as fast as he could and calling out, "nine and a half, eleven, ten, thirteen," etc. The river depth seems to average from nine and a half feet to fifteen all the way to Taku where we arrived about three o'clock. Here we tied up at a wharf at the end of nowhere, and a lot of coolies carried in baskets of coal. At nine o'clock we started again only to get stuck inside the bar where we rested easily until three in the afternoon and then made a clear run to Chefoo arriving at seven o'clock a.m., Tuesday.

Beach hotel, Chefoo.

Guarding deities on a temple door, Chefoo.

Temple garden, Chefoo, China.

The five of us went ashore in one sampan and our luggage in another, and twelve men carried it to the Beach Hotel at that time full of officers' families belonging to the U.S. fleet lying outside. The fleet left on Thursday. If the steamship agents knew anything about their business, we would have stayed on the *Shen-king*, gone to Shanghai and been in Japan now, but they told us that a steamer called the *Ohio III* running between Kobe and Chefoo was due and would leave on Thursday, so we waited as it would give us a chance to see Seoul and some of Korea. But no *Ohio* showed up, and the agents could not explain it, and we might be waiting yet if I had not got into conversation with a woman at the hotel who said that she was Mrs. Jones, wife of Captain Jones of the *Ohio III*, and that the ship had been chartered by the Harriman party and was then at Taku. When I reported this information to the agents, they were much surprised as they knew nothing of it, and then we heard of the *Chin Hua*, and you know the rest. We passed the time in Chefoo by walking on the beach and around the hill on which are the consuls and playing bridge when we were not running down to the steamship office for information. Warren was taken with a bad attack of tonsillitis and had to stay in bed and have a doctor. Woods and I were put up at the Chefoo Club by a young Englishman we met and then read the papers. One afternoon we went to a place called Temple Hill where the Treaty of Chefoo was signed by Li Hongzhang and the representatives of the Powers after the Tai Ping

Rebellion. To reach Temple Hill, we had to pass through the native city, and I believe there is more dirt and filth there than in Canton or Peking and nothing whatever of interest.

A street scene in Peking.

A street scene in Peking.

A group of Chinese children in Peking.

With regard to Peking, outside of the Foreign Concession, it is a dirty, squalid place with a slightly more acrid odor than Canton. The streets as a rule are wide and very rough. In the middle is generally the road almost twenty feet wide, and this is cut down straight on each side about two feet and sometimes three or four, and there is a ditch from three to eight feet wide; then comes the sidewalk, if you can call it such, on which are booths and stalls and then the houses, usually one-storied. There is no drainage, and the rain runs off into the ditches which remain full or partly full of foul, stagnant water. On the other hand, there are a few fine macadam roads with brick gutters almost a foot wide. These are few though, but an excellent road is in course of construction from the Winter Palace to the gate leading to the Summer Palace road. This is the road on which royalty rides to and from the Palaces. Unless one wants to visit or study, two days is enough for Peking, and he will be glad to leave and will long for the fine clean roads and people of Japan.

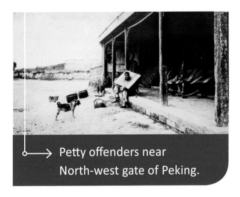

Petty offenders near North-west gate of Peking.

Street scenes in Peking.

A street scene in Peking.

Blue of different shades is the predominating color, and this is most noticeable when looking down on a curved street such as the Hatamen Road from the Hatamen. If the eye is not allowed to rest on any particular object, the general impression is of a great many blue specks, either men or the cart covers, flitting about in the street below. The women wear blue, too, but a good deal of black and a most extraordinary headdress which has the appearance of a flat piece of wood a couple of inches wide and a foot or more long, and the hair is drawn over this in fantastic ways and decorated with bright combs, pins, and flowers. They also paint their faces most vividly with rouge and white powder, with red dabs on the lips. The women wear long trousers, and the Chinese women bind the feet so that they go stamping about in a most laborious manner which must be very uncomfortable. The Manchus do not bind their feet.

The "Bund" in Shanghai.

The "Bund" in Shanghai.

Street scene in Shanghai.

Astor House Hotel, Shanghai,
Tuesday, October 3, 1905

We arrived here Sunday afternoon and had to wait down the river several miles
before a launch came to bring us up to the city. The larger steamers cannot go up
the Wusong River on which Shanghai is situated, but lie about fifteen miles down,
but smaller boats go right up. This hotel is the best and largest here and is in many
ways the best we have found though it has its shortcomings. There is not much to
see in Shanghai that cannot be seen in other Chinese cities except in the foreign
settlement, and this is the most wonderful part of the place. Shanghai undoubtedly
deserved to be called the most cosmopolitan city in the world. One can stand on
the Garden Bridge near the hotel, which, by the way, is at the corner of Whangpoo
Road and Broadway, and see the representatives of probably every nation passing
in a steady stream from early morning until late at night in every description of
vehicle from victorias and automobiles down to Chinese wheel barrows. There are
soldiers and sailors of all nations, and signs and newspapers are printed in every
language. On the river are miles of trading steamers flying all the European flags,
but the Stars and Stripes are conspicuously absent except on the fleet which is here
now. This is the metropolis of foreign cities in the East and is full of fine stone and
brick buildings and magnificent streets brimming full of life.

→ The Nanking Road in Shanghai.

The Bund along the river front is a wonderful thoroughfare with the
principal banks, clubs, and shipping companies on one side and a strip of park
on the other between the street and water. The buildings are mostly of the
English style of architecture—handsome, large, and substantial. The principal
language is English as that nation has for many years been preeminent in the
Yang-tse Valley, but of late the Germans have made great inroads. At the other

end of the Bund is the French Concession, a city in itself, and here everything is French. This is the most orderly city, from an outsider's point of view, in China. It is remarkably well policed by Sikhs, Chinese, and Englishmen. The Sikhs make very good policemen and watchmen. They are tall, handsome, aristocratic-looking fellows with a very proud air and make a striking appearance with their gaudy turbans and full curly beards. They are always dignified, never smile, and carry a heavy cane which they do not hesitate to use freely, and the coolies are in mortal terror of them.

The way supplies are delivered in Shanghai.

Waterfront along the "Bund."

A Sikh policeman in Shanghai.

Rapid transit in Shanghai.

Astor House in Shanghai.

Astor House in Shanghai.

We took a long drive this afternoon out Bubbling Well Road, the great afternoon drive here, and there were many fine turnouts and automobiles. The coachmen and footmen wear the regular Chinese livery, but we saw an exception where they were dressed in Occidental togs which seemed entirely out of place when you saw the pigtail hanging down their backs. The drive was a lovely one along a fine macadam road with beautiful houses and grounds on either side and looked more like English country than China. This is a great place, I am told, for people of both sexes with shattered reputations who find little to attract them at home and finally wander to the East where an assortment can be found in all the principal cities, but Shanghai is especially noted for practitioners of all kinds of sharp business. I caught a cold on the boat and have been feeling a bit out of sorts, but it is nothing serious and is much better today as I have only a slight cough and husky voice which gives out once in a while like a worn-out phonograph.

→ Woosung River, Shanghai.

The worst of traveling in China is the money question. The currency changes in nearly every town, and you can't use Canton money in Peking or Peking money in Shanghai, and so you lose a little every time you move, so you have to figure as nearly as possible how much you will need in each place. The standard coin is the Mexican dollar, and as our dollar bills are scarce, you are generally loaded down with several pounds of these huge pieces. There are many counterfeits about, and the Chinese when getting money at a bank test every piece spending an hour or more over a small cartload of it. As for "cash," the little brass things with the holes in them, they are carried on long strings, and in Peking, I saw a whole cart full of them going through the street. It takes from eight to fifteen

→ Small junk.

of them to make a cent, and whenever we got them in change, we would use them up on children and beggars.

Chinese junks loaded with lumber on Woosung River.

Chinese junk on Woosung River near Shanghai.

I tried to see Mr. Kahler to whom Mr. Crane gave me a letter, but he was out, and I saw some people for Roy Suffeon. I think that I shall try to see our old subscriber, Jeune Tin You, tomorrow if I am feeling well enough. We leave here on Thursday. The German we picked up from the wreck is a Mr. Besse and is quite an important man in China having been with the Government for twenty years and is now in charge of the arsenal here. He was returning from an audience with the Empress when he was blown up. He invited us to take tiffin with him at the arsenal, but sent word later that he was suffering from the after-effects of the shock and is confined to his bed. The Englishman is a Captain Dodsworth, formerly of the army and has served in India, South Africa, and the Soudan and was in Ladysmith during the siege. His trip here was for pleasure, but he was also getting notes for the Vickers-Maxim Company on the Chinese Army, all of which were lost along with his war medals, letter of credit, and everything else he had. He called today to return some money and clothes we lent him and has put us up at the Shanghai Club and will give us letters to some friends in India. He is now trying to recover damages from the China Merchants Company who owned the *Hsei Ho*. I took breakfast this a.m. with Commander Wells and Dr. Barber of the Battleship *Ohio*, and they say that Miss Roosevelt and her party who went to Korea have had as hard a time getting away as we had from Chefoo, and Morgan, the Minister, cabled to Admiral Train for a ship, but received word later that it was not needed so I suppose they must have chartered a vessel to take them through to Japan. I am glad we did not go to Korea as Wells says it is a dirty place, and Seoul has nothing of interest, and there are absolutely no accommodations for strangers. He and some other officers went to Port

Arthur and were taken all through the works there and at Dalny. When we came here Sunday, we went alongside the *Askold*, the Russian ship that has been interred here for a long time.

On Board *Liberia*,
Thursday, October 5,1905

We came on board this vessel for Nagasaki this afternoon, and she sails at high tide sometime early in the morning. I believe that Miss Roosevelt and her party join at Yokohama and the ship is to make a record-breaking trip to San Francisco taking the northern course and not touching at Honolulu. Woods and I are booked only to Nagasaki where we will look up our baggage left there by the *Logan* in charge of the U.S. Depot Quartermaster. We will then proceed to Kobe, perhaps by this steamer and perhaps by rail. I don't look forward with any pleasure to a long railroad trip to Japan, but it may be the quickest way, and as we are now behind in our schedule owing to bad connections from Peking, we want to make up as much time as possible. We will probably be in Japan two weeks or thereabouts and then sail for Burma and India. I am sorry that I could not tell you beforehand about the time I would be in different places or you could have written so that I could have received letters when I touch at Hong Kong on the way to India, but I did not expect to be so long in getting there and so gave Calcutta as my next address and will look for lots of mail there. In one of Edwin's letters, he said to call at Crok's for letters. I suppose this means Crok's in the large cities like Calcutta, Bombay, Cairo, etc. I looked up General Bronson Rea in Shanghai, as I was told in Manila that he would be there for several months, but he returned to Manila three weeks ago. I also called on Jeune Tin Yow, but he is in Peking. I saw Mr. Kahler, Mr. Crane's friend, but did not stay long as he was busy, and I was very hoarse. My cold is quite well today, and my voice is in much better form. I miss hearing from you very much, and it will be nearly a month before I reach Calcutta with a double interest. I hope that you have all kept well this summer and that business has been good. I have kept in remarkably good health for one moving about so much and living in all kinds of places, and this little cold and some prickly heat are the only troubles I have had. I have eaten most things that have been put before me except uncooked vegetables, but have drunk no water which was not distilled or bottled. There are several brands of the latter out here, many of local make and others imported. Living for travelers is not very high as the best hotels are none too good, and the next best would be about tenth rate at home. On the whole, I am glad to get away from China as it is a depressing country unless one is pursuing some particular line of study, but I am glad I have been here, and the experience is a useful one. If I am ever unfortunate enough to live here, I hope it will be Shanghai, as it is the only up-to-date city I have seen, and it is certainly a clean place, and the foreign settlement is so large that you don't have to see the Chinese town unless you want to.

This steamer is far superior to the "Manchuria" in everything except size, but it is large enough. In its furnishings and fittings, finish and arrangements of cabins and decks, I believe it is equal to anything I have seen on the Atlantic. We are all fine—that is Mr. and Mrs. Godchaux, Warren, Woods, and myself at the doctor's table. They will probably stay there after Woods and I leave. I am going to mail this on board so that it will go back with this steamer. The papers out here have scarcely any news from the States except regarding the peace negotiations, but I have seen some September copies of *Harper's, Collier's* & *Leslie's* in which are some of our pictures, but the only daily papers that come here are the San Francisco papers and none from New York. I hope that you have saved anything that comes before you about the trip. Give my best regards to my friends at home and in Yonkers and the office and with a great deal of love to you all, I am

Your loving son,
Francis

NOTES

In *Nine Years To Make A Difference: The Tragically Short Career of James A. LeRoy in the Philippines*, by Lewis E. Gleeck, Jr., the author quotes LeRoy in describing how he, "…helped Co. Edwards (Insular Bureau Chief in War Department) show off the maps in connection with Architect Burnham's provisional plans for the improvement and beautification of Manila and its environs." James A. LeRoy was Taft's principal advisor in the Philippines, and he includes descriptions of the ocean voyage and Philippines issues in his diaries and writings on the 1905 mission which he wrote before his early death from tuberculosis.

CHAPTER 3 WILLIAM HOWARD TAFT →

Letter from China to His Wife, Nellie

→ William Howard Taft, U.S. Secretary of War in 1905.

September 24, 1905

My darling Nellie,

When we returned to Manila, instead of going to the Wrights at Malacanan, I invited Miss Roosevelt and Mabel Boardman to come with me to Benito Legarda's house. You may remember that I telegraphed Legarda that I would be his guest for a few days to arrange the matter with Wright. I did this because I wanted it to be distinctly understood that I should be in a place where I could hear Filipino evidence without embarrassment to the witnesses. I also knew that Alice Roosevelt did not enjoy her visit at the Wrights because she found both Mrs. Wright and Katrina impossible. Her impressions concerning Katrina would amuse you. I have already written you the trouble with Mrs. Wright's lack of tact and real dislike for the Filipino women or contempt for the whole race brought her into over the entertainments, and I knew no way but the direct way of making Alice the guest of the leading Filipino with me to show that we had no sympathy with the apparent desire to exclude the Filipino hosts from those who should entertain the party. I fancy that Corbin had some finger in the matter for he reported to have said that the Filipino families were not of sufficient rank to entertain Senators and Congressmen. Mrs. Corbin and Mrs. Wright are both Catholics and I am sure that neither has any sympathy with the Filipino society. Legarda had made some elaborate preparations for us. I think that he must have put in new plumbing. I had a beautiful bathroom, fine bedroom and Alice and Mabel each had similar provision. He had opened a garden at one side of his house, and the last night of our stay he gave us a very handsome ball and we had elaborate meals every time we ate in the house. I saw a great number of Filipinos who called me at the Legardas who would not call on me at the Wrights, and I heard the complaints which were made about the anti-Filipino policy pursued by the present administration. I am very sorry to say so but the truth is that the attitude of the administration has changed very materially since I left and the leading men have drifted away from the policy of constantly cultivating the Filipinos and having them understand that we are in the Islands for their good and are anxious only for their good and anxious wherever possible to accord with their wishes in working out their destiny. I think Wright likes the Filipinos; I think he is anxious for a successful government, but I think he lacks first the energy to do what has to be done, second, the strength of character to resist the tactless measure that Judge Ide would introduce, and third, he does not believe as strongly as I do in the policy of conciliation. He has managed now to get the government into a condition where it is supported by no party and where the Filipinos of Manila having social aspirations are setting their faces like flint against him. Katrina is impossible. Her hair is blondined to the point such as to make its artificial color apparent and the subject of joke. She is constantly thinking of the man she is engaged to be married to, a young doctor in the army, and she is on the trip around the Islands and her conduct with Clough Anderson gave excuse for serious scandal. I was disposed first to refuse to permit Clough to go back with us on the vessel, but afterwards I concluded that as she was not under my charge it was not necessary for me to become responsible for any direct reports that I might receive of improper conduct, and while I talked to Anderson and he denied everything, I have washed my hands of the matter ever since. She is the laughing stock of the ship, walks like a bowery girl and conducts herself in every respect in a most objectionable way.

I found a great many expressions of affection from the Filipino people and have confidence that if you and I were to go back to Manila for two or three years, we could restore the old condition of things. Everywhere you were inquired for, your virtues were dilated upon everywhere. The difference between your success and Mrs. Wright's failure was made prominent. I was sincerely sorry that you were not with me not only on my account, but especially on account of the warmth of welcome which you would have received had you come.

→ Public square before City Hall.

→ Pier and arch in honor of the visit of the Secretary of War.

In my last letter, I think that I dwelt on the material improvement in Manila caused by the better streets, better houses, the improvement of the harbor and the improvement of the parks. I am also convinced that the government has been efficiently administered, that the process of elimination of the bad and poor stock has been going on, and that as a machine for the collection of taxes and the preservation of order the government has steadily improved. I am very much amused to find that Wright had become tired of Allen as the head of the Constabulary. I told him I would relieve Allen at once if he desired it, but Wright is not willing to sacrifice any personal feelings to severe methods and so he said that if I would talk to Allen perhaps things could be made better. I talked to Allen pretty frankly in the presence of Wright and Forbes. I told Allen just what Wright told me that he had been running his Constabulary as a young army with the idea of making it a Brigadier General's command and on that making a claim for a Brigadier Generalcy; that he has not made the men under him subordinate themselves, as they ought to, to the Governors of the provinces, and that with their military ideas they held themselves aloof from the men in the provinces upon whom they must depend for successful administration. It is proposed now to cut down the Constabulary from 6500 to 5000 men and thus reduce the cost considerably, and to rely more on the Scouts and on the Army whenever emergency shall arise.

Wright thinks a great mistake was made in the beginning to make Allen as high an officer as a Brigadier General. I do now know as you remember, but I remember distinctly writing to Wright and talking to him after his return pointing out that a mistake had been made in excessive rank which would attract the hostility of the Army and do practically no good, but Wright insisted that it was necessary to dignify the place. Now he thinks it would be much better to reduce the rank. Allen received a jolt in the matter which I think will get under his skin. The trouble with Allen is he is so conceited in a nice, gentlemanly way that it has been impossible almost to impress him with the necessity for watchfulness and a change.

Forbes is to be a distinct disappointment. He does not do any thinking for himself on general Philippine issues, but accepts Wright's views completely. In the face of all I told you about the falling away of Filipino support, Forbes had the temerity or ignorance possibly to tell me that there was a conspiracy against General Wright by a few Filipinos, but that on the whole he was the idol of the Filipino people. I told Forbes that I had not been there very long, but that I had been there long enough to consult the sources of Filipino public opinion and I most distinctly differed from him. I told him that I thought he (Forbes) had made a great mistake in not cultivating the Filipinos; that I had told him to do so, and that he had given no attention to them at all. He told me he had been so busy he had no time, but after he had been there for a year or eighteen months he proposed to move over among them and give them his attention. Was not that Bostonian? As if he could attend to the needs of the Filipinos some two years after he had reached there and accomplish every purpose when he did. The trouble with Forbes is he is so infernally conceited that he cannot be told anything and I am a good deal discouraged about him. I hear very conflicting stories as to his capacity. He is a hard worker but he lacks governmental experience and views everything from the standpoint of the manager of a street railway corporation, and apparently fails to understand that a government, responsible as it is to a large number of people, must have different methods of audit and accountability from that of a private corporation like a railway company. Still I am not entirely sure the he has not done good work in the matter of simplifying governmental methods, and I shall await the results of his conference with Lawshe before making up my mind. I only know that he, Wright, and Ide constitute a majority of the Commission and they are utterly lacking in the proper spirit, it seems to me, with reference to the conciliation of the Filipino elements. They seem to think it does not make much difference whether they have the support of the Filipinos or not. To me it makes every difference in the success of the government as you know.

Bacolad. The Orchestra.

Jolo. Native boats in the harbor.
August 18, 1905.

The trip around the Islands was very successful as I have already written you. The *Logan* was crowded and we came into close quarters, but on the whole we got along very well. I think the presence of Mrs. Corbin on board with Mrs. Wright created some trouble in that Mrs. Corbin did not recognize some of the ladies and attempted to run the thing on a clique principle. I tried to smooth things out and got along very well with everybody, but I found there were some sore places and that Mrs. Corbin did nothing to remove them. As you have doubtless seen, Bourke Cochran (sic), under the influence of the hierarchy of the church, has changed his position with respect to the Philippine business and is now anxious to aid us in every way possible. Cochran and Mrs. Corbin are great friends and Cochran delivered two addresses in the Philippines which greatly assisted because they showed that the Democracy was surely coming over to our view of the situation and was preparing for a possible succession to our responsibilities in such a way as to make it practicable for it to continue our policy. The natives expected that with so many varying political views, we should have a twenty-four foot ring before every native audience, instead of which there was only one voice and that was that they need not expect independence for years to come. I think that will have a thoroughly healthy effect throughout the Islands. Cochran's speeches, Shirley of Kentucky, a Democrat made a similar speech, and the other Democrats kept their peace, so that my speeches as the speeches of the Administration were more or less accepted as the speeches of the delegation. Then they had a day for complaints, and the wildest enemies of the irreconcilables could not ask for a more pitiable presentation of the lack of knowledge of government and of its responsibilities and difficulties than was shown by the people that occupied the committee for a day in discussing the necessity for immediate independence. I have a copy of the evidence and I should like to have you read it over to see how foolish men can be without knowing it.

I left the Philippines despondent somewhat because before me was the necessity of ultimately eliminating from the Government Wright and Ide and possibly Forbes. Wright wants to go back after six months vacation and Mrs. Wright does also. When I first went there, I told Wright that my impression of the President's attitude was that he should remain there as long as he chose, though he expected that his stay would be short. I am not sure that when the President hears what I have to say that he will continue to be of the same mind.

Shuster who is ambitious to get into the Commission made a speech which set all the Wright people bitterly against him and gave him prestige among the Filipinos. During our stay in Manila, Cruz Herrera, whom you will remember as the president of the Municipal Board and the so-called Alcade, was giving

→ A memorial pavilion specially built for Secretary Taft.

an informal dinner to three or four Congressmen, at which Shuster and Leroy and some others were present, and in a running speech, or at least a speech resumed from time to time, Cruz Herrera depicted the woes of the Filipino people, charged Governor Wright with being no friend of theirs, and directly charged that Mrs. Wright had acted with respect to the coming of the delegation and their entertainment in Manila as if she desired to prevent the Congressmen from meeting the Filipinos and learning the truth. Of course this was most un-Filipinolike and ungentlemanlike for Cruz Herrera in his cups, for I think he must have been somewhat the worse for liquor, to mention the name of a lady, but everything that I have heard makes it clear that in so far as his charge against Mrs. Wright is concerned, it was fully justified by the facts. Should Wright go, there is no one for Governor General but Smith, whom I believe you do not think a great deal of, and yet Smith has carried on the Public Instruction Department magnificently, although it has the bitter opposition of the American hierarchy and although they are complaining of it. The progress that the schools are making although the funds are low is the most encouraging fact that I find in the Islands. I never have enjoyed a morning so much as that which called me to make a speech before the Normal students, some four hundred there were who were ready to go out and begin the teaching of youth and they listened and seemed to understand every word I said. It was a most inspiring audience. I promised to write down a stenographic note of my speech, but I have lost the inspiration and find it difficult to do so. During my later stay in Manila, I attended the Jesuit school and the University of Santo Tomas. They both presented me with albums.

A police band welcoming the U.S. Delegation in the Phillippines.

We set sail from Manila on the *Logan*, changing the party somewhat, but still retaining the Corbins and their staff, for Hongkong. I had expected rough weather in crossing the channel, but was delighted that only the first day out we caught the tail of a typhoon that roughened the weather some, but the second and third days were as beautiful days as we could hope to see. When we reached Hongkong we anchored near the Admiral's headquarters and the Korea was about a mile and a half down the river.

Before I finish this, I expect to go over the various persons in the party and give you some gossipy facts that may interest you and bring to your mind who the people are with whom I have been traveling.

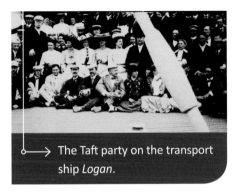

The Taft party on the transport ship *Logan*.

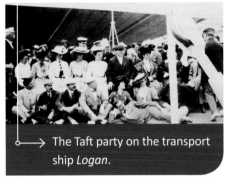

The Taft party on the transport ship *Logan*.

At Hongkong the officials were all alive to receive us. The Admiral came aboard and the Colonel Commanding and the Governor sent his Aids (sic) and we went to lunch with the Governor at the Peak and the Governor proposed to give us a dinner, the sixty-one of us. I dined at the Government House down in the city Sunday night. That night we went to Canton. There were threats made against our going to Canton and the Viceroy had issued a proclamation, but the Viceroy invited us to come and take dinner with him at the Manchu Club at Canton. There was some discussion as to whether we ought to go, but I thought we ought to go and so did the majority of the party, and this was further reinforced by a telegram from the President directing me to go and talk over the matter of the boycott which was then on. We concluded we could not take the ladies, but there was an American gunboat which did take Mrs. Newlands, Alice, Mabel Boardman, and Amy McMillan. They got there early in the morning and went to the Consul's house and had a rest, but none of them were able to go to the city. We went out on the railway from Canton north and then we crossed from one end of the city to the other on the river and took lunch with the Treasurer of the Province on account of the illness of the Viceroy. We had a regular Chinese feast which I cannot say was unpalatable and really had a very interesting experience. I made a speech along the lines of the telegraph which I had received from the President and hope it has done some good though of that I cannot be certain. We came back from Canton and spent the next day in Hongkong at lunches and other functions and topped off with a dinner at the Government House. Some of our party by this time had grown careless of invitations and embarrassed the Governor a good deal, but he gave us a very handsome dinner and then we attended a handsome supper and ball given by the Hongkong Club on the Bund, and the next day we sailed. The *Logan* was going to Peking to change the Legation Guard and bring back the Company of the 9th Infantry and take up a company of Marines. The Corbins took occasion to go on this trip and I sent Alice Roosevelt and those of the party who desired to go numbering about twenty-eight. Meantime the rest of our party, numbering about sixty, have come along with us in the *Korea*. As my particular part of the party went in the *Logan*, and the livelier part I may say, it made this trip seem rather dull and without important event. We went to Shanghai and there I had some conversation with important people over the boycott, as indeed I had in Hongkong, and I think I now can give to the President something of the inside of the matter. If I had desired, the President would have ordered me to go to Peking to look into the matter, but I was in a hurry to get home that I concluded to give up the novelty and fascination of that trip. Mrs. Newlands became the chaperone of Alice, and she and the Senator, together with Mabel Boardman and Amy McMillan now constitute her party.

At the horse races in Hong Kong, September, 1905.

At the horse races in Hong Kong, September, 1905.

When we were in Shanghai the news came to us of the riots in Tokyo growing out of the dissatisfaction of the people with the settlement of the war by the peace which Mr. Roosevelt had brought about, and it was supposed that these riots were directly against foreigners, but investigation showed me clearly that they were directed rather against the ministers in power, and that the riot grew out of a very unwise interference by the police with the people who were meeting to protest against something which they did not like and which they had a perfect right to do. The Japanese authorities were very anxious that we should get no false impression about the Japanese and their feelings for Americans and I am bound to stay we found no evidence of anti-American feeling. Our welcome was not of the wildly enthusiastic character of that we had before, but we were not seeking it, did not make ourselves prominent in the same way, did not have Alice with us and were travelling rather incognito. The Minister of War sent his Aide and the Prime Minister sent his Secretary of State to explain. The Governor of Tokyo and the Mayor of Tokyo, and the Governor of Yokohama and the Mayor of Yokohama, all came to make their statements, and I sent a telegram to the President which perhaps you saw. They were as friendly as possible, and made the short stay which we did make in Yokohama pleasant. Of course we went the ordinary way by Nagasaki, Kobe and Yokohama. I went to dinner with Harris at Nagasaki, and had dinner in the Grand Hotel in Yokohama given by Nagasaki to me and my staff informally. We had had an informal dinner given by the President of the Tea Guild that day, and whatever the cause, we were all made sick so that the next morning there were twelve of us who had to report being roused in the night with a diarrhea and in some cases cramp and colic. I suppose it was some poison tomain (sic) that had gotten into the food, perhaps the Maryland terrapin which we were favored with on the menu. Nagasaki seemed particularly pleased with the letter of thanks which I wrote him and which he told me to read to the Emperor and Empress, and the Empress stayed an hour while he detailed to her our trip to Japan, so much interested was she in our doings. When we first landed this time, Nagasaki said that he came directly from the Emperor who had expressed his great pleasure in our landing again and hoped for a pleasant journey etc.

→ View from Imperial Hotel. Tokyo. July 1905.

Since we left Yokohama—and I am writing on Sunday September 24th, we hope to arrive in San Francisco on Wed. September 27th— I have done nothing on any account except to write to you and to play bridge. I enjoy the game very much even at half a cent a point. I have had bad luck in holding hands and have not played the game very well either and yet I have enjoyed it and reluctantly come to take up the work which I had planned to occupy my whole trip with. The ladies have done a great deal of shopping and the people on board are not excited about customs. I am more or less troubled because I have a number of presents, the values of which I do not know and in many cases the value of which amounts to nothing. I think I shall exercise some discretion in those that I offer for duty. The truth is that as an official heretofore, I have been recognized as a kind of Commissioner and they have allowed everything to go through. I presume they would this time

Image of Jinzo, carved in rock. Hakone.

if I insisted, but going in with a great number of Congressmen, all of whom have something dutiable, I think it might amount to a scandal of a political character if the courtesy of the port were extended to so large a party in allowing a free entry. I shall have some things to declare and so will many others. If we land on the 27th, I hope we may catch a train and a special on the 28th, and reach Washington by the fourth of October, so that Arthur can put in his time getting the house ready for you. This will be a change in the plan originally made between us and I hope a grateful change. It will enable me to run over to New York and welcome you as you come in to the New York harbor. It is my purpose when I reach San Francisco to cable you of the date of my arrival and in that way you will know the probability of my meeting you in New York. I cabled you from Yokohama stating that we hoped to reach San Francisco on the 27th of September. I hope you received the cable.

You say in your letter that you think that if I had not gone to the Philippines, I would be Secretary of State. I doubt this. I have a letter from the President which I enclose for your reading which is characteristic of him. I am not able to say why

Mr. Root accepted the position. I saw a letter from him to General Corbin in which he would naturally express his views on this subject and he said nothing except that Mrs. Root regarded his coming back to the State Department as coming back to the penitentiary. I had supposed that the reason of his change was that Mrs. Root had changed her mind about Washington. It is certain that Edith Root dislikes New York very much and has not been the social success that she hoped to be. I get this from Alice. Mrs. Roosevelt does not like Mr. Root, so Alice tells me, and preferred to have me as Secretary of State, but of course she yielded to the judgment of the President. Her reason for disliking Mr. Root is a funny one. The President and Mr. Root as you remember used to go out on long walks and the President insisted on climbing precipices. He carried poor old Root through the same places until Root got out of patience. One day when Root was not along, the President in his wild career had a severe fall which lamed him, and when Mrs. Roosevelt told Root about it, Root laughed and said he was very glad. Mrs. Roosevelt was very indignant on the subject and did not see why he should express himself in such a brutal manner.

Alice is a curious girl, frank in the same degree that her father is, but I am afraid that her associations with Nick Longworth and with girls of a fast set have made her very rapid, at least in her talk. I know that she and Nick indulge in conversations on subjects that are ordinarily tabooed between men and women much older than they and indeed are usually confined to husband and wife. I don't think she loves Nick and I don't think he loves her. I think his attentions to her are largely for the purpose of giving him a kind of prestige and notoriety which he enjoys. I think he has a bright manner and a quick way of saying bright and new things that attract Alice very much, but she seems entirely aware of Nick's cold, selfish nature and of his coarseness, and speaks with great uncertainty as to whether they are to be married or not. If so, she says she will take a year in Europe at any rate to see whether the spell will last. She said that she had not written home on the subject and she would not say anything or commit herself definitely and ultimately until she had reached home. Alice is an honest girl. Of course greatly self absorbed. It would be hard to be otherwise. She is not a selfish girl when the issue is clearly presented to her, but she seems to have a kind of double existence, a Doctor Jekyll and Mr. Hyde arrangement. She made a very good impression wherever she went because she seemed to be so young. She was pleasant and while she did not gush, she nevertheless in public conducted herself in an attractive and dignified way. I think she made an excellent impression on the Filipinos. I know that Legarda and Tavera were much pleased, and while in some instances I had to take a good deal of care to prevent her shocking some of the Filipino brethren at the meals etc., on the whole she got through very well. I think Alice is a girl who could be trained to have a strong character, but I am very sure that her present association with Nick is bad for her and I am afraid there are some associations in New York of the same class that are equally demoralizing. Alice is always very nice to me; followed any suggestions I had to make with great alacrity and left very little so far as our personal relations were concerned to be complained of. At some times she did seem to be oblivious to the comforts of other people, but on the whole, considering what she is, what she has gone through and who she is, I do not feel that she is subject to great criticism. Certainly she made herself popular in the party and they all expressed themselves as quite pleased with her manner and her interest in things. She grew very tired of the functions which were given her in Japan and she threatened to go home with us and not go to Peking, because she feared the same thing in Peking. I doubt if she received as much attention there as she did in Japan, but I have no doubt she will have had a pleasant experience there.

Of my staff, you know Colonel Edwards. He has given a great deal of attention to this trip and its success is largely due to him. He has mannerisms as you know and assumes a good deal that one has to get used to without losing patience over it.

General Bliss went out with us. He is a taciturn, very able man, but played very little party in the company.

Captain Thompson, one of my Aides, is a very hard worker and a very efficient worker, but he is somewhat loud in his voice and manner, repeats his jokes two or three times in order that they may be appreciated and is somewhat elephantine and clumsy in his manner, but a very good fellow.

Kyoto. School children cheering the Taft party.

Captain Kelly, I took out, because he knew Spanish. He is a quiet, gentlemanly, hard working fellow and has done his work well.

Major Edie, whom we took as our medical officer, has done excellently because he understood our troubles whether proceeding from a diet of food or liquor and has kept the party in good condition.

Then there was with me Alice Roosevelt, Mabel Boardman and Amy McMillan. Mabel Boardman, you know. She is a girl of very high character and quite attractive to me and wears better than anyone else on the trip. Amy McMillan is a nice girl. She is dainty, beautifully dressed always, ladylike under all circumstances, a little bit self absorbed at times, a little bit disposed to girlish enthusiasms and manor (sic) after an age when those things may be profitably laid aside, but she is really a very nice girl and I am glad to know her better.

Senator Warren, of Wyoming, the father of Mrs. Pershing, a widower, is a very good natured, accommodating man. I think he has considerable ability in achieving things. He is not an interesting man, but he allowed himself to be made the defendant in a mock trial and showed such excellent good humor over some darts that were thrown at him that might well have aroused his ire that I think he won the respect of everybody.

→ School girls dancing and singing near Sanbo-in Temple, near Kyoto.

Senator and Mrs. Nathan E. Scott. Senator Scott is from West Virginia and I think you know him. He is a loud-mouthed, porcine, coarse, some purse-proud man, who made his money himself and brought himself up from a very humble condition to that of a millionaire and a Senator. He is good natured, he is generous with his money, though somewhat hoggish in his desire for accommodations. He is disposed to raise a row on the slightest provocation if he does not think himself properly treated, but there are some things about "Scotty" that commend themselves. He is a violent anti-civil service reformer; he is a straight out Republican, he is a stand-patter, he is for the flag in an appropriation. Mrs. Scott, his wife, is a lady of saturnine expression when unaroused. She has a deep voice and is herself disposed to complain especially on the sea which does not appeal to her, yet she too is very generous and her feelings are very easily aroused in favor of her kind. The Senator after threatening to go to Fairbanks or to Foraker, took me around the ship the other day and said he would say I was a liar if I ever told this to anyone, but that he intended to carry the West Virginia delegation for me and to contribute five thousand dollars to my preliminary presidential campaign. I thanked him and told him I did not intend to organize a preliminary campaign.

Senator and Mrs. Dubois. I do not know as you know Senator Dubois. He was a Yale man in '73; he went out to Idaho, got into politics there and came back as delegate to Congress and when they let the territory in a state he was made Senator. He was later out for a term or two and then was elected again. He within the last four years married his present wife. I do not know that he had one before. She was a school teacher, a large fleshy, rather fine looking woman, who now has all the didactic expressions of a school marm, with a voice to raise the dead. She has added to that the charms of a hysterical person. Her nerves are in a constant jar and she likes to have people come and sympathize and hear her complaints, but she is an impossible person. She has the faculty of assuming that when men show her things they desire to make her presents and she has in that way obtained four or five presents which the men did not intend to give at all. She is sick half the time and she so raised the devil with Fred that he had to go on a drunk and nearly got delirium tremens so the family is at odds. She was thrown out of a carriage in Manila and severely shocked. I doubt, however, whether the thing was so serious as Mrs. Dubois likes to represent. Mrs. Dubois has a story by which she by her heroism saved the baby in the fall, whereas Mrs. Stafford tells me that the baby was thrown out some thirty or forty feet from where Mrs. Dubois fell so she had nothing to do with the saving. I think you must have met her in Washington. She has spoken of it. She is a woman who does not know when to keep her mouth shut and she is rather the butt of the entire party. In a sense the Scotts have made themselves unduly prominent, especially the Senator, in their insistence upon rank. Coming across Lake Lanao in a launch, Mrs. Scott objected seriously to the use of the lamp to assist Colonel Wiley, a member of Congress from Alabama, from a position of seriousness and danger which he had achieved by falling down a hatchway. Her objections reached Colonel Wiley, and suffering as he was he resented it, and the suggestion made thereafter was that the Scotts did not object to Wiley's falling down the hatchway, but that what they did object to was that he should have preceded a Senator of the United States. However, I rather like Mrs. Scott. I think she is a good woman and that she controls the Senator for his own good.

→ The national flags of Japan and U.S.A. in the streets of Tokyo.

Senator Foster, from Louisiana, is one of the pleasantest, most delightful gentlemen on the trip. He is a real gentleman, and he was accompanied by his two friends, Mr. and Mrs. Godchaux. You remember the Godchaux' in LA. We did not see this one and his wife. She is a very sweet woman and he a very quiet gentlemanly man. They went to Peking as did Senator Warren.

Senator Patterson of Colorado is a curious man. He has the reputation for all sorts of corrupt bulldozing methods in Colorado, and he conducted the cross examination of me when I came home from the Philippines the first time and abused me afterwards on the floor of the Senate for misrepresenting conditions in the Philippines though he afterwards apologized somewhat. He is now representing the Democratic party of Colorado who threaten to punish him for contempt. He is a man of very decided ability, but he is quite uncertain and you never know where he is coming out. Personally and on such a trip as this, he is a pleasant member, and he it was I think who influenced the other Democrats into saying nothing which would interfere with the pleasant tenor of our ways through the Philippines. He is a widower.

Senator and Mrs. Francis G. Newlands, you know. Mrs. Newlands, as you know, is one of my great favorites and is certainly a very sweet woman and nothing that occurred on the trip led me to change my view.

I ought to say that someone in the *Washington Post* reported that Mrs. Dubois was to be the official chaperone of Alice, and Mrs. Dubois took this matter seriously and said the reason why she did not sit at the official table where Alice was was because Fred declined to put on evening dress every night. As nobody appointed her official chaperone, except the reporter of the *Washington Post*, this made her appear rather ridiculous.

Senator Chester I. Long is a serious minded Senator from Kansas, without his wife, one whom we count on to aid us in the Senate. He is on the Philippine Committee and has a very good understanding of Philippine matters. Mrs. Newlands, Miss McMillan and Miss Boardman all promise a number of entertainments for the Taft party in which they propose to include you so that you must be prepared to meet these people of whom I now write.

Mr. and Mrs. Sereno E. Payne are in many respects the pleasantest people aboard. He is the Chairman of the Ways and Means Committee of the House, which makes him the leader, and Mrs. Payne is delightfully pleasant, always good humored and always interested.

Harbor at Nagasaki.

I think it not too much to say the same of General and Mrs. Grosvenor, though Mr. Payne's manner is perhaps better than that of General Grosvenor, and General Grosvenor has sometimes made complaints but subsequently apologized.

Colonel and Mrs. Hepburn of Iowa are of the same party, he being the head of the Interstate Commerce Committee, and Payne, Grosvenor and Hepburn represent the strong elements of the Republican party. They are of much higher standing proportionately than the Senators we have in the party.

Representative and Mrs. George W. Smith. Smith is an anomaly. He has been returned for six terms from a Congressional District in Southern Illinois. He is a drunkard. His face blossoms with whiskey humors and he has gotten drunk several times though never in pubic, and yet he continues to come to Congress from session to session and his people at home support him. Although his seniority entitles him to the Chairmanship of the Postal Committee, Speaker Cannon would not appoint him.

Representative and Mrs. De Armond. Mrs. De Armond shows some signs of having been a village beauty. She is a bright woman, a little complaining and a good deal disposed to talk. Some people don't like her but I rather think she is a nice woman. De Armond is the strongest man on the Democratic side of the House. He is one of the most beautiful speakers I have ever heard. From his lips the words flow with a force, smoothness and ease that I have not seen equaled even by Bourke Cochran. De Armond is very much interested in my candidacy for the Presidency and has walked many miles on shipboard to show why I must not interfere with the boom certain to come.

Representative and Mrs. William A. Jones from Virginia, a Democratic member and bitter opponent of our policy. His wife is a lively Virginian, somewhat younger than he, though she must be thirty-six or seven. She uses some rouge, but she is a very shapely form, is very active, dances well, is greatly interested in everything she sees and has the sort of beauty that some women think attracts men. Her husband is one of those amiable men, stubborn beyond expression. He is the most difficult man to explain a proposition to that I know of. If Jones had the lively characteristics of his wife and saw as many things as she did, I think he would be a more useful Congressman and one much more progressive. She has been to call on you she told me and said that you were gracious.

Representative Henry A. Cooper left his wife at home. He is the Chairman of the Philippine Committee and you know him. He is a curiously timid man in some respects about danger and can easily be dissuaded into a belief that danger is near when it is far away.

Representative F. H. Gillett, of Massachusetts, you know. He was at our table and he makes a pleasant companion for he is one of the most conservative timid men with respect to doing things I have ever met. He is always asking *cui bono*? He is discouraged about the Philippines and many other things. He comes from the region of the *Springfield Republican*, with which he does not agree, but which affects his views.

Representative Charles Curtis of Kansas wishes to be Senator. He is part Indian, and while I do not think he would adorn the Senate Chamber, he would do as well as many.

Representative George E. Foss is Chairman of the Committee on Naval Affairs and has delivered one speech on that subject in Congress ever since the beginning of his career in that body. He is a man of handsome presence, easy delivery and it goes all right.

Representative and Mrs. E. J. Hill. He is from Connecticut and is one of the most active men for getting information I ever knew. His wife shares him in this faculty. The difficulty with Mrs. Hill, and I like her, is that her voice is so modulated as to keep everything on the same tone. The consequence is that everything she says becomes trying to ones ear and makes people attempt to escape her.

A road in Kyoto, shaded by a bamboo forest.

Representative William M. Howard of Georgia is a quiet man but one of the best men on the boat.

Representative and Mrs. M.E. Driscoll are a pleasant pair of people. He has had a curious life. His father and mother were Irish and he was born shortly after they landed in Syracuse. They moved into the country and he lived on the farm until he got his education and then studied law. He has been to Congress once or twice and they like to send him because he is Irish. He wrote something in a letter for publication about Alice and the President telegraphed to know whether members of the party are expected to write personal matters to the newspapers. He was much cut up and made an apology which the President accepted. It was in jest on his part but something he ought not to have done.

Rep. Charles F. Scott is a newspaper man now in Congress from Kansas. He spends much of his time in writing the results of the trip. He is one of the most level headed men in the party and I count on his assistance.

Representative Wiley is a Colonel from Georgia and a Colonel who is an expansionist in every bit of his make up. He wants nothing to do with anti-imperialism. He says he is a Democrat by location only. He is going back to explain to his people what a wealth we have in the Philippines.

Representative W. Bourke Cochran, you perhaps do not know. He is a very curious individual and you will meet him next winter. He was born of Irish parentage and received an education with his brother who was sent to France to become a priest, so that he speaks French as he speaks English. He has the genius of oratory, but he is wholly lacking in character. He was the tool of Tammany for a long time and then made his money by a system of blackmailing corporations which led to his public condemnation in New York. Then you may remember when McKinley ran in '96, he made his great reputation as an orator by the speeches he made in favor of McKinley. Then in 1900 because the authorities would not pay him the enormous price that he received for speaking in the campaign of 1898, he went over and spoke for Bryan on the anti-imperialistic issue, and now here he is again back to us. He is an agreeable man in manner and in an effort to entertain. He has the air in discussion of a pseudo-philosopher and reduces everything to a syllogism, but like many pseudo-philosophers, the trust is that he reaches his conclusions from very different motives than from pursuing general principles and then he hunts the general principle upon which to base the conclusion, which for private reasons he wishes to reach. He has built a very handsome house in Washington and now the Roots have rented it. He is a great friend of the Pattons in Washington and a great friend of Mrs. Corbin. He affected great interest in Alice Roosevelt. She hates him because he attacked her father in the last campaign in a most mud-slinging and undignified way and so when he laid himself open she attacked him in a way that I cautioned her against later on. She called him a man who posed as an anglophobe in public and was an anglophile in private, as a stage orator, a man who was always playing to the galleries with no principles, but always affecting to be moved by one. His good nature, for he must have some, prevented his getting angry, though he spoke to Corbin,- but I cautioned her against it in the future. His social aspirations are very funny. He had an English valet with him. He delights to talk about his correspondence with Lady Mary and Lady Gravis etc. I could talk further about Bourke, but I shall leave something for our conversation.

Representative and Mrs. George A. Loud. These are nice people from Michigan. Loud is a lumber merchant of a family that has had money by lumber. He does not seem to be very refined but he has a good education. Mrs. Loud is a thin-faced, not attractive woman at first, who was recently married. She left a baby three months old to come on this trip because it was feared that she was going into a decline. The trip has done her good. She is a nice woman.

Representative Shirley of Louisville and Mrs. Shirley, his mother. Shirley is a fellow with crooked legs, but rather a fine man with capacity. I have heard him argue in the Court of Appeals and he has done it well. He plays bridge and is quite conceited in his game. He has the Kentucky disposition to blow, but on the whole I think he has a very fair prospect for a successful political life. His mother is the typical Kentucky matron, loving her boy and talking a great deal about him, but she comes of good stock and is a nice woman.

Representative Newton W. Gilbert is a new member of Congress from Indiana, gentlemanly and apparently successful in a political way. He took occasion to confide to me that while he would have to be for Fairbanks, he would not be for Fairbanks enough to hurt if a pinch came.

Representative W.B. McKinley of Illinois is a street railway constructor and owner and he has been most generous with his gifts to the ladies of the party.

Mr. and Mrs. Herbert Parsons are people whom I am anxious to have you know. He is the son of John E. Parsons and she is the daughter of a beautiful New York belle who married Clews, a New York banker. They were of our particular party on the Manchuria and added much to our pleasure. Mrs. Parsons is a bright woman who attends in some way as an instructress at Columbia. She was brought up in fashion, but seems to break away from it some. They are well to do and will take a house in Washington.

Of the unofficial party, you know Clough Anderson. He has been conducting himself in a way that I do not think is either proper or dignified but that is his business.

Mr. Atherton Brownell is a newspaper correspondent who I have very little knowledge of or sympathy with.

Mr. Thomas Cary was of one of the best families of Buffalo and came in through Edwards. He is a good fellow anxious to please everyone, but I was not particularly impressed with him.

Mr. Louis Chapin is a young man just graduated from Yale and a cousin of President Gilman of John Hopkins University.

Mr. Charles Clark is the editor of the *Hartford Courant* and an old Yale friend of mine and a Bones man. He has enjoyed the trip. His daughter Miss Clark is a very sweet attractive girl.

Mr. Ward E. Copley was added because of the request of Senator Alger. He has been gentlemanly.

Prof. A. O. Coolidge left us after we went through the Philippines and he is going around the world the other way. He is professor of Russian at Harvard and is agreeable.

Miss Mignon Critten was a companion of Jake Schmidlapp's daughter, and Shirley became very attentive to her and I understand they were engaged.

Mr. Stuyvesant Fish, Jr, is a son of the Stuyvesant Fish whom we saw in Washington this winter.

Mr. Francis W. Frost is another newspaper man of whom I know little.

The Godchaux' I have spoken of.

Colonel James D. Hill came in the interest of the Louisiana sugar people to look into sugar matters and seems a very nice fellow.

Garden of Rakuraku-en Inn. Hakone.

Mr. R.B. Hobart is a friend of Coolidge, with whom he is travelling around the world.

Mr. C. T. Jobes is the son of a man who has had business with the Insular Bureau. He is young and I do not know much of him.

Mr. W. Johnson is the representative of the *American Exporter*, a trade journal.

Mr. Burr McIntosh is our photographer and general entertainment man. He really is a great institution. He writes poetry and doggerel and gets up all sorts of entertainments and carries them on himself. He wrote a poem which I enclose with this which is sung to the tune of Mr. Dooley.

Jack Schmidlapp you know as you do Charlotte.

Mr. E. G. Stillman was on board for a time but lived up to his name.

Fred Warren was the son of Senator Warren and conducted himself properly.

Roger Wetmore, the son of Senator Wetmore, is shallow and a great disappointment to this father. He has the reputation of getting drunk, but I am bound to acquit him of that so far as this trip is concerned.

Professor Arthur H. Woods is a tutor at Groton. The President asked me to take him.

Harry Woods, you know. He seemed to enjoy himself.

Mr. Lafe Young is the correspondent of the *Chicago Tribune* and the owner of an Iowa newspaper. I declined to allow him to go across Mindanao with us, at which he took umbrage, but he subsequently climbed off. He seems to be a man of wide information and of great influence in Iowa.

Mrs. Nagle, who came into our party with Mrs. Pershing, joining us at Yokohama, is really a very nice woman from Denver, Colorado. She is pretty and dresses well. She has had an unfortunate domestic experience in that she married a wealthy railroad man who got drunk periodically and disgraced himself publicly, until one day in the Waldorf, she said she would leave him and she did. She has a divorce. She has been sought after by a number of people, especially by our old friend John Wesley Gaines. She has announced the matter so publicly that her ambition that she has rejected him did not partake of the character of news.

I have thus gone over all the party that you might know and perhaps carry some of their personalities in your mind when you meet them as you undoubtedly will during the next winter in Washington.

On the whole, the trip has been a great success. Everybody says so and we have been singularly free from friction and quarrels which were to be expected in a trip of one hundred days with ninety people of such different views and character. Burr McIntosh has taken a great many photographs and I hope to select a number though they are expensive to show you where we have been and how we looked. I am now impatiently waiting for the end of the trip so that I can start east to greet you on landing.

CHAPTER 4 INTERVIEWS →

Margo Taft Stever

INTERVIEW WITH ERIC BESCH, APRIL, 2009

Eric Besch, a descendant of Francis W. Frost.

(S—Margo Taft Stever, B—Eric Besch)

S: I was interested in learning more about F.W. Frost. I was wondering if you could go over his biography.

B: He was the youngest son of a fellow named George H. Frost. George was the first person to kind of make it in the family. He moved from a working yeoman farmer level to a professional level. His father was from Vermont, son of a Revolutionary War soldier who fought at Bunker Hill as a corporal and a sergeant, and his mother was the daughter of a fellow named Daniel Frost who fought at Bunker Hill. His commander was a guy named Moses Smith, and Daniel ended up marrying Moses Smith's daughter. It goes from Francis to George and then George's father was Ebenezer, and Ebenezer's father was Daniel, and Daniel's father-in-law was Moses Smith. He was a captain in the Revolutionary War and fought at various battles including Saratoga. Daniel Frost married a woman named Lydia Smith. She has common forbear with Joseph Smith, the founder of Mormonism, and as a result, that part of the Smith population is exceedingly well-researched, as Mormon's tend to be, into genealogy. That was a real boon. Lydia had several children and the oldest was another boy named Daniel, named after his father. He apparently was a bit of a bully and harassed his little brother Ebenezer, so Ebenezer lit out for the territories.

At that point in time, that was New York state for him, just due west of where they lived in Glover, Vermont. He made his way starting about the age of thirteen taking care of horses for the American army during the War of 1812. He became a farrier and a blacksmith, and he married in New York State and had two children. His wife died, and within a month, he married again having two small children. He didn't waste time with the use of courtship, and with this second wife had four boys, and then he crossed over the St. Lawrence into northern Ontario, but not way north, just below where Montreal is located. He started a forge there and worked for a while. And then they were developing the canal that runs from Ottawa to Kingston.

In the wake of the War of 1812, the Canadians felt that their shipping routes were vulnerable along the St. Lawrence, and they wanted an alternative route, and they created a canal system between Ottawa, connecting the Ottawa River to Kingston—Lake Ontario there—with the idea of protecting the shipping. The canal system passed through the town of Smith Falls, and so it was a little bit of an up and coming place, but still very much wilderness, still very much living among the local Indian tribes. That was a touch- and-go relationship. Apparently, for the most part everyone was happy, but not always the case. In fact, where we live now is called Rita Ferry, but it was called Oliver's Ferry. Oliver ended up being done in by Indians having himself killed an Indian, so it was in revenge. Even though it was the 1820s, there was still a fair amount of wilderness.

The canal also bought Yellow Fever into the area so there was a fair amount of disease as well. But he started his workshop and started applying metal sheeting to the local farmers' wooden plows that turned out to be essential for success because of the rocky soil of the area. A lot of these farmers were people from Ireland and Scotland who came over—part of working for the canal and this sort of thing. The canal engineer was a guy named Bye who had served in the British Royal Engineers in India, so one of the locks is called Punta Male, which is the name of a small town apparently in India where he had worked. But his soldiers and engineers brought malaria with them from India to the northern reaches of Canada.

Ebenezer Frost was a bit of an innovator, a very shy man, very hard-working. He lived along the river and controlled an area of the river that he used for fresh water, but he didn't use it for power. At the time, the farmers who wanted their work done would come into town, and he would help their horses up to a trundle and used that to work his bellows and other machinery. His daughter from his first wife married a local carpenter who made a lot of the furniture for the people who lived in the town. Together, they began a school for the local kids, and all his sons went there until they were of a certain age and then started to go to Ottawa for schooling. He apparently believed very much in education so that the oldest of the second wife's children was able to go to McGill and study engineering. He graduated just as the Civil War was on the horizon, and after he had a couple of years experience and the Civil War was in full swing; he was a Canadian engineer with a fair amount of experience, and, therefore, very sought after because all the American engineers were fighting the Civil War and building fortifications for the Union Army.

At the same time, Chicago was growing incredibly fast because of the demand of the Union Army for beef. He went to Chicago where he was a general civil engineer. There were a lot of railroad roads being laid out so he became an everyman working on that kind of thing, but there were clearly not enough trained engineers around, so he would find talented laymen and write up little cheat sheets about how to survey a railroad bed, and how to put together a temporary bridge, and how to do all the different things that they had to do. He would come around and inspect their work and that sort of thing. But these little cheat sheets turned out to be very useful, and other engineers asked to have copies of them as well and so he made a bunch of copies, but then he asked for a little input to cover his printing costs and before long, he was spending a lot of time and making a fair amount of money. He realized that he could make a business out of this, out of printing information about engineering. When he would send out his little information sheets, they would write a little note back thanking him and saying on step five of sheet number seven, really you should add this step, sub-step two, and so they would improve it. So he would write little articles about the improvements, and some of the dynamic changes in engineering. It was really growing in leaps and bounds at that time.

Many of the metal bridges in North America were being built. So it was a pretty innovative time, and he ended up documenting a lot of the North American innovation in the engineering realm informally, at first, and then formally. He ended up marrying the daughter of a hardware representative from a company of a British iron monger who had outlets in New York and in Chicago. A guy named Hunt was from an upstanding company socially connected in England on the verge of upper middle- class status. They had a lot of artists and had gone to schools for a time with a fair number of Episcopal ministers in Oxford and Cambridge. But he managed to pull off his social ascendancy from a blacksmith's son to a professional engineer, and, in fact, in his final years, he became a fairly erudite and well-traveled fellow. At that point in time, he had a son by his wife, Louisa Hunt, and then he decided to take a leap of faith. With two hundred dollars, he sent his family, his wife and child, to his father's place in Canada where his brothers had expanded his father's business into a true manufacturing industrial complex, with some big manufacturing innovation, that had been successful. His third brother became a member of the Canadian Parliament and then was called to the Canadian Senate.

So he sent his family up there while he went to New York City to establish his printing company for the engineering news that he was doing. He founded that and grew it carefully and then brought his property in Plainfield, New Jersey. Originally, he lived on Broadway. Then, he moved his family to Plainfield and brought them from Canada. He always kept our Canadian connections from our experience there although the family had only one generation born in Canada; the rest of the time everyone had been born in the United States. By this time, Francis was not yet born, but was on the way. His sons were too young to take it over in a direct way, but they all worked in the business.

Even after he retired, he sold the business to a fellow named Hill, and then Hill later partnered… He brought Hill in as a partner and then eventually sold the rest of it to Hill, and then Hill eventually partnered with a guy named McGraw. To this day, as you know, McGraw-Hill is still a very large publishing house. They continue to publish, and they merged with another engineering paper that they had, the *Engineering Review* I think it is, so that now they had the *Engineering News Review*, an amalgam of those two early papers, my great-great grandfather's being the better of the two. It's still true today that *Engineering News and Review* is considered the premiere technical engineering paper in the country. That publishing connection has been important. It was a big deal in the family. They paid close attention to it.

His brother, Francis, was a senator. Part of the reason why their company, Frost & Wood, in Smith Falls, was successful was that he was an erudite writer in both French and English and was able to put together some excellent copy and do some innovative marketing. For example, they would have 122 tie-offs with the other local manufacturers to show how the Frost & Wood product was superior, and he was able to write in a folksy and technically sufficient way so that the local farmers who read it would be intrigued and would be inclined to buy their products. And, eventually, Frost & Wood became a world manufacturing company. My mother remembers seeing contracts for plows and reapers from the Russian Czar's ministers. She remembers seeing a newsreel from Russia, and they were reaping wheat probably down in the Ukraine and seeing the Frost and Wood logos on the catcher boards of the wheat shearers—the big cutters that cut down the wheat and separated the grain from the stocks.

S: So Francis W. Frost was too young to work in the company before his father turned it over to Hill?

B: Yes, I am not sure exactly of the timing, but I believe that's the case. Now, they still were closely connected. His older son was Charles, who was my great-grandfather, Charles Hamilton Frost—George's son and Francis's older brother. He was trained in newspapers. He went to Yale. He married a Canadian who had gone to Johns Hopkins and studied there and was among the second graduating class of females from Johns Hopkins. She is from a fairly well established Canadian family—in the line of Hemmings from the town of Hemmingford, which is named after them. He had served as Agricultural Minister and as a member of Parliament from Quebec. He had a fairly substantial family.

One of his sons, T.L.B. Hemming, was a three-star general in the British Army as a Canadian and was very involved with the mobilization and training for World War I. Those people were well established and again included a lot of religious types—ministers and that sort of thing. Hemming was a very innovative guy, and he had a model farm in Quebec. He was interested in trying new things. So the sense of innovation and not necessarily religiosity, but the Calvinistic or Puritanical, not Puritanical in the sense of morally Puritanical, although I am sure they were very Victorian, but the sense that good things follow hard work and effort—that was strongly inculcated in the generations.

They were not inclined—I think that they were still close enough to modest roots, at least the Frosts were—that they had a sense of how important hard work was and that what goes up can come down, and that only through diligence and fortitude does one maintain his position in society—this kind of hard-fought sort of thing. I think that was given to his sons as well, even though Charles went to Yale. The letters between the brothers are warm and, on occasion, playful, but they also had a firmness of purpose. No one drank (alcohol); that was something that just didn't happen. There was no hint of scandal or infidelity—very stolid. The women who tended to become the wives of Frost men were competent and talented in their own right in a much different way. Edward married Scribner, Barbara Scribner.

S: Was that another brother, Edward?

B: Yes, that was Francis's third brother.

S: Was he younger than Francis?

B: Francis was the youngest. So that type of background infused the family, and it may come out in the letters that Francis wrote to his father. His father loved to travel and was very eager about learning new things. When he traveled, he always looked at engineering types of work that were in the area, and he said that he could see how things were done so that he could continue to be innovative throughout his life. And even on a practical level, he was involved after the fire in Chicago; he was one of the engineers who remade the city. He was involved with changing the direction of the river that runs through Chicago…

S: What year was the fire?

B: I think that was 1879. But we have a Hunt portrait that was scorched. What they did was they had taken all the valuables out of a building and were moving to the city and it got too close to a building that was already engulfed and one of the portraits that we have was marred and scorched by the fire. During that time, once again, he sent the family to Canada while the town was being rebuilt. And he was involved with doing that. So he was involved with the westward expansion, the rebuilding of Chicago. In the small town when he moved to Plainfield, he designed their sewer system. When he saw an engineering project, George felt that he should know about it. So Charles, his son, went and worked with Frost & Wood, his uncle's manufacturing company. He represented them in New York for a while, I think.

But he also worked with the newspaper, *The Engineering News and Review*, as did all the boys. At a certain point of time, George ended up buying two of the three papers that were being published in Plainfield. My great grandfather, Charles, owned and ran them and then, eventually, combined the two. I know that Francis had worked with that paper. People were always on tap to pitch in to family businesses. They ended up being used as representatives here and there for not only Frost ventures, that would be the manufacturing in Canada, and the newspapers, engineering, and local publishing companies in New Jersey and New York, but also the Hunt part of the family which was involved with hardware and ironmonger stuff.

S: Ironmonger?

B: Ironmongers. That's what they called hardware men in England. There was another son who died in the 1917 flu epidemic—Edwin Frost.

S: I think that Francis refers to someone named Edwin in his letters.

B: Ebenezer had George, Charles, Harwood, Edwin, and Francis Willoughby. So going back to George Frost, he was one of six kids, and Edwin was a brother of his, and he died at 18, so that wouldn't be the flu epidemic guy. Someone died in the flu epidemic, and George's children were engaged in various enterprises in the United States. Francis had a daughter who died. So the brothers in Canada ended up having no one to pass the business on to—the Frost and Wood Manufacturing Company. They ended up eventually selling that to another manufacturing company which combined with Frost and Wood. They finally closed the plant down in 1958 or 1960. To this day, I talk with people who have said that they remembered seeing my great aunt when she used to ride around in a coach and four and had people with livery on to open the door. Francis was a senator.

S: This was Francis who?

B: Francis Frost, George's brother. He and his wife were riding around in the coach—Francis W. Frost's uncle. He was a federal senator in the Canadian Parliament. So when British royalty came from England and traveled from Ottawa to Smith Falls, they met Francis Frost who greeted them. When Andrew Carnegie came to Canada, he came to Smith Falls and met the son of one of the engineering guys who he knew, George Frost. There is a Carnegie Library in Smith Falls that was established, and I imagine funds were given by the Frosts to establish it there, so they were kind of big fish in a small pond. But they had no children and neither did Charles Frost; there was a dearth of people to inherit the business, so it ended up passing out of the family.

The same kind of thing happened in the George Frost family, the one that came to the United States. My great-grandfather had two daughters who married Alcoa junior executives when they started out, but they moved up the ladder. They had their own careers and businesses, and they weren't in the publishing business. So they ended up moving from Plainfield and went to California, and one went to New York State, so no one was there to take over the business when Charles, my great grandfather, and Francis's older brother died in 1926. The family held onto the papers for a couple of more years and then sold them to the Gannett family who at the time owned the *Utica Star* and maybe the *Syracuse Herald*. They owned two or three papers in New York State. This was their first non-New York purchase. And they became to this day a very powerful family in publishing. So that was a transition away from the local newspaper.

S: What were the birth and death dates of the Francis who went on the trip?

B: He was born on March 23, 1876, and he died on December 14, 1935.

S: But he didn't want to take over the business, or couldn't?

B: He had an import/export business that he was running, and he liked to travel a lot, and so he had a different focus. He had his own import/export business called F.W. Frost & Company at 60 Wall Street in New York.

S: Did he go to college?

B: I don't know. I don't see anywhere he did. I didn't come across it.

S: I don't think that Harry Fowler Woods did either. I think that he was offered an opportunity to either go around the world or go to college, and he chose travel.

B: I don't see any records of Francis going to college. It didn't seem to stunt his ways.

S: Did he travel before the 1905 trip?

B: I think that he probably did to England, and likely to the continent as well. To be absolutely positive, I would be hard-pressed to show. After going on the 1905 trip, he went back to the Orient a bunch of times. Because he ran an import/export business, he traveled extensively through China, Japan, and the East Indian Islands. He had gone around the world twice before he died.

S: What did he die of?

B: He had a heart attack. He had been bad health for a couple of years before he died. He died of a heart attack fairly young, and I am not sure why that is because his brother died fairly young as well, but normally we are a long-lived family.

S: Was he in shape and everything?

B: I would think so. They did do a lot of traveling, and I wouldn't be surprised if some of the traveling took a toll on their constitution. They didn't have quite a strong a handle on public health and infectious diseases.

S: Why did he go on the 1905 trip?

B: He was sent as a reporter for the family papers, and that was the cover for which—George Frost was a donor to Republican causes and was involved in politics, and so he would have had the connections to have his son included in the party. I think that his father saw it as a great opportunity, and he saw it as a great advantage to see the world and to travel with a fairly established group. I am maybe reading more into it. They were high society for Plainfield and high society for Smith Falls, but Plainfield and Smith Falls are not New York or Washington…That branch of the family had trouble during the depression. The import tax ended up crushing Francis's company.

S: Was that while he was alive?

B: Yes, he didn't die until 1935.

S: What did Francis's business import and export?

B: I think that he handled raw materials, and I know that in one point of time, George was doing import and export, too, but he was doing fine art.

S: Was that the son, George?

B: Yes, that was his son. He did a lot of traveling. Francis and his brother, Edward, traveled around the world, and he was an exporter of documents—old maps, folios, early Coptic translations of texts of the Bible. He came across what we call nowadays "Gnostic texts," but he had some really old Spanish and Portuguese maps, and he would buy and sell these papers. That was the way he made his way through the depression. They lived very frugally, so he and his wife, Scribner, would have money to buy these documents and kinds of things. International arbitrage was something the boys engaged in.

I know that after the 1905 trip, Francis was busy in New York and then in Geneva and Paris. He didn't engage in a lot of the reunion activities that occurred from time to time. Whatever aspirations he might have had, and I have to say this is a conjecture, for the Washington power crowd, he had foregone for the more realistic existence, or maybe for what he thought was the more profitable opportunity to be an importer/exporter.

S: Do you think that they did live a good life until the depression?

B: Yes, I have pictures of their house on Rallway Road. It was the days before everyone put up these mansions, and it was an impressive building for a family of three.

S: Where was it?

B: Rallway Road, outside of Plainfield. I also know that he gave donations. He traveled frequently to Japan and China for his business, and he would sponsor young and upcoming Chinese and Japanese students to travel to the United States. I have photographs of him sitting down with his wife in Japan at a banquet held in his honor for his support of these things, and occasional letters and photographs from people who had received assistance, and one of whom survived World War II. He emigrated to France where he married a daughter of some prominence whose child married a French nobleman. His descendant is some sort of Duke in France right now. I have photos of different people whom he sponsored in the United States and helped support in their education. I think that the 1905 trip was really influential in his future life both as an importer/ exporter, but also for his charitable activities if not for his social ambitions, or what they might have been. He certainly was intrigued by the Far East and stayed engaged with it throughout his life.

S: I did find the article that said that Harry Fowler Woods was the best man in Frost's wedding, but I wonder if they retained their friendship at all beyond that, or if there is any record of it?

B: I was looking through records, but the things that I came across were connections with the Blackwell side of the family and other things….In the last five years of his life, he wasn't traveling very much, and they were probably rattling around in their big house that they couldn't unload, of course, trying to make ends come together. But until that point in time, he was part of a fairly international family. His uncle spoke and wrote in French so fluent that he wrote newspaper copy in it, and he gave speeches in Parliament. That's one generation away from being a farrier…They (the Frost brothers) were fairly cosmopolitan and had a real sense of being citizens of the world.

S: That's interesting. I was just reading an article on travel sent to me by Michael Hunt, a history professor at University of North Carolina. It was written by one of his graduate students. But it puts a framework on travel in the 1900s by Americans as being imperialistic in nature, and it just seems to me that is one way of looking at it, and there may be some people who traveled for that reason. But I do think that there were so many other reasons including what you mentioned concerning the desire to learn about innovative ways of doing things and especially when people in the United States felt that the Europeans were more cultured and more learned, they would want to go to the old countries just to learn about their culture and civilization, and it didn't necessarily have so much to do with imperialism.

B: I have a photograph of my great great grandmother and one of her nieces from the Hunt side of the family on a dock with all these Egyptian sailing ships— the dirges, the one-masted triangular sailboats on which they sailed up and down the Nile, and next to her is this little, naked Egyptian boy sitting there with his penis showing and not dressed at all. She is there dressed in her dresses with several layers of petticoats and ankle-length dress with her umbrella and that sort of thing. I can't help but think that either she was totally shocked by that and overcame it, or she really was like the men. They were women of the world and had traveled enough so that wasn't a big leap for them. So it is kind of interesting to consider.

When Francis died at fifty years old, his sons were going along except for George's mishap at Princeton (he was kicked out for bootlegging)—that was probably the first indication that anything had not gone right. His other son was doing fine and had just married in 1935 in April right before Francis died (in December). So he probably had a fairly decent life though no doubt he was a little despondent at the end because of the depression, but his son went to Exeter, and I have all kinds of references to the Frost boys attending coming out debutante dances both in New York and in Plainfield. So they were actively social, engaging guys, and they rode horses…

S: A few years ago, when we first met at Yale with Professor Jonathan Spence who is, of course, a major historian of China, when he first looked at the photographs, he said the problem is going to be deciding how to use them. There is just so much here, and so many different representations of things to look at— architecture would be one, and there are just a lot of approaches.

B: I remember seeing those stone tigers and dragons. I found some photograph of some of those same objects in modern day Beijing, and the photographs are out on a lonely plain, it seems, totally surrounded by barren countryside. In the photographs of 1905, they were on the side of a densely built up street.

S: We did a little bit of that in the "Looking East" exhibition teachers' manual. We have a friend whose brother is a photographer in Shanghai, and he did some before and after photographs—then and now photographs… Actually, if you have a photograph of Frost—I know there is the photograph of Frost having dinner at the Great Wall, but if you have a photograph of him taking pictures, that might be one thing to look for…

B: It's sleuthing personalities and motivations and why they tick that I find very interesting.

S: Exactly.

B: Very often, I can relate the last hundred or last hundred and fifty year history to family members who are involved at least peripherally in trends like mechanization or manufacturing processes or one of the things that Francis did—he was able to arrange for timed payments like holding peoples' notes, farmers' notes, and paying on time. This was Francis's uncle. So when we were talking about the credit meltdown and what is going on now and how it effects business to my eleven year old, and explaining it, I used the Frost & Wood narrative as an example of how, if you want people to buy your products, you have to make buying easy for them, and help them figure out how to get the money, and this sort of thing. This connects with history. This brings history home in a real way, and it is exciting for me to do that for my children.

S: One thing that Francis does in his letters is he expresses the point of view of a person of the times in relationship to China. He starts off by saying the best part of the trip is over when they approached China, but his letters about China are fascinating, and he goes into great detail. But he definitely viewed China as dilapidated and sort of Third Worldish…

B: Well, it had a junta at the very top absorbing huge amounts of income with a lifestyle that was very insular and not accepting to foreigners, and there was nothing in it for the foreigner except to stand outside and be jealous to a certain extent, while the rest of the population lived in abject poverty—it was kind of the North Korea of its day.

S Also, they had just lived through the advancement of the United States when you think of Frances Trollope who had come to Cincinnati and had written a scathing book about the horrible manners and culture of the Americans and how in just fifty years, the Americans had come up to being much more advanced, and here they are going to China and once again running into "noxious smells" and the downtrodden human condition.

B: It is interesting that Francis wanted more of it since he continued on his own with a small coterie of friends including Harry Fowler Woods to even more obscure places, and he repeated this for the rest of his life. He made a profession out of it.

S: One thing that he said in one of his last letters is that no one would want to come back to China unless they had to. He was glad that he was leaving to go to Japan, and then it is interesting that he himself continued to return to China and built a business around that kind of travel.

INTERVIEW WITH MICHAEL HUNT ON 1905 U.S DIPLOMATIC MISSION TO ASIA, APRIL 27, 2009

(Michael Hunt—H; Margo Stever—S)

H: The indemnity piece….There are ways in which the scholarship has changed a little bit, and some of the things that are policy related, U.S. policy toward China, in combination with Japan, so on and so forth, those issues, historians still give them attention, but there hasn't been much fresh work, and where a lot of the fresh work is going, some of the themes that I highlight in the *Ascendancy* book, and that is the growing role of the U.S., not simply as a great power, but also as a cultural model and economic powerhouse. We are rewriting the turn of the century period less in terms of the emergence of a great power and more in terms of the U.S. in the context of early globalization, and the U.S. kind of playing a role in that, or figuring in a very important way. Another way of saying it is that I can hardly remember the indemnity article and the policy issues that absorbed me early on. That is where the scholarship was at that time. A lot of the shift is towards what the *Ascendancy* book tries to do and pulling in some of those threads.

→ Michael Hunt, Everett H. Emerson Professor Emeritus, University of North Carolina-Chapel Hill.

S: Yes, it is interesting that you wrote that article in 1972. I was looking at the *Tragedy of American Diplomacy*, and that was written around the same time, and it seems so long ago.

H: Yes, I am not sure that I want to comment. (Laughter) Yes, I think that the first copy of *Tragedy* was written in 1959, and I picked up a copy in the early 60s in Baltimore, and looking back on it autobiographically (I've done a short autobiographical piece), that was a long time ago—a half century.

S: In your indemnity article, you mentioned something about the slaughter of Christian missionaries in 1905 as one of the reasons for Americans being reticent to return the indemnity to the Chinese for self-strengthening.

H: There are a number of threads that are playing out at the same time or interweaving here. One is you've got the missionary presence, and they had just recovered from 1900 and actually had developed even in the 1890s a fairly big voice in Washington. I think probably the missionary, and I would disagree with the people who stressed economics, that really the missionary voice is more powerful in Washington beginning in the 1890s and maybe until the 1920s or thereabouts. Of course, you've got the immigration issue which blows up in 1905 particularly simmering from the 1870s and 1880s at least on the Chinese side. And then you've got the China policy, protecting our interests in China, and the trade issues which are also there which are to some extent linked to the policy interests, kind of preventing other powers from carving up spheres of influence that would hurt U.S. trade and investment. It is a complicated set of factors going on here. I don't remember whether I attribute one thing over another in explaining why we did it. But it seems to me that one of the key things looking back is that the indemnity remission did reflect a kind of missionary faith that China could be changed, that this was a U.S. obligation. The missionaries had taken that view even before the *Open Door Notes*, John Hay had issued those, this kind of view that China was going to become a cultural frontier, not just an economic frontier, but also a cultural frontier for the U.S. I think that was very powerful. I think that Roosevelt was a complicated character, and I don't think that Roosevelt shared that view when he became President, but I think that Taft certainly did, and Wilson later had that view. And McKinley was certainly open to the idea that the missionary presence needed to be respected, defended, and promoted. Probably the missionary dimension of that both in the literal sense of the missionary speaking out for Chinese education, and missionaries were incredibly important in Chinese education at this point. A lot of the schools that operate even today such as Zhejiang, the university in Guangzhou, St. John's, and so on and so forth, and many others—this is a powerful interest group or presence, and on top of that even broader faith that is part of U.S. nationalism that American presence can transform, has a good transformative effect.

S: When I read your article (on the Chinese indemnity), you certainly showed how the United States might have been involved in using the indemnity as a way of kind of creating an influence by the United States and not allowing the Chinese to use the money for their own purposes. But I also thought what you are saying now that the idealistic aspect probably did enter in for some people, that it wasn't just an imperialistic, cynical, exploitative ploy, but also…

H: But, of course, the two are not mutually exclusive. If you think back to the Philippines, there the notion that both taking the Philippines and the pacification in which Taft played a very prominent role—that was in part a belief that the Filipinos were not ready to manage their own affairs, that they needed tutelage and instruction, and this was part of the playing out of the new American mission. Americans did not want to call it imperial, but it was hard not to. The dimensions of it, the features of it, it was obviously a very imperial kind of enterprise, but in a sense a very—the Americans would have liked to have seen it at the time, a very enlightened, imperial—well, "uplifting" was the term that was used.

S: It is so interesting to look at it from the perspective now when at the time it seems as if the Chinese were trying to cling to what was an old way of life, and now looking back we realize that everyone is on this sort of treadmill of impending destruction wrought by the industrial revolution with global warming and everything else, so it is just really so complicated to look at anything anymore it seems to me.

H: Exactly, this is what keeps the stories going, that we are always reappraising the past in light of recent developments; it is kind of eternal employment.

S: I was wondering if you have any ideas about the possible significance of the 1905 diplomatic mission to Asia and why it hasn't received much attention?

H: Thinking back on it again, the big significance is the fact that tourism is growing—this is the beginning of not exactly mass tourism, but tourism of the middle class. Reasonably well-to-do middle class are beginning to travel in the latter part of the nineteenth century. This idea of the world coming on the horizon for a lot of Americans is becoming much more pronounced. You could think of even the way officials like Grant's tour after his presidential period, he goes on a world tour. As I recall, it is treated with a great deal of attention by the press. So in one way it's kind of Americans learning about a broader world, and in another way it's Americans looking at the way the world sees us, and what we can do to the world, or with the world. So part of it is kind of a discovery of the other, and part of it is thinking about how we can relate to the world. And I think that these tours, Mark Twain did the same thing, and I think that this was just widely practiced, this kind of world tour, or tours to foreign lands. And the reason that it's so important is this is something new because you've got steamships, and you've got for officials the telegraph as well now which allows for dependable, rapid, safe travel. And many people wouldn't have thought about doing it earlier because it would take so long, it would be so risky, it would be so unreliable. So what this party in 1905 is doing is building on a tradition or pattern of exploring the broader world. And I think those pictures that you've got really are testimony to that—I mean they are sort of capturing this world and saying here's what's out there and maybe trying to explain it, or trying to figure it out themselves, or whatever. So this is kind of the cultural dimension of the rise of this great power. I don't think that their interview with the Empress Dowager played a great role. I don't think that the tour had much of an impact on the boycott.

S: Taft did negotiate in Canton, and Stacey Cordery made the statement in the *Alice* book, or the conjecture that Alice's venturing forth somehow split the boycott because someone made an insulting poster of her being carried by turtles instead of coolies that was supposed to be very insulting because the artists were nearly murdered, but she intervened to make sure that they weren't killed.

H: I wouldn't buy that at all. I think that the imperial officials in Beijing had a very ambivalent attitude toward the protest, toward virtually all the early twentieth century nationalist movements because on the one hand, they endorsed demands that Qing officials wanted which was more autonomy and more control over foreigners, less foreign interference, but on the other hand, they reflected a kind of challenge of Qing authority because these were movements that they did not directly control. They were usually run by local gentry, maybe local officials, even, and this was my vague recollection, that the Qing finally decided that this was a movement that was getting out of hand, that was causing too much foreign protest, that was raising too many fears about a social movement or a national political movement that might lead to subversive channels, so that the Qing began to apply pressure to the protest movement. I think that the protests always consisted, or the boycott specifically consisted, of a variety of groups some of which were primarily concerned with the welfare of the overseas Cantonese in the United States, and others saw this as a vehicle for making a nationalist appeal. That would be one basic division right there. And I think that division was there from the very outset—some who were more radically alienated from the Qing and were ready to use this protest movement to weaken the dynasty and others who were ready to settle for some concessions from the United States, and that would be enough. I would be skeptical of that explanation.

S: I just started to read *In Search of Justice*, by Guanhu Wang, and it talks about how the boycott is a transnational kind of movement that starts in the United States and also China and involves different societal groups, and obviously the beginning of the nationalist movement in China.

H: That's actually a very important point because I think that again highlights the way in which globalization occurs, and I think that we are beginning to see the migration itself as part of a series of major migrations that occur in the course of the late nineteenth and early twentieth century, and one of them is this kind of transatlantic migration again that steamships make possible. The second is this Chinese Diaspora which really booms in the late nineteenth and early twentieth century mostly down to Southeast Asia, but to the North America and South America as well. And the third is to maritime Russia across the heartland of Russia, and when you look at movements of people during this era, those are the three biggies that really constitute millions of people on the march. So in a way the U.S. boycott is one little element in this larger process of migration and also tension because a lot of the tension is with Southeast Asia where increasingly nationalist regimes and resentment of overseas Chinese cause problems and cries for China to protect them and so forth. So you see the way in which globalization us impinging on the U.S./China relationship here.

S: The other thing about the 1905 trip is that the Taft/Katsura agreement is viewed as an important precedent for the Portsmouth peace negotiations. No one apparently found any correspondence between Roosevelt and Taft, so it is sort of unclear about how the whole thing precipitated, and it seemed as if it almost happened in a spontaneously with Taft ending up in these negotiations. He did cable Roosevelt and said, "I hope that this is OK," and Roosevelt said that it is exactly as he would have done it. But that might have been an important negotiation.

H: Yes, I think you are right. I think that is probably the single most important political or diplomatic aspect of the trip. My reading is that this is a Roosevelt policy, and I say that for a couple of reasons. One, Roosevelt's speeches once he becomes president in his statements and even in his letters shift toward a more modest Asian policy in which he says really Japan is going to have to contain the Russians, and that is before 1905, and then they are also the country that is going to have to civilize China. We don't want to do that. So he really was moving towards a kind of sphere of influence policy so the Taft-Katsura and the Root-Takahira Agreement of 1907 are, I think, the kind of fruits of Roosevelt's move towards a sphere of influence. And it also helped deal with the Philippines, and a lot of this comes back to the Philippines. The Philippines was not defensible, and they knew it. The Navy was constantly trying to figure out how they could defend the Philippines. They just couldn't do it. Rather than becoming a kind of an outpost allowing for a more aggressive expansion of American policy, it really becomes a "heel of Achilles," was Roosevelt's term. One thing that tends to support seeing Roosevelt and not Taft behind it is that when Taft becomes president he aligns with Knox in this rather aggressive China policy, and Roosevelt actually challenges him on it. Roosevelt is out of office, but he says, "Look, you are going too far. Do you really want to risk war with Japan over China? China is not worth it to us."

S: I've only been studying 1905 to tell you the truth, and I'm not a historian. But I wasn't sure what Taft did in China with that policy that you are discussing. He was trying to get more trade with China, wasn't he?

H: Well, the name that is given is "Dollar Diplomacy." That is the name most people know it by, and I think that it is primarily attributed to Knox, and I am not sure to what extent Taft really was enthusiastic about it, but at least he supported it. And it caused real friction between him and Roosevelt. And the idea was that the United States would not want to get boxed out of China. This was sort of a continuation of the John Hay policy that if the United States did not play a major role, then we would get elbowed out.

S: Out of the amazing market that China represented?

H: It's not only that, but also the key to controlling the market is increasingly becoming, or at least they think that it is becoming these loans that are being made to China for railways and for other concessions that involve loans or else direct loans to the Chinese government, and so the U.S, Knox and Taft, take the position that the United States has to have a role in these loans or otherwise, we will lose a voice in China's future. And so they put together a bunch of banks to serve as sort of a chosen instrument for the United States, and Roosevelt just thinks that this is nuts because he doesn't think there is much of a market in China. He doesn't think it is worth antagonizing Japan, and he doesn't think it is worth going to war to defend our interest in China. This is just peripheral, and Taft and Knox are getting themselves way too deep and way too far down the road to conflict in the Pacific. So he doesn't like it. And Taft and Knox say we have this policy called the "Open Door" in the Pacific, and it obligates us to defend China and defend our trade. So it is a real kind of growing division between Roosevelt and Taft over this issue once Taft becomes president. So that would be the other, and that is how we got started on this on the 1905 agreement, and what is behind it, whether it was Taft or not.

H. I assume that you have Taft relations?

S: My great-grandfather, Peter Rawson Taft, II, was William Howard Taft's half-brother.

H: It's too bad to have to be pro-Roosevelt. (Laughter) There must be millions of Tafts running around.

S: There must be.

H: A long time ago, I went to Cincinnati to give a Yale alumni talk, and I think that I haven't quite gotten over how many Tafts I met. They just kept popping up. And I said that there must be lots of them.

S: I was just in Cincinnati this past weekend. We just got back yesterday. We were at a memorial service, but in my family alone there are six children, and there have got to be a lot of us. Just through this project, I've gotten reconnected and I've met a number, so it's been interesting.

H: Have you looked at the Taft papers at the Library of Congress?

S: Yes, and have you read a lot of William Howard Taft's letters?

H: Yes, I think that I did, and again it's vague now, but I don't remember them being terribly revealing.

S: Well, I've read a lot about the trip, and actually I found that a lot of his letters to Nellie, incredibly long letters, were fascinating. In fact, I sent some of them to the Chinese professor, Shen Hong, with whom I am working, and he thought that one in particular was like the prologue of Chaucer's *Canterbury Tales* because Taft describes each member of the trip.

H: These letters weren't published at the time?

S: They are just in the William Howard Taft papers; they are not published.

H: Do you know how much coverage the tour got?

S: Because Alice Roosevelt was on the trip, there was a lot of coverage. Just about every day, there was an article. The other thing that I was going to mention is that these photographs are some of the only known images of the Forbidden City during this time because they were the largest group of the first Westerners who were allowed to go into the Forbidden City, and they all had their hand-held camera. There were hordes of Americans with cameras, and they were all taking pictures, so I think that we may have some pictures of the Forbidden City that the Chinese don't have at least during this particular moment in history.

H: This may be another way in which new technology and tourism are playing a role as you get these, and I had not really thought about this, as you get these really very easily managed cameras, and suddenly you got all these images flowing back. I mean before you know you had the elaborate gelatin or whatever, and you had to have a small party to take a picture, and it was very elaborate, but whereas now you had…So this was actually a multiplier then of people who were going abroad who wanted to talk about or show what they had been able to do. I wanted to mention this to you. The National Geographic Society, I think that it was created in the 1880s or the 1890s, and it was a sign of the growing American interest in the world. It was founded in the United States. The book you could go to if you wanted to get started on this is *Reading National Geographic*, by a couple of anthropologists. Katherine Lutz is one of the authors. University of Chicago published it.

S: O.K. Great.

H: I think that there's at least a capsule history of the early years in there, and it actually talks about this question of race and how the view of foreigners—to what extent is that kind of racialized, both in the way the pictures are taken, and in the way they are viewed at the time. It might be an interesting starting point in thinking about this question. There is also one other book that I wanted to mention to you, *Consumers' Imperium: The Global Production of American Domesticity, 1865-1920*. University of North Carolina Press, 2007) by Kristin Hoganson. And it's about growing interest in exotic home decoration and the growing interest in exotic goods to decorate homes. Again, it's part of this kind of Americans seeing themselves in a broader world and beginning to draw on fabrics and furniture design and atmospheric stuff for their rooms. Basically, this is women doing it, but it reflects the larger, broader interest and kind of sensitivity to the world out there which I think is critical for the kind of newer aspect of the 1905 tour. My wife and I were up in New York in the fall and we went to a home, Alana, Frederick Church's home. It started off with a very conventional design, and he got interested, I mean this is about the same time, 1870s, 1880s, I think, maybe just a little bit earlier, and got very interested in Middle Eastern motifs, and actually as a result did a tour of the region of the Mediterranean and farther into the interior of the Middle East and came back and just was going crazy to build this house that captured all these designs that he had encountered. I think that is really ramifying, this sense of the world being opened up by travel, by steamship,

Americans as a new part of this bigger world. I think that's really the backdrop, for me the most important part. You were talking about the photographs, and I actually think there has been a lot of interest in historical photographs, and the Chinese are obviously interested in this as well. It's not just the U.S. that has been pushing it. And I have seen a number of collections of photos that have been published from the late nineteenth and early twentieth century capturing visually what was going on; a lot of it just daily life in China.

There is a way of seeing the trip as an American engagement with the world, and for the Chinese it also has its own similar kind of cultural attraction—this is the way in which the world is capturing us, helping us recreate that link. And I think that a lot of Chinese still thinks of this as the century of humiliation, but they are also interested for broader reasons because they themselves can see the way in which the late nineteenth century really marks the beginning of their country's transformation culturally, socially; you get these burgeoning metropolises such as Shanghai, in particular, with engagement in trade and foreign education. You mentioned the end of the examination system and a growing interest in foreign education. American missionaries were there primarily putting their investment, putting their effort at university, at college level.

S: And there was significant innovative medical work by missionaries.

H: Yes, so it is a complicated period in that sense. Looking back, it's not the humiliation, but the transformation that got China to where it is now.

S: I read what you said in *American Ascendancy* about the development of sea power, and you've talked about tourism and the steamer, but I don't know if you have any other thoughts about the visual impact of the huge steamers and battleships as opposed to the delicate junks and the Filipino's skinny boats.

H: You raised that question about how the Chinese would have reacted, and I suspect that the reaction already played out much earlier when the British naval vessels attacked the defenses in the 1830s and 1840s. That was really when they began to recognize the differential between their own power and foreign power. The Chinese, I think, were already beginning to acquire naval vessels around this time, so I don't think that it would have been a real mind blower to see these ships. They were already very aware of the nature of the difference, I think. The same thing has already happened in the 1850s in Japan, in the 40s and 50s. You know there are those wonderful Japanese woodblock prints of the Perry expedition.

S: I was just looking at a print of one of those at the Beinecke Library at Yale.

H: You see the Japanese coming to terms with the size of these cannons and the size of the ships. So I think that this is older, the recognition of the might of foreign navies is something that has already been assimilated and is already driving the proposals for reform and even for revolution at this time. You know we've got to close this gap, we've got to modernize, we've got to be strong. You know the term Chinese historians always refer to is wealth and power, "fu chong," this already by the late nineteenth century is becoming the standard refrain that Chinese nationalists are invoking. We need to become strong and powerful and prosperous and wealthy and be able to stand up against the foreigners.

S: I just finished *The Man Who Loved China*, by Simon Winchester. I was wondering why you think the Japanese surpassed the Chinese at this time in technological innovation and discoveries. At the end of the book Winchester mentions that the Chinese stopped trying, and he theorizes why that occurred. But I was wondering why you thought that the Chinese slowed way down during this period to the point where someone like F. W. Frost would come in and say that the best part of the trip is now over as he approaches China.

H: That's actually a revealing comment in all sorts of different ways. I think that historians used to worry a lot about the question of the contrast between Japan and China, and why one did so well, and the other got so bogged down.

S: Yes, for a period of time.

H: Yes, in this period, and historians have kind of debated that, and I don't think that it's actually something that they worry about much anymore. I think one of the major responses is fairly easy. Japan is pretty small so the scale of control is not as great as China, and on top of that, the elites are able to come to a consensus about the need for drastic reform. That's known as the Meiji Reforms, and they are able to organize the state to push those reforms through, and it's a very strong, purposeful kind of consensus-based state at least among the elites. China doesn't have anything like that. It's divided; it's unwieldy; it's a foreign dynasty. The divisions about how to move ahead—foreigners are much more implicated in the life of the country where Japanese have largely kept the foreigners out until the 1850s, and even then they are not nearly as penetrated as the Chinese are—so I think that they are really quite different cases. Probably, the key difference is that the Qing state, the Manchu state, was not as effective as the Japanese state. The Japanese were able to put together a modern state. It looks a lot like the states that are arising in Germany and France at the time. The Chinese state is still very rooted in its imperial origins, Confucian orthodoxy, and limited control at the local level.

S: Do you think that their views exemplified by the Boxer Rebellion with conceptualizing harmony with nature as antithetical to industrialization, do you think that there was a stronger sense of that in China than in Japan?

H: No, I wouldn't say that the Chinese were more in harmony with nature, or that was a preoccupation. In fact, the Boxer rising, Joseph Esherick gives the best account of that period, of that phenomenon. His argument is that it's disruption in the countryside, loss of status and land, and so forth, on the part of peasants. That is the heart of it, and that then feeds into divisions in the imperial court about whether you accommodate or resist foreigners. So here again we come back to the problem that the Qing don't have local control within their own counsels about how to proceed, so I think that there are much more specific rather than general or psychological views of nature or the world. I think that there are actually more specific kinds of things that are in play here in the Boxer period, and in the Boxer years, and in this period generally.

Your questions lead off into all kinds of literature, some of which I know pretty well, and some of which I used to know pretty well, and some of which I am not incredibly familiar with, but you are getting into all kinds of really interesting questions. You could spend a lifetime doing the reading on all these topics.

S: I know. I know.

H: At some point, you have to produce something.

S: These F.W. Frost letters are going to be translated, and they start and end saying that no one would want to come back to China unless they had to. Interestingly, Frost did become an importer/exporter and went back to China several times. That's what Frost became, and they are interesting letters and very descriptive.

H: How would you characterize the reactions of other members of the party? Were they sort of put off by China?

S: Well first of all, the party split in two after Canton. Taft and a group of the older members of the group returned to the United States after visiting Shanghai. Many of younger members, who Taft said were the more interesting in the group, including Alice Roosevelt, Nicholas Longworth, and my great grandfather, H.F. Woods, F.W. Frost, and a number of other people, went to China. But anyway, the very fact that Taft didn't stay to the end of the mission says something. He obviously must have been tired and exhausted, and his wife wasn't with him, and he must have wanted to get back, and he wanted to run for president, or whatever he was planning to do. But actually Alice Roosevelt in her autobiography, *Crowded Hours*, writes about her reaction, and she has a lot of compelling descriptions and says that she wants to go back to China. But F.W. Frost and Woods went to Canton, and I think that China was a serious kind of third world country, if you will, and from Frost's descriptions, just smelling the horrible smells in the cities was a trial. I think that the United States had become more developed. Did you ever read Frances Trollope's, *The Domestic Manners of the Americans*? I'm from Cincinnati, and she hated the United States, and particularly Cincinnati, where she lived. It was written around fifty years or a little earlier than 1905, and it's a scathing description of the United States from an English person's perspective. And Frost's descriptions of China were of China. He was used to a higher standard of living, and suddenly he was thrust into this rougher kind of life.

H: The language of the time was the "sick man of Asia," this country that was kind of falling apart, I guess. The missionaries, I don't think, saw it that way, but for ordinary Americans, this was pretty shocking.

S: And Frost definitely does allude to the glory of the past, and he gives all these examples of how beautiful China must have once looked, and what it looks like to him at that point which is just decrepit, and how in certain places, once a year, they would clean up for the moment when the Dowager Empress came by, and then they would let it get all overgrown again.

H: This would reinforce the U.S. view that China was a mess, and how was it going to be saved? I don't know if your people were saying that in their letters, but that was a widely held view—that countries in this kind of mess needed outside help to get it out of this collapse that China had fallen into. The photos tended to reinforce that picture. You get the photos of the city lanes that are mud and pools of water.

S: Yes, Frost talks a lot about the roads. Apparently, they were incredibly difficult at times.

H: Between cities, the roads would have been bad. Trains were just getting started at this point.

S: Frost and Woods broke off from the Roosevelt party, and they went to the Great Wall. And Frost talks about how they were waiting for a boat, and they were told that this boat was going to arrive, and they were waiting and waiting, and then they found out that Harriman just commandeered the boat. So in other words, he was able to buy a boat from out of its schedule, and this kind of thing must have led to disorder.

H: Let me suggest again the Lutz book, *Reading National Geographic*, because I think that would be a good introduction to thinking about how to read these images and give you some idea about them, because I think often we take photographs as self-evident, you get what you see, but in fact they are really more interesting evidence than that, and more complicated evidence, for what the person who took the photo was trying to do and how it might have been viewed or read or interpreted by other people. And that is in a sense what we were doing just now— talking about how these photos would have fit into broader preconceptions, or maybe reinforced broader preconceptions, or maybe challenged them.

S: Do you have any books to recommend on sea power?

H: In the U.S. specifically?

S: Or just in this era.

H: There is nothing that comes to mind as kind of a general treatment. The very things we were talking about earlier were coming into play for navies—the shift toward the role of technology—bigger guns, more armament, larger ships, more ships, naval power as a kind of form of rivalry. It is really the leading edge of this kind of technologically driven military development, and it continues right on down to the present.

S: And did you hear the recent proclamation of the Chinese that they are going to work on developing their sea power.

H: Yes, I think that's right. I think that they've been moving in that direction for some time. One of the hallmarks of being a modern state is that you have got to have this kind of naval power, and the rockets, and the bombs, and all the rest. It sort of goes back to this earlier period—it wasn't just simply amassing an army or floating a few wooden boats, but getting much more complicated. In fact, the U.S. Navy is the first one that becomes more professional precisely because they are dealing with all these technical technological issues that come into the fore. That bibliography that I mentioned also lists general works so you might find something in there on early late nineteenth early twentieth century naval power.

S: This is really helpful. Thank you so much.

INTERVIEW WITH STACY CORDERY, MAY 24, 2009

(Margo Taft Stever—MS; Stacy Cordery: SC)

MS: I know that you interviewed my Aunt, Angela Campbell, and I think that you cited your discussion with her in your book.

SC: Yes, about Paulina.

MS: Your book has certainly generated a huge amount of interest. First of all, I was wondering if you might be able to tell me what you think of the significance of the 1905 U.S. diplomatic mission to Asia?

SC: I am going to reiterate, Margo, that you are the expert on that, not me. I know a little bit about Alice Longworth, and not so much about the larger diplomatic issues. As a Roosevelt scholar, the 1905 stuff was important, but I don't think it was the centerpiece of Roosevelt's foreign policy. Future events are going to show the importance of Asia in world affairs, particularly where the United States was involved. So like so many other things that TR did,

→ Stacy A. Cordery, Professor of History, Monmouth College.

I think that historians will say that looking ahead what he did during his administration turned out to be really important. It either put off war for a few more years, or, maybe, it allowed more time for Americans to understand better, or for diplomats to do their job better. So I think that the importance of the 1905 trip had to do with what we all talk about, the "balance of power" in the Far East, as it was called then. Roosevelt was very concerned that Russia not be too strong, and he certainly admired Japan. He had learned foreign policy at McKinley's knee, and McKinley was the author of the "Open Door." I think that in the big picture of Roosevelt's presidency, the 1905 congressional trip out there was an important piece of diplomacy, and that is why I was interested in the fact that he let Alice go along.

MS: I just read for the first time in a recommended book titled, *Admirals, Generals, and American Foreign Policy*, by Richard D. Challener, that Roosevelt had contemplated sending a large number of troops into China because of the boycott as a way of trying to impress the Chinese with American strength, and yet he, for some reason, decided not to and allowed Alice to go. I was interested in the chronology because I hadn't known about this until I read the book.

SC: Well, Alice was the speaking softly; the troops would have been the big stick.

MS: I wonder why he decided not to send them in? I guess some change of strategic idea.

SC: Presumably, that would be killing a gnat with a rifle; too much power. As I said in the book and in the article, I think that she played a role in disarming the boycott.

MS: I was interested if you had citations for her actually splitting the boycott because that was fascinating to read about?

SC: I would have to track down my footnotes, but it was such a long time ago when I wrote that.

MS: But I was wondering if you have any ideas about why the trip didn't receive much attention when you look back at history books; it is as if people don't even know about it, and, suddenly, now there is so much attention. Do you know why there is so much attention now?

SC: You know I teach history so I can tell you that one of the answers to your first question is that there is only so much time for....You know the record is full of amazing events that never get covered because we only have a fifteen week semester, or whatever, and I think that history…the older I get the more I am convinced that history is a record of who is able to sell the best, most inflammatory (laughter) as you put it, sorts of topics to publishers. Otherwise, how does it get out there? Social history has come a long, long way in exposing us to other viewpoints, other stories, the forgotten people, and so forth, but at the end of the day, at least in our era, who controls history?....I think it's the "History Channel" and "History Book of the Month Club," and if you look, it's all military history. There are social and diplomatic history aspects to this trip that are very important, but that don't make great films because there are no bombs dropping, or cars exploding, or whatever. And so I think that diplomatic history is very, very, very difficult to tell in way that can be appreciated by high-schoolers, or college students, or television audiences, or film audiences. At bottom, this was a diplomatic mission, so where are the fireworks? There was pretty nuanced stuff going on here. Maybe, Bradley will be able to tease out and focus on the boycott, or the fame of Alice being there, or the love affair of the first daughter. I mean I don't know what he will be able to do, but I think that one answer is that there is only so much time to cover things, and this wasn't deemed important. And two, it takes a lot of background explaining and contextualizing to do justice to diplomatic missions. Why is it important now? I don't know. I think that some of it is because of your photographs and the exhibition. I think that maybe there's been a resurgence in U.S.-Asian relations. I don't really know.

I am not a diplomatic historian so I do not follow this sort of stuff. You probably have got a much better sense of why if it's getting more press now, why that is.

MS: I only have ideas, but I am not a historian, so I probably have a less valid conceptualization than you do.

SC: I really doubt it.

MS: It's interesting to see the balance of power, and the Herculean changes during this particular millennium, and thinking of the huge amount of turbulence, and some kinds of considerations such as sea power, and questions about sea power, and all sorts of things that are very much in the forefront of what is happening now, and what was happening then. Anyway, it is an interesting puzzle to try to figure out.

SC: It is, and you know, issues of piracy. TR had to deal with those, too. There are some modern parallels to his presidency, but if you think about the presidents to whom we pay the most attention, they are fundamentally war presidents. TR, to his credit, managed to avoid a war. So, founding fathers, they have all their books, and then war presidents have all their books. That is not to say that Roosevelt is lacking biographers, but the other thing, interestingly, for me is that when I look back at presidential greats, and the ones that students come into my classroom knowing or thinking that they know a lot about, Roosevelt missed his anniversary, TR 1901, September 14, 1901, and that was three days after 9/11, so all the conferences about TR, all the gathering out there at Sagamore Hill and the Hofstra Conference, those were all cancelled because of 9/11, and so he never quite got that big celebration that would have put him on the front pages of the newspapers, and, I think, brought about a resurgence in all aspects of TR's presidency including his diplomacy, and, maybe, that's part of the answer to your question as well. I mean the books came out, but when the scholars were all ready to come together, and all the big names were going to be there on the East coast, 9/11 happened, and it just never came off.

MS: That's amazing.

SC: Oh, also, can I just say one more thing? I think in academia, diplomatic history maintains its position—it's a nerdy kind of a field, so most graduate students wouldn't chose to go into diplomatic history, and there are very few. When you look at the job ads, diplomatic history is always one of the smallest, smallest draws, so there are not a ton of jobs, and I think that diplomatic historians of the caliber of Bob Devine, for example—there seem to be fewer of them every year—and so I think that diplomatic history as a field is not as evident as it was forty years ago. That might be part of it, too.

MS: Interesting. I did try to contact Lewis Gould; he said that he doesn't do interviews anymore.

SC: Yes, he's retired.

MS: But he's about to put a book out on Taft, you said?

SC: Yes, but this is what happens. He's retired like everyone I know who's retired. He's five times busier in retirement than when he was teaching.

MS: Oh, yes.

SC: There are two books that came out on Roosevelt this year, and he's writing a biography of Helen Taft.

MS: Someone published a biography of Nellie Taft a few years ago.

SC: That was Carl Anthony.

MS: Yes.

SC: They will be different books. He has found out all sorts of important things about her, and the importance of music in her life, and what she did on the cultural scene in Washington, D.C., that is pretty interesting. But he's also working on an annotated collection of their letters. Taft was absolutely besotted with his wife, and he could write four and five and eight and ten page letters to her.

MS: We found one about the trip that is twenty-seven double-spaced pages long.

SC: That's the sort of stuff that will be… I am sure the annotation will be very useful, and I am sure will tell us lots of interesting stuff because no one beyond scholars like you have bothered to read the letters between the two Tafts.

MS: I felt like he would have been a great novelist, actually, after reading some of his letters because they just had such interesting perceptions about people, and it will be good that Professor Gould is publishing that book because I think that a lot of people don't realize the complexity of his views. I was talking with Michael Hunt, and he didn't seem to realize that Taft had the views that he had about the Philippines that were reflected in the letter, and I sent him the whole letter because he is doing a book on the Philippines, and the pacification of the Philippines. I think Taft was empathetic in a lot of ways that people might not recognize.

SC: I agree. I think that they liked their time living there, too. Nellie did some good things when she was there given the era and given her own background. But I think that they came away with really fond memories of the Philippines.

MS: Yes, for sure.

SC: They must have been treated well by the people there. Nellie could really get on a high horse, but what I remember thinking was she was not lording over this people as a white conqueror up there. I always kind of liked the Tafts.

MS: They were more progressive, if you will, than many politicians of that era because they believed that educated people were equal, which was probably one of the most progressive views of the times—even many of the anti-imperialists were actually staunch racists.

SC: My interpretation of Roosevelt's social Darwinism is that any nation, any people, could and would rise and fall in power, and it just so happened that he was alive at a time when Caucasian America seemed to be in the driver's seat or white Europe seemed to be in the driver's seat, but that didn't mean—I mean this is why he was so concerned about Japan—he knew Japan had a formidable past when Japan had been at the top of the pecking order. So keeping Japan and Russia in balance was important, and my take is that Roosevelt, like Taft, believed that just because fortunes favored Europe at that moment didn't mean that Asia wouldn't be, or one particular country, wouldn't be next, so you had to be on guard. So, fundamentally, if you believe that next year, or next decade, Japan could be at the top of the heap, then you have to believe that the Japanese people were more capable of things that more racist Americans at that time didn't or couldn't believe Japan could have been capable of.

MS: People were so surprised that the Japanese dominated the Russians in the Russo-Japanese War. There was a cataclysmic change in people's views of race which were beginning to change in a huge way during that time. This probably had a lot to do with why the boycott happened and the exclusion laws and everything like that. Do you have any other views on the boycott?

SC: I was interested in Alice's role in this. I was interested in that poster. I was interested in the fact that Alice kept that poster until the day she died on the wall of her house. I was interested in any quote, anything that I could tease out or find anywhere to suggest that Alice was being treated as a representative of the United States because I wanted to know about her beyond her celebrity. I wanted to know about how seriously Roosevelt was in sending her as a kind of a diplomat, or as a quasi-diplomat, and that is what I was looking for, and I was trying to see if I could build a case for Alice as not exactly a new woman, but a different kind of woman. It was too early for the new woman of the twenties, but Alice as a diplomat taken seriously in a culture that prized the family. Roosevelt didn't let her go to England, to the coronation, when there was all that hullabaloo about Alice being seated along with the other royalty in England—Roosevelt could have none of that. But sending her to Asia was a different thing.

MS: And she was allowed to stay at the Summer Palace.

SC: She was, but there was controversy about that as well. I think that poor Taft walked a fine line every step of the way between making decisions that would cause Alice to seem undemocratic at home, and making decisions that would make the host or the host country angry because Taft would have rejected these overtures that were to say how highly we regard the daughter of the President, and so forth. So I think that Taft had the hardest line by far. You can see that he worked with diplomats in the countries in which they traveled to try to get it right. In the Summer Palace being borne aloft by bearers in the private gardens, you can just imagine part of Taft was going, "This is great; this is what TR wanted. Terrific stuff here!" And at the same time, going, "Oh, no! How's it going to play in New York?"

MS: What do you think about the fact that Taft didn't stay with the rest of the Taft party, with what I have called the Roosevelt party, in China, but he did some initial negotiations on the boycott, and then half the Taft party went back with him to the United States. It is interesting that the younger, and what Taft called the more vibrant part of the Taft party, went to China.

SC: I don't know if, at the end of the day, Roosevelt thought that was so important. I don't know. Again, I am not an expert on that boycott, and, maybe, wherever you got that cite about Roosevelt wanting to send troops over would tell you more.

MS: Because Roosevelt wanted to run Taft for President, maybe Roosevelt wanted Taft back in the United States because he needed to start working on a campaign.

SC: And checking on that kind of timing would be useful, I'm sure. I don't know. Have you read Henry Tsai's book, *China and the Overseas Chinese in the United States*? Henry Tsai has got an article in *The Historian* called, "Reaction to Exclusion: The Boycott of 1905 and Chinese National Awakening."

MS: I haven't seen those.

SC: Those are the sorts of things I looked at for this chapter along with Roosevelt's letters.

MS: It's really interesting to read about the role of women and what was happening during that particular moment in China with the Christian missionaries influence and the liberation of women...so much was changing with the way they were unbinding their feet, and the whole education, and everything like that. The Empress herself didn't bind her feet. Because women were considered more attractive if they were hobbling around, she was wearing these really high platform shoes to remain in fashion.

SC: In pictures, some of the women Alice saw were in western dress. I don't know what to make of that. You're the Chinese expert, not me. I do know that Alice went back and forth between wearing what she called native costumes on that 1905 trip, and then native people in Western dress. There's probably something someone could write about that.

MS: Yes, in the 1905 photographs from the Harry Fowler Woods collection, the Western men have a diverse look. Some of them look like they are wearing Revolutionary War clothing, and then some of them almost look like they come from the 1920s, and it's very odd to see, but I guess it just depended on what they were doing, or where they got the clothes, or something like that. Because I think that they borrowed clothes from some marines at one point. Did you ever see a picture of the poster that you referred to?

SC: I saw the poster in Alice's granddaughter's home.

MS: Oh, so you met her?

SC: I did.

MS: I was trying to figure out because we were really interested when we had the exhibition in finding some things to show that were from the trip. And I thought that she would probably be the person…

SC: She has dresses that were made from the fabric that the Dowager Empress gave her on her wedding. She still has bolts of that material.

CHAPTER 5 CONCLUSION

The Photographs Reveal Significant Events in the Late Qing Dynasty
By Hong Shen

TWO OBJECTIVES OF THE 1905 U.S. DIPLOMATIC MISSION

The primary reason the United States chose this critical moment to send a government delegation to Asia was to solve two major problems. From February 1904 to March 1905, Japan and Russia had pitted themselves against each other in a bloody war in the region of northwestern China. The Russian army and navy had suffered two disastrous defeats at the bay of Port Arthur and Tsushima Strait, and Russia was forced to negotiate peace with Japan. Nevertheless, both sides were unwilling to abandon their respective interests in northwestern China, and their negotiation had reached an impasse.

Determined to intervene, President Theodore Roosevelt dispatched Secretary of War William Howard Taft on the diplomatic mission to Japan, in order to persuade the Japanese government to send a delegation to Portsmouth, New Hampshire, to negotiate with its Russian counterparts for a peace treaty. After the intervention by the U.S. government, Japan and Russia

The U.S. Government Delegation led by Taft arrived in Manila on August 5, 1905.

eventually reached an agreement. In the subsequent Portsmouth Peace Treaty, ratified by both governments, Russia acknowledged the special position of Japan in Korea, and surrendered its power in Port Arthur and Liaotung to

Japan. The Russian Manchuria Railways were also put into the hands of the Japanese. Both sides agreed to withdraw their armies from Manchuria within eighteen months. For the successful intervention in the dispute between Japan and Russia, as mentioned, President Roosevelt won a Nobel Prize for Peace in 1906.

The second thorny problem the American delegation had to deal with was the 1905 Chinese boycott of American goods. The spark that ignited the Chinese boycott movement was a series of U.S. Congress exclusion acts against the Chinese immigrants..On May 6, 1882, the U.S. Congress enacted the first notorious exclusion act against the Chinese, imposing many discriminatory restrictions on the personal freedom of Chinese workers. These included setting deadlines for them to leave the country; forbidding new Chinese workers to enter the United States; even requiring those Chinese who had already become legal residents to obtain permission for re-entry before they left the United States; re-examining the official documents issued by the Chinese government to those visiting the U.S., authorized by the U.S. customs officers; disallowing the Chinese immigrants the rights to become U.S. citizens, etc.

In 1888, 1892, and 1902, the U.S. Congress issued a series of new exclusion acts, amending and enlarging the original items of the Chinese Exclusion Act, with the result that the restrictions on Chinese immigrants became even more severe. For example, any Chinese worker who left the United States would not be allowed to return; the original privilege of the Chinese for personal protection was canceled; even those teachers, students, tourists, merchants, and officials, whose privileged status had been acknowledged by the Chinese Exclusion Act, would often be deliberately cross-examined and ejected when they were visiting the United States.

These restrictions and discriminatory acts had caused great indignation and resentment among Chinese in all walks of life, and the Sino-U.S. relationship dropped to the freezing point. Since the Chinese boycott movement spread to different parts of China, large amounts of American goods transported to China were kept in overstock in the harbors of various open port cities. Both the U.S. diplomacy and export industry had suffered a heavy blow. In order to improve the Sino-U.S. diplomatic relations and to end the Sino-U.S. trade impasse caused by the Chinese boycott of American goods, President Roosevelt sent his daughter, Alice Roosevelt, with the 1905 government delegation as an envoy of good will. One of her intentions was to establish a personal relationship with Empress Dowager Cixi, with whom

Sara Conger, wife of the American Minister Edwin H. Conger, had already developed a friendship.

That friendly gesture was exactly what the Empress Dowager desired. In 1902, since her return to Peking from exile in Singan, the Empress Dowager had tried her best to improve the diplomatic relationship between the Qing government and the Western powers, especially the United States. With this aim, she took the initiative to invite Sara Conger, wife of the U.S. minister and the wives of other European ministers to be her guests in the Forbidden City, and she also sent her foster daughter to lead a group of other princesses and their mothers to be guests of the U.S. minister in the American Legation. All of these activities had paved the way for Alice Roosevelt and other members of the U.S. government delegation to visit the Imperial Summer Palace and the inner Winter Palaces of Chuxiu and Changchun in the Forbidden City, where the Empress Dowager Cixi lived.

Newspaper articles about the 1905 U.S. diplomatic mission and the visit of Secretary Taft and Alice Roosevelt to China in *Shen Bao*, a leading Chinese newspaper in Shanghai document an interesting coincidence: at exactly the same time the U.S. diplomatic delegation led by William Howard Taft was invited to visit China and Miss Roosevelt met the Empress Dowager Cixi in Peking, the Qing court also sent five of its ministers abroad to visit the United States and other Western powers.

The earliest news report on "The Visit of the U.S. President's Daughter Is Expected" appears on page 4 of *Shen Bao* on September 6, 1905. On the same page are two other news reports that "The Viceroy of Canton's Plan to Send Officials Abroad," and "The Attendants of the Ministers Going Abroad Entered the Imperial Court." On the next day, also on Page 2 of *Shen Bao*, there is "A List of the Attendants of the Ministers Going Abroad," as well as the news, "The Date of the Ministers Going Abroad to Leave the Capital Is Approaching." On page 4 of the same newspaper, we read the news report that "The U.S. President's Daughter Has Arrived in Guangdong." Another news report on *Shen Bao* of September 10, 1905 claims that "The Two Ministers of Dai Hongci and Duan Fang Set Their Date to Leave Shanghai for the U.S.A." and the date was set on September 12, 1905. Again on page 4 of the same newspaper, there is the latest news that "The U.S. President's Daughter Has Arrived in Shanghai." Reading these parallel news reports, it appears possible that the 1905 US diplomatic mission to China was a meticulously arranged exchange of government delegations.

One direct result of William Howard Taft's negotiation with the Qing officials in Guangzhou and Shanghai, as well as Alice Roosevelt's friendly visit to Peking, was a greatly-mitigated diplomatic situation. Immediately after the visit of the U.S. government delegation, the Qing court issued an edict forbidding any kind of demonstrations for the Chinese boycott against American goods. On returning to Washington, D.C., Taft made a detailed report to President Roosevelt about the result of his visit to China. Miss Alice Roosevelt, who returned to the U.S. with a full load of personal gifts from Empress Dowager Cixi, Yuan Shikai, and others, would certainly recount to her father the good will of the Qing government to improve the diplomatic relationship with the United States. It was only logical that President Roosevelt would order a reassessment of the Chinese Exclusion Act and decided to return nearly half of the Boxer indemnity of 1900 to China. On the basis of this Boxer indemnity, the Tsinghua Academy, the predecessor of Tsinghua University, was established to train the Chinese students selected for studying in the United States. The year 2011 marked the centenary of Tsinghua University, one of the top universities in China, thereby creating a special historical significance in the re-examination of the 1905 U.S. diplomatic mission to China.

Even after a century, the 1905 visit of the U.S. government delegation to China can be regarded as a prototypical example of how the animosity and diplomatic impasse in Sino-American relations could be solved peacefully through exchange visits of diplomatic missions and face-to-face negotiations of high-level officials. It is regrettable that Chinese and American historians have not as yet given enough attention to this important event in the history of Sino-American diplomacy.

ITINERARY OF THE U.S. GOVERNMENT DELEGATION IN CHINA

The Qing government adopted an apparent double standard in receiving the U.S. government delegation led by William Howard Taft and later by Alice Roosevelt. On the one hand, they gave an unprecedented high-grade reception to the American delegation, but on the other, due to the pressure of the indignant attitudes that produced the boycott of American goods all over China, the Qing government took a very low profile in reporting on the 1905 U.S. diplomatic mission in news media. For example, almost no feature articles about this important visit are found in *Shen Bao*. Brief news reports of this event are printed occasionally here and there. On page 4 of *Shen Bao*, September 6, 1905, for instance, there is a three-line news report:

> "*The Visit of the U.S. President's Daughter Is Expected*: It was reported yesterday that the U.S. president's daughter would pass Shanghai on the ninth of September. Governor Jiang has sent a high official, Yaozhong Luo, to Shanghai to receive her with all the formalities."

→ Page 1 of *Shen Bao*, September 7, 1905.

→ Page 4 of *Shen Bao*, September 7, 1905.

Again, on page 4 of *Shen Bao* the next day, another brief news report features the expected visit of Alice Roosevelt:

> "*The U.S. President's Daughter Has Arrived in Canton*. According to a cable from Hong Kong on September 7, the daughter of the U.S. President Roosevelt and her counselor Mr. Taft, have arrived in the capita city of Canton. The officials of the Viceroy's yamen and officers of both navy and army will treat them with a banquet. Fireworks will also be set off this evening as a sign of welcome." Translated from *North China Daily News*.

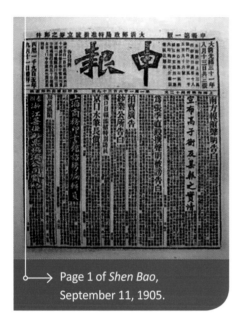

→ Page 1 of *Shen Bao*,
September 11, 1905.

→ Page 4 of *Shen Bao*,
September 11, 1905.

A few days later, on page 4 of *Shen Bao*, September 10, 1905, another news report witnessed the U.S. delegation's arrival in Shanghai:

> "*The U.S. President's Daughter Has Arrived in Shanghai.* About 1:30 yesterday afternoon, Miss Alice Roosevelt and Secretary Taft arrived in Shanghai on a U.S. warship, and they landed on the pier of the Japanese Company of Ocean Liners. They were welcomed by the U.S. consul general and other American merchants. After a short rest in American Consulate General, they went to Astor House for lunch at 2:30 pm."

Nevertheless, on page 4 of *Shen Bao* the next day, another news report included the following correction:

> "*The U.S. President's Daughter Has Gone to Peking.* We reported yesterday that Miss Alice Roosevelt and Mr. Taft, secretary of war, had arrived in Shanghai. According to the latest news, Mr. Taft was accompanied by five senators and twenty congressmen, and many other male and female attendants. The president's

daughter, however, had gone directly from Hong Kong to Peking. She has not been to Shanghai. Yesterday's news report was a mistake that needs to be corrected."

→ Page 1 of *Shen Bao*, September 13, 1905.

→ Page 2 of *Shen Bao*, September 10, 1905.

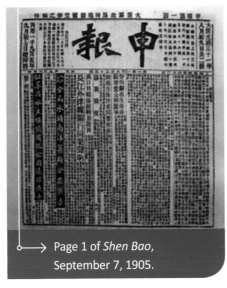

→ Page 1 of *Shen Bao*, September 7, 1905.

→ Page 3 of *Shen Bao*, September 13, 1905.

As reported, the U.S government delegation, before its entry into mainland China, had divided into two parts. As a leader of the delegation and a high-ranking government official, Secretary Taft undertook the more difficult diplomatic mission and led five senators and twenty congressmen to Canton and Shanghai to negotiate with the local officials on how to end the Chinese boycott against American goods. Alice Roosevelt, as the U.S. president's private envoy of good will and a distinguished guest of Empress Dowager Cixi, was not involved in such diplomatic negotiations. She and her attendants took a steamship and traveled directly to Peking, the capital of China, via Tientsin.

In one of the photographs taken by Harry Fowler Woods, Miss Alice Roosevelt and her entourage arrived in Tientsin where they were greeted ceremoniously by an honor guard and a military band from Yuan Shikai's New Army. Alice is pictured climbing up Empress Dowager's private train, ready to go to the capital city of China as the military band lined up on the railway station platform and even performed the national song of the United States, "The Star-Spangled Banner." Because Alice Roosevelt represented her father, U.S. President Theodore Roosevelt, she was treated as a head of State.

Among the 250 snapshots he had taken within China, there is not one of William Howard Taft, probably because he was involved in high level diplomacy directly upon entering China and then departed for the United States. The major photo opportunities for Harry Fowler Woods occurred when he accompanied Alice Roosevelt after the group split. When Woods and Frost left the Roosevelt Party for their grand tour of Burma, India, Egypt, and Greece, Woods took the six photographs of Canton's Five Story Pagoda and the Pearl River, as well as twenty-three photographs of Shanghai. Besides the Bund and the Nanking Road, there are also photos of the Woosong River, Shanghai Harbor, the pier of the Japanese Company of Ocean Liners, and the Astor House where the Americans had their first lunch in Shanghai, etc., as described in the news report of *Shen Bao*. On pages 2 and 3 of *Shen Bao*, September 13, 1905, there are two more new reports about Alice Roosevelt's visit in China:

> *"The U.S. President's Daughter Has Arrived in Beijing.* According to a news report from Peking on September 13, Miss Alice Roosevelt has arrived in Peking. She will pay a visit to the two empress dowagers. It is said that she will leave Peking on September 17." Translated from *North China Daily News*.

> *"A Detailed Account of Miss Alice Roosevelt's Arrival in Canton.* In the evening of September 5, 1905, the

U.S. president's daughter arrived in Canton by a night steamboat. Early the next day, she landed with Mr. William Howard Taft, U.S. Secretary of War, seven senators, twenty-four congressmen, and three ladies. At first they took a rest at the American Consulate General at Shameen. The governor sent the Commissioner of Foreign Affairs to receive them with full ceremony. The Commissioner and the U.S. Consul General accompanied the American delegation, with the exception of Miss Alice Roosevelt and the ladies, to pay a visit to the stone embankment walls along the Pearl River. They were warmly welcomed by Mr. Ye Shimei, the chief engineer of the Highway Bureau; Mr. Lian De, the General Manager of the Bureau; and Mr. Huang Zanyan, the General Director. When passing Foshan and the three lakes southwest of Shizidou, the Americans and their hosts all stopped and got down from their vehicles to take pictures. While they were on the way, one American congressman mentioned to Mr. Huang about the Chinese boycott of American goods, explaining that even Americans themselves considered the Chinese exclusion acts unjust, and that there were proposals to amend these acts. During their visit in Canton, they saw insulting posters aimed against Americans, which were inappropriate in etiquette. Mr. Huang replied that this was done by ignorant people, and the Chinese authorities had already issued orders to forbid such acts against Americans. The U.S. congressman nodded in agreement. Soon afterwards, they changed onto a steamboat and sailed to the House of the Eight Banners in Canton, in order to attend a welcoming banquet. Viceroy Cen Chunxuan was absent because of his illness, all the other officials of the Viceroy's yamen attended the banquet. The banquet ended in two hours."

The second and more substantial news article accurately reports that Alice Roosevelt traveled by boat close to Canton, but she did go with Taft and the delegation into Canton. Her adventures near Canton are described within these page, in other recent books, and in the letters (published in this book for the first time) of Francis W. Frost. In consideration of the strong animosity of the Cantonese citizens against Americans during the Chinese boycott movement, the female members of the delegation were not permitted to go near the city of Canton, but just stayed for a short while in the foreign settlement at Shameen, observing Canton from a short distance.

After they returned to Hong Kong, and Secretary Taft departed with a large segment of the traveling group, Alice Roosevelt led the remaining members of the U.S. government delegation, including Woods and Frost, north to Peking by sea route, and they arrived in Tanggu via Port Arthur and Tagu. Then they changed to a special train to Tientsin and Peking. Alice Roosevelt's leadership was especially notable since this is the first time that a woman led a diplomatic mission for the United States. Secretary Taft led his part of the now split delegation to Shanghai by a steamship after they had finished their visits to Hong Kong and Canton. There he again negotiated with the mayor of Shanghai on how to end the Chinese boycott of American goods. After that, the U.S. government delegation left Shanghai for Japan and then traveled back to the United States.

Upon their arrival in Peking, Alice Roosevelt and her retinue did not stay together. As distinguished guests of Empress Dowager Cixi, Roosevelt and a few of her female chaperons were invited to live in the ducal palace of Prince Qing. After an audience with Empress Dowager at the Imperial Summer Palace, they were invited to stay overnight as a sign of preferential treatment. The other members of her delegation stayed in the only two hotels for foreign guests, Grand Hotel des Wagons-Lits on the Legation Street inside the wall of the Tartar city and Hotel du Nord in the Chinese city.

Yuan Shikai, Viceroy of Chihli and a powerful reformer in late Qing Dynaty, did not let this excellent opportunity slip through his fingers. He sent to every member of Alice Roosevelt's delegation a letter of invitation and offered a grand banquet in Tientsin to welcome the visit of the U.S. government delegation.

After visiting the imperial palaces in the Forbidden City, Harry Fowler Woods and Francis W. Frost decided to set off for a journey to visit the Great Wall, the Ming Tombs, and the imperial hot springs in T'ang Shan, instead of going to Tientsin to attend the grand banquet. They also planned to take a steamship to Chefoo in Shantung and from there changed to another steamship to Korea and Japan. Unfortunately, the steamship they waited for had changed its route to another place. They had no choice but got on another steamship to Shanghai, then from Shanghai to Japan. From there they traveled to Burma, India, Egypt, and Greece, and both men created albums, records, and letters from their voyages and adventures.

THE PEOPLE AND SCENERY OF PEKING
ONE HUNDRED AND SEVEN YEARS AGO

A street scene in Peking.

One of the Woods photo albums contains 253 photographs of the 1905 U.S. diplomatic mission in China. The central part of this album is 165 photographs taken in and around Peking. The contents of these photographs cover almost every aspect of the city life, including the daily routines of ordinary people outside Ch'ien Men, as well as the mysterious imperial court inside the Forbidden City. In similar fashion with the foreign athletes, officials, and spectators of the 2008 Beijing Olympiad, the members of the 1905 U.S. government delegation led by Alice

Roosevelt were full of curiosity about Peking. Besides the audience with Empress Dowager Cixi and Emperor Guangxu, their main purpose in Peking seemed to be nothing but sightseeing. As the photographs of Harry Fowler Woods show, within the short period of four or five days, their footsteps covered almost every corner of this great city, encompassing the classic scenic spots like the Temple of Heaven, the Imperial Academy, the Lama Temple, the Great Bell Temple, the Yellow Temple, the Five Pagoda Temple, the Drum Tower, the Bell Tower, etc., as well as those well-known scenic spots in the suburbs of Peking, such as the Nankou Pass, the Great Wall at Ba Da Ling, the Ming Tombs, and the Imperial Hot Springs at T'ang Shan.

The photographs of the old city of Peking taken a century ago now seem to be ages old. The main streets of the old capital city were wide and straight. Many memorial archways spanned the street. The facades of those ancient shops along the streets were so attractive and charming, but they can no longer be found anywhere in the modern city now filled with skyscrapers. Camel caravans or rickshaws rather than automobiles populated the streets.

→ Hotel du Nord, a hotel for foreigners in Peking, 1905.

In 1905, the old city of Peking sported no five-star hotels but two hotels specially catering to foreigners. Some members of the American delegation, including Harry Fowler Woods and Francis W. Frost, resided in one of them, the

Hotel du Nord. From the Woods photographs, we can see that the hotel has a quaint façade, visually demonstrating the impact of the nations occupying China during this period. The courtyard was actually in the typical Peking style, with a western style gateway, and the French name of the hotel mounted above. The rickshaw drivers, surrounding a foreigner outside the hotel on the right, seemed to be mainly doing business with them.

Within the gateway of the hotel, there was a hidden world of its own, a tidy compound of traditional Chinese houses of grey bricks and tiles built around a courtyard. Even the ground of the courtyard was paved with bricks in beautiful patterns. It was in mid-September, a spell of hot weather after the "Beginning of Autumn" prevailed in Peking. An awning spread over the courtyard as a sunshade. In the middle, there were two flower beds with some Chinese roses in full bloom. The traditional-style wooden window lattice formed beautiful visual patterns, dense above but sparse below, with window papers pasted from the inside. Various pictures of folklore appeared on the window papers. This courtyard was both graceful and quiet; the comfort of staying here must have been superior to residing in those small family hotels in Beijing during the 2008 Olympiad.

Included in the Woods photographs of Peking are many historical sites that no longer exist. One photograph shows a group of old houses which look like a Taoist temple, yet on a horizontally inscribed board, the following words appeared in both English and Chinese: "Chinese Imperial Post Office." So this is the original site for the office buildings of the Chinese Imperial Post Office, which used to be a branch of the Chinese Imperial Customs during 1905-1907. The address here would have been Xiao Bao Fang Lane on Chong Wen Men Nei Boulevard. In order to prepare for the 2008 Beijing Olympiad, a museum of postal service in China was built on this site. The museum holds a collection of photographs of old buildings in China's postal service, but unfortunately there is no photograph such as this one of the original office buildings of the Chinese Imperial Post Office.

Among the photographs in the Woods China photo album, the most impressive ones are those of Empress Dowager Cixi's Imperial Summer Palace, her winter palace of Xi Yuan (Middle and South Seas) and the Forbidden City where Emperor Guangxu once lived. As distinguished guests of Empress Dowager, Alice Roosevelt and other three ladies in the American delegation were carried into the Forbidden City by eunuchs on sedan chairs, while all of the other men followed behind on foot. Similarly, the American delegation marched in the ceremony of the 2008 Olympiad. Unlike the Chinese delegation, whose march was uniform and trim, the Americans in 1905 walked in groups of three or four, gazing right and left, with cameras in their hands. Every now and then, they would leave the procession and take pictures of what had previously been a forbidden place—the Chinese Imperial Palace. For seasonal reasons, giant awnings spread over the courtyards within the Forbidden City. The scale of these sunshades is so great that the imperial courtyards look like the Olympic stadiums or gymnasiums. After the audience at the Summer Palace, the Qing imperial court also treated the American guests from across the Pacific Ocean to a banquet at the Sea Palace Hall of Xi Yuan (Middle and South Seas). From one of the old photographs within the Sea Palace Hall, one can spot a banquet room decorated with western-style crystal chandeliers, western furniture, ornaments, tableware, and a fine billiard table outside the banquet room. It may be possible that Empress Dowager Cixi had a passion for watching western sports, as depicted in the Chinese television serial, *An Expedition of Heroes*.

Another impressive sight in the Woods China photo album is the bird's-eye view of the city center of old Peking, shown in three photographs taken from the top of the Drum Tower, which is located on the axle line of the city. The view of the first photograph overlooks a boulevard towards the east, with one of the eastern city gates, Tung Chih Men, barely visible on the horizon. Though the main streets of 1905 Peking were both wide and straight, the city consisted of only dirt roads which would turn muddy and slippery after rain. Since there was no sewer system, shallow trenches on the edges of the streets drained sewage waste water away. As a result, they became smelly stagnant pools which would breed both maggots and mosquitoes, as well as pollute the environment. Most of the resident houses in the city of Peking were low and shabby, but the facades of the stores and shops along the streets were exquisite and luxurious. The view of the second photograph overlooks another boulevard towards the south, with Ti An Men, the Coal Hill, and Pei Hai Park in the distance. This boulevard used to be one of the most prosperous commercial streets in old Peking, with various stores, shops, and restaurants lining both sides of the street. The third photograph reveals a full view of the Bell Tower north of the Drum Tower. The Bell Tower, which has not changed much since the days of Marco Polo, is one of the oldest architectural features in Peking.

Finally, it should be emphasized that the Woods China photo album includes a group of twenty photographs of the Great Wall. Some of these images show the magnificent Great Wall in perspective; others represent the details of the walls and beacon towers, showing the real conditions of the Great Wall in 1905; still others are either group photos or photos of individuals taken on the Great Wall. Researchers on the history of the Great Wall will understand that such a group of original photographs representing this remarkable wall in 1905 are extremely rare.

EXHIBITING THE PHOTOGRAPHS

Before the publication of *Looking East* by Zhejiang University Press in 2012, the 1,100 photographs of the 1905 U.S. diplomatic mission to Japan, the Philippines, and China in the collection of Harry Fowler Woods never appeared in book form and were known to only a few people. After the death of Harry Fowler Woods in 1955, they were kept in a remote Adirondack camp owned by the Woods family. During the summer of 2004, James Taft Stever, a 23-year-old college student majoring in history and a descendant of Woods, concluded that the five photo albums potentially had historic value. James possesses a master's degree in political history from Brown University. His mother, Margo Taft Stever, and James spent several years doing research on the collection of the H. F. Woods photographs. At the same time, they raised money from different sources in order to engage Ira Wunder to restore and scan these photographs into electronic images. In 2007, an exhibition, "Looking East: William Howard Taft and the 1905 Mission to Asia—The Photographs of Harry Fowler Woods," with more than seventy selected images, was held at the Nippon Club in New York City. The exhibition immediately created a sensation. Several influential newspapers, including The New York Times, published lengthy reviews of the exhibition, delivering the message about the rediscovery of these valuable historical photographs.

During October 24–26, 2008, the School of International Studies, Zhejiang University, University of Copenhagen, and University of Edinburgh jointly held an International Symposium on Sinology and Sino-Foreign Cultural Relations and Exchanges in Hangzhou. As one of the organizers of the international conference, I was fortunate to be able to read an abstract of their paper describing the photographs and the 1905 mission and to discuss with Margo Taft Stever the possibility of an exhibition of the 253 photographs Woods had taken in China, plus fifty more representative photographs taken in the United States, Japan, and the Philippines, to be held on the main campus of Zhejiang University during the conference. As it happened, Margo was also thinking about the possibility of holding an overseas exhibition of these photographs, especially in mainland China. We soon reached an agreement on featuring this exhibition in Hangzhou, and the H. F. Woods Camp Trust donated the exhibition of digitally restored photographs to Zhejiang University.

The exhibition of H. F. Woods photographs opened in Hangzhou on October 24, 2008. After our intense but orderly preparation, with strong support from the university authorities and the leadership of the School of International Studies, the exhibition of "Looking East: William Howard Taft and the 1905 Mission to Asia—The Photographs of Harry Fowler Woods" was successfully displayed at Zhejiang University during late October and early November, 2008. The visitors to this exhibition consisted mainly of the students and faculty of Zhejiang University, but some of the other visitors included citizens of Hangzhou who were interested in history and old photographs. Researchers and scholars also came from Beijing and abroad especially to see the exhibition. A few local newspapers sent their journalists to the opening ceremony to write news reports.

Encouraged by the exhibition's success, I seized the first opportunity to suggest to Margo Taft Stever that we should collaborate on publishing a book about these photographs in China, and she responded with enthusiasm. After returning to the United States, she and James carefully studied the William Howard Taft Papers at the Manuscript Division of the Library of Congress, Harvard University, and elsewhere, and Margo interviewed several American historians who specialized in Sino-American diplomatic relations, asking them to express their views on the significance of the 1905 diplomatic mission. She also visited several members of the Woods family, as well as a descendant of Francis W. Frost, to find out more information about the story behind the H. F. Woods photographs. She did succeed in finding letters written by Francis W. Frost and William Howard Taft during their visit in China and more photographs of this journey in F.W. Frost's possession. Based on these efforts, Margo and James expanded their conference paper into this book on the 1905 U.S. diplomatic mission to Asia.

Meanwhile, I also did some library research on the Chinese records of the diplomatic mission and set about reading, collating, and translating the archival source materials which the Stevers mailed to me, and I began to design the structure of this book. Those who have conducted archival research will understand how difficult it is to read and identify the handwriting in old manuscripts. The handwriting in those informal letters or diaries are sometimes nearly illegible. Many proper nouns or special terminologies relating to various aspects of the social life in Japan, the Philippines, and China are difficult to understand. Furthermore, the spelling of these proper names, terminologies, and place names can be irregular. Without sufficient knowledge of the 1905 U.S. diplomatic mission to Asia, it would be almost impossible to read and translate these archival materials into Chinese for the Chinese language version of this book which was published by Zhejiang University in 2012.

Margo Taft Stever and I collaborated to address these problems. After careful word-for-word identification and arduous research, we eventually resolved almost every problem that we came across in the manuscripts.

Our collaboration has opened a new approach to the study of Sino-Western cultural relations and exchanges. It seems probable that a large number of old photographs of China similar to those of H.F. Woods exist outside of China. Apart from the collections kept in libraries and archives, a large number of similar photographs are no doubt scattered among hundreds of different families, in albums either hidden and forgotten on high shelves, or put away unheeded at the bottom of a chest. I believe that, with China's global emergence, interest in the history of China will continue to heighten in Western countries, and more and more hidden old photographs of China will be discovered. If they are not found in the near future, because of the chemical composition of the old photographic paper, they will become silvered, and the images will disappear. Chinese and international researchers should make every effort to find and preserve these photographs, which carry invaluable historical memories, and return them, as the Woods family has done, back to the places where they were taken, to fill the monumental gaps in our nation's historical recollection. The publication of *Looking East* is the culmination of our efforts.

AFTERWORD

By Xuemao Wang

Not long after I first arrived at the University of Cincinnati and became the dean and university librarian in 2012, a longtime friend of UC and an enthusiast of the international connections of Cincinnati to Asian communities brought me the Chinese-language edition of this book. After briefly skimming it, I was immediately attracted to the rich historical photographs—images that I had never seen before, even in China. I learned the book was published by Zhejiang University Press in China, and my friend encouraged me to think of publishing an English-language edition.

My enthusiasm and curiosity towards what happened in 1905 during William Howard Taft's first and largest American government delegation to China were just part of my driving interests in the book. I wanted to know why this significant historical event was rarely known by people in both countries and barely mentioned by historians from both countries. Certainly, I am also interested in the book's implications for today's and future generations to understand this significant historical event. I was convinced that in order to achieve these goals, I should consider the possibility of publishing the book on this side of the world.

In preparing to do so, I took a trip to Zhejiang University in Hangzhou, China in 2013 to meet one of the book's authors, Dr. Hong Shen, as well as to discuss matters regarding publishing terms with Zhejiang University Press. Following that visit, I organized an international authors forum by inviting Shen and the other author, Ms. Margo Stever, to Cincinnati for a joint presentation. The forum drew a large participation from the University of Cincinnati community and was very successful.

In recent geopolitical affairs, East Asia is catching people's greater attention and concerns, especially with recently increasing tension between the countries of China, Japan, Vietnam, the Philippines, and others. Over a century ago when President Theodore Roosevelt sent then Secretary of the War Taft to Asia, he had the clear goal of America playing a role in resolving regional tensions. The mission in the 1905 voyage had two very important aims: ending the Russo-Japanese War through diplomacy and demonstrating the powerful influence in the Philippines by the United States. By bolstering the president's administration policy in China of

"Open Door," the result would be an increase in its competitive advantage in trade. President Roosevelt understood America's position in balancing world power and in easing conflicts by sending a diplomatic delegation to learn how the United States could be more effective on the global stage.

The current U.S. administration has instituted a key Asian policy known as pivot or rebalance. The key points of this policy is aimed at "strengthening bilateral security alliances; deepening our working relationships with emerging powers, including with China; engaging with regional multilateral institutions; expanding trade and investment; forging a broad-based military presence; and advancing democracy and human rights." Nowadays, sending a large delegation to the Far East no longer requires a "Manchuria" solution. The globalization and new technologies have made people's communication ever easier. However, neither globalization nor technologies can replace the human role in understanding, inter-exchanging, and inter-dependency especially when it comes to resolving conflict.

Today, the University of Cincinnati has launched an ambitious global outreach. In Asia, we have engaged with most of the countries and regions, particularly China. The recent successful academic program with Chongqing University is just one example. Recent enrollment data shows that UC's international students have reached 3200. Students from Asian countries have reached 2700, and students from China alone have reached 1100.

It is my hope that the publishing of this book in English will help raise a greater global awareness of this important and under-promoted historical and diplomatic event. With additions added to this book regarding William Howard Taft's relationship with the University of Cincinnati, I hope this book will help engage UC alumni around the world, particularly in East Asia where the fast-growing alumni base is important for the university's future. History can teach us how we may wisely assess current affairs and how we may rationally foresee the future. *Looking East: William Howard Taft and the 1905 Mission to Asia, The Photographs of Harry Fowler Woods* is an invaluable resource for not only understanding history, but also our present and future.

Margo Taft Stever earned degrees from Harvard University and Sarah Lawrence College. In addition to her historical writing, her published collections of poetry include *The Lunatic Ball* (2015); *The Hudson Line* (2012); *Frozen Spring* (2002); and *Reading the Night Sky* (1996). Her poems, essays, and reviews have been published in numerous magazines and anthologies, including *Salamander, Blackbird, Prairie Schooner, Rattapallax, The Webster Review, New England Review, Minnesota Review, Connecticut Review, Poet Lore, West Branch, Seattle Review,* and *No More Masks.* She is the founder of The Hudson Valley Writers' Center and current co-editor of Slapering Hol Press. Stever was a prime mover in the restoration of the historic Philipse Manor Railroad Station for the Center's home. She is a great-granddaughter of Harry Fowler Woods and Peter R. Taft (half-brother of William Howard Taft) and is a relative of Nicholas Longworth and R. Clough Anderson, who were also travelers on the 1905 mission. Stever oversaw the restoration of the Woods photographs and directed the Harry F. Woods 1905 photography exhibition at the Ohio Historical Society. *Photo courtesy of Ben Larrabee.*

James Taft Stever is a great-great grandson of Harry Fowler Woods and a relative of both William Howard Taft and Nicholas Longworth. He holds degrees from Hampshire College and Brown University. Stever first recognized the historical significance of the Woods photographs and co-authored the museum catalog that accompanied the initial public presentation of the restored images in addition to contributing to the text of this book. A former member of the Peace Corps, Stever worked in Kyrgyzstan and currently lives in Concord, New Hampshire, where he owns and operates Generation Farm, an organic vegetable, herb and fruit farm. *Photo courtesy of Marley Horner.*

 **Hong Shen** is a professor of English at Zhejiang University, China. His research is in English literature, Sino-Western cultural relations and exchanges, and missionary studies. He earned his degrees from Peking University, and has been a visiting scholar at University of Oxford, Harvard University, University of Toronto, and University of Bristol. Shen has published thirty-three books and more than one hundred articles, including studies in *Mierdun de sadan yu yingguo wenxue chuantong: Miltton's Satan and the English Literary Tradition* (2010); *Xihu baixiang: Diversified Images of the West Lake* (2010); *Tiancheng jiyi: Memories of A Heavenly City* with Roy Sewall (2010); and *Yishi zai xifang de zhongguoshi: China's History Found in the West: The China Reports in The Illustrated London News* (2014).

Jeffrey Harrison, a great grandson of Harry Fowler Woods, is author of five books of poetry, including *The Singing Underneath*, chosen in 1987 by James Merrill for the National Poetry Series; *Incomplete Knowledge*, runner-up for the Poets' Prize in 2008; and *Into Daylight*, published in 2014 by Tupelo Press as the winner of the Dorset Prize. A volume of selected poems, *The Names of Things* (Waywiser Press, 2006) was published in the United Kingdom. A recipient of Guggenheim and NEA Fellowships, he has published poems in *The New Republic, The New Yorker, The Nation, The Yale Review*, and many other magazines and anthologies. He has taught at a number of colleges and universities, and at Phillips Academy, where he was Writer-in-Residence. He lives in Dover, Massachusetts.

Kevin Grace is the head of the Archives & Rare Books Library at the University of Cincinnati and teaches in the University Honors Program.

"20,000 Moros in Parade for Taft," *The New York Times*. August 21, 1905, 9.

Alden, John D. (Commander, U.S. Navy). *The American Steel Navy: A Photographic History of the U.S. Navy from the Introduction of the Steel Hull in 1833 to the* cruise *of the Great White Fleet, 1907 to 1909.* New York: American Heritage Press, 1971.

"All Americans Are Under Ban," *Atlanta Constitution*. July 21, 1905, 4.

"American Boycott Forerunner of Cry by the Chinese of the Death to Foreigners," *Atlanta Constitution*. September 14, 1905, 1.

"American Schools Menaced By Boycott," *Atlanta Constitution*. July 14, 1905, 14.

Anderson, William P. *The Anderson Family Records*. Cincinnati: W.F. Schaeffer & Co., 1936.

Anthony, Carl Sferrazza. *Nellie Taft: The Unconventional First Lady of the Ragtime Era*. New York: Harper Collins, 2005.

Baer, George W. *The U.S. Navy, 1890-1990: One Hundred Years of Sea Power*. Stanford, Calif.: Stanford University Press, 1944.

Bartlett, Mark. *The President's Wife and the Librarian, Letters at an Exhibition*. New York: The New York Society Library, 2009.

Boehle, Rose Angela. *Maria: A Biography of Maria Longworth*. Dayton, Ohio: Landfall Press, Inc., 1990.

Boot, Max. *The Savage Wars of Peace: Small Wars and the Rise of American Power*. New York: Basic Books, 2002.

"Boycott Forbidden," *Washington Post*. July 2, 1905, 5.

Bradley, James. *The Imperial Cruise: A Secret History of Empire and War*. New York: Little, Brown and Company, 2009.

Brands, H.W. (ed.). *The Selected Letters of Theodore Roosevelt*. New York: Cooper Square Press, 2001.

Brough, James. *Princess Alice: A Biography of Alice Roosevelt Longworth*. Boston and Toronto: Little, Brown and Company, 1975.

Burton, David H. *William Howard Taft Confident Peacemaker*. Philadelphia: Saint Joseph's University Press, 2004.

Cable, William H. Taft to Elihu Root, July 29, 1905, "Agreed Memorandum of Conversation between Prime Minister and Myself," Library of Congress Manuscript Division, William H. Taft Papers, Series 2.

"Canton Cordial to Taft," *The New York Times*. September 5, 1905, 6.

Challener, Richard D. *Admirals, Generals, & Foreign Policy:1898-1914*. Princeton, N.J. Princeton University Press, 1973.

Chambrun, Clara de. *The Making of Nicholas Longworth*. New York: Ray Long and Richard R. Smith, 1933.

Chang, Jung. *Empress Dowager Cixi: The Concubine Who Launched Modern China*. New York and Canada: Alfred A. Knopf, 2013.

"Chinese Attack Flag," *Washington Post*. August 23, 1905, 4.

"Chinese Empress Cordial: Chats Informally with Miss Roosevelt and other Americans," *The New York Times*. September 16, 1905, 7.

"Chinese Forcing the Boycott Fight," Los Angeles Times. July 28, 1905, 12.

"Chinese Going for Americans," Los Angeles Times. July 20, 1905, 11.

"Chinese in Hawaii Aid the Boycott," *The New York Times*. July 14, 1905, 6.

"Chinese Very Bitter Against This Country," *The New York Times*. June 28, 1905, 4.

Cist, Charles. *Sketches and Statistics of Cincinnati in 1851*. Cincinnati: William H. Moore & Co., 1851.

"Conger to Go to Orient to Fight Chink Boycott," *Atlanta Constitution*. August 19, 1905, 5.

"Corbin at Peking," *Los Angeles Times*. September 13, 1905, 11.

Cordery, Stacy A. *Alice Roosevelt Longworth: From White House Princess to Washington Power Broker*. New York: Viking, 2007.

Dalton, Kathleen. *Theodore Roosevelt: A Strenuous Life*. New York: Random House, 2002.

Dickens, Charles. *American Notes*. New York: St. Martin's Press, 1985.

Duffy, Herbert S. *William Howard Taft: A Biography*. New York: Minton, Balch & Co., 1930.

"Empress Dowager and President's Daughter," The New York Times. September 24, 1905, Magazine, 1.

Endy, Christopher. "Travel and World Power, Americans in Europe, 1890-1917," *The Economist*. August 1, 2009, 28.

Everett, Marshall (ed.). *Startling Experiences in the Three Wars: War in China, The Philippines, South Africa*. New York: Educational Company, [no date], Probably late 1800s.

"Extends the Boycott: Anti-American Movement Has Spread to Siam," *Washington Post*. August 1, 1905, 4.

Fairbanks, John K. *China Reinvented: Images and Policies in Chinese-American Relations*. New York: Vintage Books, 1976.

Fairbanks, John K. and Merle Goldman. *China: A New History*. Cambridge, Mass.: Harvard University Press, 1992.

Feifer, George. *Breaking Open Japan*. New York: Smithsonian Books in association with HarperCollins Publishers, 2006.

Felsenthal, Carol. *The Life and Times of Alice Roosevelt Longworth*. New York: Saint Martin's Press, 1988.

Fish, S. *1600-1914*. New York: Privately Printed by J. J. Little & Ives Company, 1942.

Francis W. Frost Photography Albums and Letters, Beinecke Rare Book and Manuscript Library, Yale University, New Haven, Connecticut.

"From Nightmare to Dreamer: An Official Apology for the Past Marks a Success Story," *The Economist*, August 1, 2009, 28.

Gamwell, Lynn and Nancy Tomes. *Madness in America*. New York: Cornell University Press, 1995.

Gleeck, Jr., Lewis. Jr. *Nine Years to Make a Difference: The Tragically Short Career of James A. LeRoy in the Philippines*. Manila, P.I.: Loyal Printing, Inc., 1996.

Go, Julian. "Introduction: Global Perspectives on the U.S. Colonial State in the Philippines," collected in *The American Colonial State in the Philippines*. Durham and London: Duke University Press, 2003.

Goodwin, Doris Kearns. *The Bully Pulpit: Theodore Roosevelt, William Howard Taft, and the Golden Age of Journalism*. New York, New York: Simon and Schuster, 2013.

Gould, Lewis L. *My Dearest Nellie: The Letters of William Howard Taft to Helen Herron Taft, 1909-1912*. Lawrence, Kansas: University Press of Kansas, 2011.

Gould, Lewis L. *The William Howard Taft Presidency*. Lawrence, Kansas: University Press of Kansas, 2009.

Griswold, Whitney. *The Far Eastern Policy of the United States*. New York, New York: Harcourt, Brace and Company, 1938.

"Harry F. Woods Dies at 95; Formerly Active Paper Executive, Active in Art, Philanthropy," *Cincinnati Enquirer*. February 21, 1955, 26, cols. 7 & 8.

Harry F. Woods Photography Albums, Beinecke Rare Book and Manuscript Library, Yale University, New Haven, Connecticut.

Hirsch, Robert. *Seizing the Light: A History of Photography*. New York: McGraw Hill, 2000.

Hoganson, Kristin. *Consumers' Imperium: The Global Production of American Domesticity, 1865 1920*. Chapel Hill: The University of North Carolina Press, 2007.

Hunt, Michael. *Ideology and U.S. Foreign Policy*. New Haven and London: Yale University Press, 1987.

___. "The American Remission of the Boxer Indemnity: A Reappraisal," The Journal of Asian Studies, Vol. 31, No. 3 (May, 1972), 539-548.

Hunter, Jane. *The Gospel of Gentility: American Women Missionaries in Turn-of-the-Century China*. New Haven, Conn.: Yale University Press, 1984.

"Imperial Ban Put on Boycott," *Atlanta Constitution*. September 2, 1905, 2.

Isaacson, Water. *Einstein: His Life and Universe*. New York: Simon & Schuster, 2007.

Ison, Mary M. "Uriah Hunt Painter and the 'Marvelous Kodak Camera,'" *Washington History*, Fall/Winter, 1990-91, 32-33.

"Just One Ship Sighted by Taft Party in Voyage from Honolulu to Yokohama, Japan," *Cincinnati Times-Star*. Ohio Historical Society, No. 110, Volume 145, August 19, 1905, 2.

Kennedy, Paul. *The Rise and Fall of the Great Powers*. New York: Random House, 1987.

Kinzer, Stephen. *Overthrow: America's Century of Regime Change from Hawaii to Iraq*. New York: Henry Holt and Company, 2006.

Knerr, Douglas G. "Housing Reform and Benevolent Capitalism: Jacob G. Schmidlapp and the Cincinnati Model Homes Company, 1911-1920." *Queen City Heritage*, 43 (Summer 1985).

"Legation Guards Changed, Marine Officer Displaces Infantry Captain in Peking," *The New York Times*. September 13, 1905, 4.

Leonard, Lewis Alexander. *Life of Alphonso Taft*. New York: Hawke Publishing Company, 1920.

Lind, Michael. *The American Way of Strategy*. New York: Oxford University Press, 2006.

Lloyd, Carpenter Griscom Papers, Library of Congress, Manuscript Division, 4.

Longworth, Alice Roosevelt. *Crowded Hours: Reminiscences of Alice Roosevelt Longworth*. New York: Charles Scribner and Sons, 1933.

"Luck, Says Mrs. Longworth," *The New York Times*. October 1, 1905, 14.

Lurie, Jonathan. *William Howard Taft: The Travails of a Progressive Conservative*. New York, New York: Cambridge University Press, 2012.

Lutz, Catherine A. and Jane L. Collins. Reading National Geographic. Chicago: University of Chicago Press, 1993.

Mahan, Alfred Thayer. *The Influence of Sea Power upon History, 1660-1783*. New York: Hill and Wang, 1957.

May, Ernest. *Imperial Democracy*. New York: Harcourt, Brace & World, 1961.

Mead, Walter Russell. *God and Gold: Britain, America, and the Making of the Modern World*. New York: Alfred a. Knopf, 2007.

Miller, Stuart C. *Benevolent Assimilation: The American Conquest of the Philippines, 1899-1903*. New Haven: Yale University Press, 1984.

Minger, Ralph Eldin. *William Howard Taft and United States Foreign Policy: The Apprenticeship Years, 1900-1908*. Chicago: University of Illinois Press, 1975.

"Miss Roosevelt at Peking," *The New York Times*. September 13, 1905, 4.

"Miss Roosevelt May Not Go," *The New York Times*. August 17, 1905, 1.

"Miss Roosevelt's Ball Closes Manila Visit: Taft Guests at Most Elaborate Affair in City's History," *The New York Times*. August 13, 1905, 4.

"Miss Roosevelt's Pluck in Face of Peril in the Orient," *Washington Post*. February 9, 1905, 6.

"Miss Roosevelt To Pay $25,000 Duty on Gifts," *The New York Times*. October 18, 1905, 9.

Musto, David F. *The American Disease: Origins of Narcotics Control*. New York: Oxford University Press, 1999.

Needham, Joseph. *Science and Civilization in China*. 24 vols. Cambridge: Cambridge University Press, 1954-2004.

Ness, Gary C. "Proving Ground for a President: William Howard Taft and the Philippines, 1900-1905. *The Cincinnati Historical Society Bulletin*, Vol. 34, No. 3, Fall 1976.

Nimmo, William. *The United States, Japan, and the Asia/Pacific Region, 1895-1945*. Westport, Connecticut: Praeger Publishers, 2001.

Ninkovich, Frank. *The United States and Imperialism*. Malden, Mass.: Blackwell, 2001.

___. *The Wilsonian Century*. Chicago and London: The University of Chicago Press, 1999.

Painter, Mark P. *William Howard Taft: President and Chief Justice*. Cincinnati: Jarndyce & Jarndyce Press, 2004.

Pringle, Henry F. *The Life and Times of William Howard Taft*. New York: Farrar & Rinehart, Inc., 1939.

Record of the Yale Class of 1867. New York: J. G. C. Bonney, 1867.

"Retired Firm Head—Funeral Services Set for Harry F. Woods, 95," *Cincinnati Times-Star*, February 21, 1955, 14, cols. 2 & 3.

"Robert S. McNamara, the Architect of a Futile War, Is Dead at 93," *The New York Times*. July 7, 2007, A20.

Rosenberg, Emily S. *Financial Missionaries to the World: The Politics and Culture of Dollar Diplomacy, 1900-1930*. Durham and London: Duke University Press, 2003.

___. *Spreading the American Dream: American Cultural and Economic Expansion, 1890-1945*. New York: Hill and Wang, 1982.

Ross, Ishbel. *An American Family: The Tafts, 1678 to 1964*. Cleveland, Ohio: World Publishing Company, 1964.

Rozik, Stacey A. "The First Daughter of the Land: Alice Roosevelt as Presidential Celebrity, 1902-1906," *Presidential Studies Quarterly*. Winter 1989. Vol. 19, No. 1, 51.

Russel, Charles Edward and Rodriguez, E.B. *The Hero of the Filipinos*. New York: The Century Company, 1923.

"Seeking to Learn Losses in Boycott," *The New York Times*. August 23, 1905, 20.

Schaller, Michael. *The United States and China: Into the Twenty-First Century*. New York: Oxford University Press, 2002.

Shen Bao. 18 Hankow Road, Shanghai, September 3-13, 1905.

Simpson, Jeffrey. "Cultural Reflections: Period Photography Richly Document the Complexity of Chinese Life in the 19th Century," *Architectural Digest*, August, 2008, 147.

Spence, Jonathan. *The Search for Modern China*. New York: W. W. Norton & Co., 1990.

Spence, Jonathan and Annping Chin. *The Chinese Century: A Photographic History*. London: HarperCollins, 1996.

Stever, Margo Taft. Interview with Michael Eric Besch, Collateral Descendant of F. W. Frost. April 22, 2009.

___. Interview with Michael Hunt on 1905 U.S. Diplomatic Mission to Asia, April 27, 2009.

___. Interview with Stacy Cordery on 1905 U.S. Diplomatic Mission to Asia, May 24, 2009.

"Sultan of Sulu Offers to Wed Miss Roosevelt: Says His Filipino People Wish Her to Remain Among Them," *The New York Times*. August 22, 1905, 7.

"Taft Arrives at Capital," *The New York Times*. October 2, 1905, 6.

"Taft Leaves for America, Found No Hostile Feeling Among Japanese, Chinese, Lost Fifteen Million by the Boycott," *Los Angeles Times*. September 18, 1905, 12.

"Taft on Exclusion," *Washington Post*. August 29, 1905, 1.

"Taft Party in Hong Kong," *The New York Times*. September 3, 1905, 1.

"Taft Party's Itinerary," *Washington Post*. August 29, 1905, 1.

Takaki, Ronald. *Iron Cages: Race and Culture in 19th Century America*. New York and Oxford, Oxford University Press, 2000.

Teague, Michael. *Mrs. L: Conversations with Alice Roosevelt Longworth*. New York: Doubleday & Company, Inc., 1981.

"That Chinese Boycott," *Los Angeles Times*. July 13, 1905, 14.

Theodore Roosevelt Papers, Manuscript Division, Library of Congress, Reel 56, 57, 59, Series 1.

"Tribes Gather to Greet Taft Party," *The New York Times*. August 24, 1905, 9.

Trollope, Frances. *Domestic Manners of the Americans*. New York: Alfred A. Knopf, 1949.

Tsai, Shi-shan Henry. *China and the Overseas Chinese in the United States, 1868-1911*. Fayetteville: University of Arkansas Press, 1983.

Tuchman, Barbara W. *Sand against the Winds: Sitwell and the American Experience in China, 1911-1945*. London: Macdonald Future Publishers, 1981.

University of Cincinnati Archives, Archives & Rare Books Library (photographs of Taft brothers, Taft Statue, and Taft in Cincinnati).

"War Department Gets News," *The New York Times*. March 10, 1906, 4.

Wang Guanhua. *In Search of Justice: The 1905-1906 Chinese Anti-American Boycott*. Cambridge, Mass.: Harvard University Asia Center and Distributed by Harvard University Press, 2001.

"Washington Girl Won," *Washington Post*. September 6, 1905, 5.

Wei, Deborah and Kamel, Rachael. *Resistance in Paradise: Rethinking 100 Years of U.S. Involvement in the Caribbean and Pacific*. Philadelphia: American Friends Service Committee, 1988.

Whitaker, Robert. *Mad in America: Bad Science, Bad Medicine, and Mistreatment of the Mentally Ill* New York: Basic Books, 2002.

William Howard Taft Papers, Manuscript Division, Library of Congress, Reel 25, Series 2; Reels 51, 52, Series 3.

Williams, William Appleman. *Empire as a Way of Life: An Essay of the Causes and Character of America's Present Predicament along With a Few Thoughts about An Alternative*. New York and Oxford: Oxford University Press, 1980.

Winchester, Simon. *The Man Who Loved China: The Fantastic Story of the Eccentric Scientist Who Unlocked the Mysteries of the Middle Kingdom*. New York: HarperCollins, 2008.

Wolff, Leon. *Little Brown Brother*. Garden City: Doubleday, 1961.

Woolman, David S. et al. "Fighting Islam's Moro Warriors-P," *Military History Magazine*, April 2002.

Worcester, Dean C. *The Philippines, Past and Present*. (2 vols.) New York: The Macmillan Company, 1921.

A

Anderson, George 66
Anderson, R. Clough 4, 7, 206, 225

B

Battle of the Clouds 40, 42
Beard, George M. 17-20
Boardman, Mabel 77, 80, 82, 205, 212-213, 218, 221
Bonaparte, Charles 69, 80
Boxer Protocols 50, 54-55
Boxer Rebellion, 3-4, 22, 36, 48-53, 59-60, 67, 69-70, 79-80, 93, 134, 139, 145
Brownell, Atherton 225

C

Carnegie, Andrew 16
Cary, Thomas 225
Chaffee, John W. 80
Chapin, Louis 225
Chinese boycott, 4, 55, 60, 63-68, 70, 75-77, 79, 127, 260
Chinese 1896 delegation to United States 21
Chinese Exclusion Acts 27, 43, 60, 66, 260
Chinese immigrants in the United States 60-62, 67-68, 70
Chinese newspaper reports on the Taft Delegation 261-269
Clark, Charles 225
Cockran, William Bourke 30, 117, 119, 155, 209, 222, 224
Conant, Charles A. 57
Confucian Temple, 145
Conger, Edwin H. 55, 62, 67, 261
Conger, Sarah 260-261
Coolidge, A.O. 226
Cooper, Henry A. 222
Copley, Ward E. 225
Corbin, Henry C. 8-9, 78, 80-82, 93, 117, 119, 133, 135, 155, 205, 209, 213, 216, 224
Critten, Mignon 4, 226
Curtis, Charles 223

D

De Armond, David A. 222
Driscoll, Michael E. 223
Drum Tower 10, 147
Dubois, Fred T. 219, 221

E

Edwards, Clarence R. 114
Emperor Guangxu 72, 147, 155, 157
Empress Dowager Cixi 4, 49, 53-54, 58, 65, 71-72, 82-84, 117-118, 133-135, 142, 155, 157, 164, 260-262, 268, 270-271
En Hai 52, 54

F

Fearson, James S. 67
Fish, Stuyvesant, Jr. 9, 82-83, 226
Fish, Stuyvesant, Sr. 9, 226
Forbes, William Cameron 207-208, 210
Forbidden City 54, 72, 84-85, 160, 261
Foss, George E. 223
Foster, Murphy J. 220
Frost, Francis W. 4-13, 26, 30, 38, 47, 50, 54, 57, 76, 79, 82, 85-86, 113-202, 226, 268-275
Frost, George H. 7-8

G

Gilbert, Newton W. 225
Gill, Edwin 62
Gillett, Frederick H. 117, 155, 222-223
Gracey, Samuel 64
Great Bell Temple 153
Great Wall 10, 84-86, 119, 133, 138-139, 160, 164, 173, 177-178
Griscom, Lloyd Carpenter 34-35, 88
Grosvenor, Charles 5, 221
Guggenheim, Isaac 67

H

Hall of Classics 147
Hanna, Hugh H. 57
Harriman, E.H. 56, 67, 86, 88, 187

Hay, John 21-22, 26, 49, 55
Hepburn, William Peters 221-222
Herrera, Cruz, 210
Hill, E.J. 223
Hill, James D. 226
Hobart, R.B. 226
Holcombe, Thomas 81, 93, 95, 133-134, 139, 190
Howard, William M. 223
Hubbard, Thomas 67
Hulbert, Matilda 18
Huntington, H.E. 67

I

Imperial Gardens 34

J

Jen Ching Literary Society 64
Jenks, Jeremiah 57, 60
Jobes, C.T. 226
Johnson, W. 226
Jones, William A. 222

K

Katsura, Count Taro 37
Kelly, William 114
Komura, Baron 36

L

La Follette, Robert M. 24
Lay, Julius G. 65, 68, 127
Lee, Harris 80-81, 95, 134, 139, 190
Legardo, Benito, 205, 216
LeRoy, James A. 30
Liang Ch'eng 56
Llama Temple 13, 84, 86, 144-145
Lo-Sang Gyal-Tsen 65
Long, Chester I. 221
Longworth, Nicholas 3-4, 7, 26-27, 31-32, 34, 42, 77, 79, 88-89, 117, 155, 216-217
Loomis, Francis B. 66, 74
Loud, George A. 224-225

M

McIntosh, Burr 12, 30, 77, 226-227
McKinley, William 13, 16, 21-22, 44, 49, 55, 224
McKinley, William B. 225
McMillan, Amy 77, 80, 82, 212-213, 218, 221
Mahan, Alfred Thayer 23-26
Metcalf, John 19
Ming Tombs 10, 84, 86, 183
Morgan, J. Pierpont 16

N

Nathan, Matthew 78, 124
Needham, Joseph, 10-11
Newlands, Francis G. 28, 73, 77, 82, 117, 155, 213, 221

O

O'Brien, Frederick 39
Open Door Policy 13, 22
Opium War 12, 60

P

Pagoda Temple, 153
Parsons, Herbert 225
Patterson, Thomas M. 220-221
Payne, Serreno E. 221
Pershing, John J. 155
Portsmouth Peace Treaty 36, 259

Q

Qing Dynasty and government 48, 50-51, 54-55, 60, 65, 68-72, 77, 262-263

R

Righteous Harmony Movement 48
Rockhill, William W. 22, 55-56, 58, 60, 63, 65, 67-70, 72-73, 78, 80-82, 139, 158
Rockwell, Alphonso D. 19-20
Rodgers, James L. 66
Roosevelt, Alice 3-4, 26-34, 36, 38-39, 72-74, 77-80, 82-85, 87-89, 93, 115, 117, 155, 158, 160, 201, 205, 212-213, 216-218, 221, 223-224, 260-268

Roosevelt, Edith 19, 30-31, 216
Roosevelt, Theodore 3-4, 19-20, 22-24, 28,
    31, 36-38, 44, 46-47, 53, 55-57, 59,
    67, 69, 72-73, 77, 80, 87-88, 115, 210,
    212, 215-216, 223-224, 259-260
Root, Elihu 58, 60, 69, 88, 215-216, 224
Russo-Japanese War 3, 13, 25, 36, 46,
    71, 259

S

Sammons, Thomas 65
Schmidlapp, Charlotte 4, 227
Schmidlapp, Jacob G. 4, 227
Scott, Charles F. 223
Scott, Nathan E. 218-220
Sherley, Joseph Swagar 209, 225
Shikai, Yuan 56
Simpson, Jerry 24
Sino-Japanese War 21, 60, 70-71
Smith, Arthur H. 59-60
Sith, George W. 222
Spanish-American War 20
Stillman, E.G. 227
Sugimoto, T. 5
Sultan of Sulu 38-39, 117-118
Summer Palace 82, 154-155, 157,
    194, 261
Sun Yat-sen 72
Sze Tak Shun 65

T

Taft, Alphonso 18
Taft, Harry 19
Taft, Horace 19
Taft, Hulbert 18
Taft, Louisa 18
Taft, Nellie 5, 31-32, 38
Taft, Peter Rawson, II. 18-19
Taft, William Howard, 3-5, 26, 31, 33-34,
    36-38, 47, 53, 57, 60, 62, 73-76, 78-
    81, 87, 115, 259-269
    address at Miami University 27-28, 62
    governor of Philippines 4, 43
    letters to wife Nellie 204-227
    and Moros 38-42

secret deal with Japanese, Taft-
    Katsura Agreement 37
Takahira, Kogora 36
Temple of Agriculture 147
Temple of Heaven 82, 147
Thomas, Sidney Gilchrist 16
Thompson, J.K. 114

V

von Ketteler, Baron Clemens 50-51, 54-55,
    144-145

W

Warren, Fred 155, 218, 227
Wetmore, Roger 227
Williams, S. Wells 60
Wilson, Woodrow 53
Winter Palace 85, 154, 160, 164-165,
    194, 261
Wood, Leonard 69
Woods, Arthur H. 227
Woods, Harry Fowler 4-13, 22-23, 79, 85-
    86, 90-93, 227, 266, 268-275
Woolman, David S. 40
Wright, Katrina 205-206
Wright, Luke 38, 205-210
Wu Ting-Fang 82-83, 157-158, 162, 164

Y

Yellow Temple 108, 151-153
Young, Lafe 227
Yuan Shikai 65, 85, 160

"I am in favor of helping the prosperity of all countries because, when we are all prosperous, the trade of each becomes more valuable to the other."

—William Howard Taft
in 1909, the first year of his presidency and four years after his diplomatic mission to Asia.